THE FEMALE BODY
AND THE LAW

THE FEMALE BODY
AND THE LAW

ZILLAH R. EISENSTEIN

UNIVERSITY OF CALIFORNIA PRESS
BERKELEY   LOS ANGELES   LONDON

University of California Press
Berkeley and Los Angeles, California

University of California Press, Ltd.
London, England

© 1988 by
The Regents of the University of California

Library of Congress Cataloging in Publication Data

Eisenstein, Zillah R.
  The female body and the law / Zillah R. Eisenstein.
    p.   cm.
  Includes bibliographical references and index.
    ISBN 0-520-06309-0 (alk. paper)
  1. Sex discrimination against women—Law and legislation—
United States.   2. Women—Legal status, laws, etc.—United
States.   3. Body, Human—Law and legislation—United
States.   4. Feminism—United States.   I. Title.
KF4758.E38 1988
346.7301'34—dc19
[347.306134]   88-27890
                                                        CIP

Printed in the United States of America

1   2   3   4   5   6   7   8   9

For my daughter, Sarah, and her father, Richard

Contents

Acknowledgments

Many people shared their time and knowledge with me to enable me to write this book. Ruth Milkman provided me with helpful bibliography on protective legislation; Alice Kessler Harris provided me with needed materials on the Sears, Roebuck and Company trial; Isabelle Katz Pinzler was completely generous in providing information on the American Civil Liberties Union position on special legislation. Herma Hill Kay, David Lyons, Richard Stumbar, Isabelle Katz Pinzler, Joan Bertin, and Patty Zimmerman read parts of the manuscript and made important criticisms. Carla Golden and Patty Zimmerman discussed many of the issues in this book with me on our daily runs. Miriam Brody, Mary Fainsod Katzenstein, and Rosalind Pollack Petchesky read the entire manuscript and made invaluable suggestions. Nancy Moore, reference librarian at the Cornell Law Library, gave me endless assistance. My student Sarah Richmond referenced queried footnotes, and my colleague Ken Lehrman located several hard-to-find Supreme Court citations for me. Kathleen Frankovic of CBS/News Polling made poll data easily available to me. Jonathan Plotkin assisted me in figuring out my new computer. Lauren Kenworthy, legislative assistant to Representative Howard Wolpe, obtained data on the Reagan administration social service cutbacks for me, as well as kept me updated on policy changes within the administration. And, as always, I thank my students at Ithaca College, especially those in my "Politics of the Body" seminar.

I also want to thank the staffs of Cornell Infant Care Center and the Ithaca Child Care Center, especially Jane Foti, Mary Ann Iacovelli, Rose Spinelli, and Diane Tripodi, for the wonderful care of my infant/toddler daughter. And I thank Lisa White for her help in the domestic realm. I thank my mother, Fannie Price Eisenstein, for everything.

My final thanks go to Donna Freedline for all her secretarial help; Dorothy Owens for her generosity in editing, typing, and retyping the manuscript; my editor, Naomi Schneider, for her earliest inquiries about this project, which helped transform it into a book; and Barbara Ras and Susan M. S. Brown for their final editorial attention.

Introduction

"Sex equality" is an elusive phrase. Depending on context, it can be vitally significant or virtually meaningless. It categorizes women according to both difference and sameness—indicating that women are either completely determined by their biological sex or entirely free of it—but in both cases men set the standard. In neither instance does the female body displace the silent privileging of the male body. If equality is not to be relegated only to economic or legal uses, we must recognize the specificity of the female body. This refocusing necessarily challenges the idea that treating women like men is equivalent to treating women and men equally.

I will argue here that no Western viewing of sex equality explicitly theorizes the specificity of either the male sex/body or the female sex/body. By focusing on the body, therefore, I intend to reconceptualize the meaning of equality and, with it, the meaning of difference. In particular, my focus reintroduces the pregnant body in order to decenter the privileged position of the male body. This approach contrasts markedly with the dominant discourses, which use pregnancy to differentiate women and subordinate them to men.

I do not mean to imply, of course, that equality requires that everyone is, or should be, pregnant. This implication would be problematic on two counts. First, pregnancy cannot apply as a standard for everyone, especially not for males. Second, it posits the kind of homogeneous view of the body that is the trouble to begin with. The ultimate significance, then, of the pregnant body for developing a theory of sex equality is that it *reminds* us of at least a *potential* difference between females and males that makes sameness, as the standard for equality, inadequate. In a more general sense, it reminds us of diversity. My refocusing, therefore, does not establish a new homogeneous standard but rather denies the validity of having one at all. If diversity is privileged in and of itself, it undermines any *one* preferred standard.

In Western theory, as in law, the female body is most often assumed to be like the male body when the equality of women and men is being asserted; by the same token, the female body is most often explicitly said to be "different" from the male when the equality of women and men is being denied. In neither locus is the woman both integral and homologous, nor is the male/man ever considered to be the "different" one. Woman is not recognized as both female—as a physical creature whose sex can be biologically categorized—*and* gendered through the culture—as an individual who can be socially categorized. Instead, gender is regarded as biologically determined: the female *is* the woman; the pregnant body *is* the mother and perhaps wife. So being a wo/man or being fe/male is "different" from being a man or a male. It is a lesser variation. The female body is engendered with "difference": sexual (as biological) identity is not specified; and the resulting "equality" both assumes and silently denies the man or male as the standard.

It will help here to explicate the peculiar relationship between sex and gender. For my discussion, "sex" represents the biological female, and "gender" designates the cultural interpretation of what it is to be female. As we shall see, the distinction is problematic. Yet, if we reject received opinion that the two are one and the same, then we must acknowledge both what distinguishes them and what interrelates them. Just as biology is never devoid of its cultural definition and interpretation, so sex itself, as a biological entity, is partly defined in and through culture. And just as biological constitution is never irrelevant to the definition of individual identity, so gender is never completely distanced from biology. Biology is, in part, gendered—which is, in part, culture; and gender is, in part, biological—which is also, in part, cultural. If we accept these premises, then we must realize the pregnant body is never merely that: it is also, in part, gendered as the mother's body. And herein lies the problem. Gender is a mix of both woman's unique biological potential and its cultural reduction to her determined function. The female as "mother" is constituted of both these meanings, and a third as well. In this third meaning, some of her potential uniqueness is seen as dwelling *within* the engendered biological "part" of her being.

Gender, as an idea, registers the role of society and culture in defining the (biological) "female" as a "woman." The problem arises when this definition of "a woman" is in turn subsumed under "the mother," when culture is supposedly determined by biology rather than constituted as part of it, when culture is not recognized as definitive in interpreting the body. In sum, when the pregnant body is conflated with the "idea" of the mother, we are left with the *en*gendered meaning of sex "difference," which attributes the hierarchical opposition of "woman" and "man" to nature. To recognize that sex and gender are interconnected and that differences between women and men exist is not the same as to accept the *en*gendered definition of "woman" and "man." Rather, this recognition entails the acknowledgment that, considering female bodies and the specific placement of women in society, some women are more different from men than similar to them, and some women are more similar to men than different from them. Recognizing that gender differences exist is a way of acknowledging that biology exists, but gender differences need not be reduced to or determined by biology. Certain gender differences may not be sexually determined at all. In contrast, the supposition of *en*gendered sex "difference," pretending differences between the sexes are natural, not cultural, homogenizes each sex and both genders—ostensibly, this supposition establishes gender on the basis of biology. To presume engendered sex "difference" is to assume that sex and gender are one. And in the engendered view of "difference," differences among women are silenced and difference between men and women privileged; the sameness among women is presumed and the similarity between men and women denied.

Rejecting the engendered form of "difference" allows us, consequently, to refocus attention on the particularities that exist within female bodies and women's lives. This focus in turn allows us to elucidate a fuller meaning of *unen*gendered difference. Each difference becomes a moment on a continuum expressing the specified meaning of commonality, likeness, sameness. Instead of sameness expressing a silent hierarchy of male privilege, it comes to encompass females *and*—in the plural terms of their common differences—differences of race, economic class, age. We thus pluralize the meaning of difference and reinvent the concept of equality.

The idea of engendered "difference" has historically been used repeatedly to deny women equality with men. Today neoconservatives and New Right antifeminists are actively using the discourse of "difference" to deny women their equality in the public realm as well as in the family. One version of this discourse is also used by revisionist feminists to reject the radically egalitarian commitments of the feminist movement of the 1970s. In spite of these developments—and in some sense because of them—it is important to redirect the discourse on equality toward an egalitarianism that affirms the biological particularity of the female body without endorsing the historical contingencies of its engendered form. Because it is not possible to distinguish sex and gender once and for all, the discussion must remain open and incomplete. At the same time that we criticize the dominance of the phallus—as the symbol of the male body in a social order that privileges the bearer of the penis—we must acknowledge that our criticism remains inside "phallocratic" discourse simply because that discourse is dominant.

In sum, this book is about sex equality—what it means and what it might mean. Accordingly, the book is just as much about sex "difference"—what it means and what it might not have to mean. Ultimately, the book considers the differences of the body and the problem they pose for a notion of equality. As I have stated, I intend to shift the focus away from the phallus and toward the pregnant body. The pregnant body decenters the phallus without centering itself; instead, it allows a heterogeneous viewing of equality that recognizes the particularity of the human body and constructs a notion of diversity that is distinctly compatible with equality.

Given these concerns, this book is also about symbols, language, and power and how they operate in relation to sex "difference," gender "difference," and sex equality. I locate this discussion within liberal law(s), as practiced in Western industrial societies. I view law(s) as an authorized discourse—as a language constituted by a series of symbols that is located in not merely the realm of the "ideal" or the "real" but a place somewhere in between. It is this "in between" that I want to understand and articulate as a realm of power that is both homogeneous and concentrated, heterogeneous and dispersed; that encourages a mix of diversity rather than a set of dualistic oppositions. Hence, my frequent use throughout of the plural in terms such as "law(s)," "difference(s)," and "body(ies)." Through this practice I attempt to dislocate our identification with homogeneity, unity, and similarity. There is no one body, only bodies, only differences, as well as pluralized conceptions of equality. A note of caution: by pluralizing equality I do not mean to condone the idea of "separate but equal" or that of "separate spheres." To the contrary, I mean to argue that the concept of equality is best reconstructed through a completely pluralized notion of difference(s), one that rejects a politics of inequality and demands a radical egalitarianism.

Chapter One

Politics and/or Deconstruction: Thoughts on Method

My purpose in this chapter is to explain my method and theoretical assumptions about power, my epistemological starting points. I will discuss the role of language in constructing and reflecting relations of power and how language affects the way we think about equality, difference, and gender. Before we can formulate a new theory of sex equality, we need a new method for thinking about the female body and its gendered expression. The process of defining this method began for me as a socialist feminist in the early 1970s, shifted through that decade in response to developments in radical feminist and Third World feminist writing, and takes place now in a critical exploration of deconstruction. My concern here, however, is not to catalog the contributions or specific histories of these politics but to utilize them as I discuss the importance of the body in clarifying the meaning of difference(s).

My method questions the validity of distinguishing between materialism and idealism. If materialism is conceptualized as the study of "real" human beings within societal structures, then these human beings need to be recognized, among other things, as males and females. This recognition involves naming the bodies as male and female along with acknowledging the language that both names and reflects cultural interpretation. These recognitions challenge the neat delineations between idealism (most often identified with liberalism) and materialism (identified with Marxism). With this challenge, oppositions such as biology and history, nature and culture, difference and sameness come under scrutiny as well. Such a radical epistemology—one that denies duality and its hierarchical, oppositional conception of difference—begins to shift political discourses, which *begin* to shift the relations of power. This epistemology provides a new point of entry for studying law. It identifies law as neither mere superstructure—outside the "real" relations of power (as many Marxists would have it)—nor the structure of power itself (as many liberals hold). Thus, this perspective allows us to rethink the contours of power.

It is difficult to find a starting place to discuss relations of power given the premise that "for humans, language plays a major role in generating reality. Without words to objectify and categorize our sensations and place them in relation to one another, we cannot evolve a tradition of what is real in the world."[1] The scope of "reality" (and with it the realm of the "ideal," against which reality is most often positioned) becomes much less clear. If language helps to constitute the real by describing and naming it, then interpretation contributes to how the real is known.[2] Thus language as an aspect of thought is a part of what is real and does not fit strictly into the oppositional category of ideal. If power belongs to the realm of the real, and the real is partially constituted in and through language, then we need a way of thinking and rethinking the notion of politics (as the activity of power). I do not mean to reduce this notion to a politics of language, or to replace the structural aspects of "reality" with such a notion, but rather to assert that the dualism of the real and the ideal is overdrawn. The realms of concrete facts and nonconcrete ideas do not exist in complete opposition. Instead, they are mixed within a continuum. The recognition of how language is used to name, to represent, to think,

1. Ruth Hubbard, "Have Only Men Evolved?" in *Women Look at Biology Looking at Women*, ed. Ruth Hubbard, Mary Sue Henifin, and Barbara Fried (Cambridge, Mass: Schenkman Publishing, 1979), p. 7.

2. There is a vast quantity of relevant literature, from which I cite only a few titles here: Rosalind Coward and John Ellis, *Language and Materialism: Developments in Semiology and the Theory of the Subject* (Boston: Routledge & Kegan Paul, 1977); Jonathan Culler, *On Deconstruction: Theory and Criticism after Structuralism* (Ithaca, N.Y.: Cornell Univ. Press, 1982); Terry Eagleton, *Literary Theory: An Introduction* (Minneapolis: Univ. of Minnesota Press, 1983); Henry Louis Gates, Jr., ed., *"Race," Writing, and Difference* (Chicago: Univ. of Chicago Press, 1985); Michael Ryan, *Marxism and Deconstruction: A Critical Articulation* (Baltimore: Johns Hopkins Univ. Press, 1982); and Elaine Showalter, ed., *The New Feminist Criticism: Essays on Women, Literature, and Theory* (New York: Pantheon Books, 1985).

relocates power in a place *somewhere in between* the real and ideal: between truth and closure and truth*s* and openness.

This place is the realm of discourse, where politics and language, homogeneity and heterogeneity, theory and practice, sex and gender intersect. My use of the term "discourse" recognizes the politics of language as a politics of interpretation of the real, of the multiplicity of truth(s). Language is as real as the thing it describes. It undermines dualism and opposition as a method; it disperses power to the various sites of interpretation. By focusing on discourse(s), we position ourselves between the interpretation and the thing being interpreted. This position is not a middle ground but rather a point historically constituted through opposition, while the dualism is challenged epistemologically.

By focusing on language as political—as being structured in and through a series of hierarchical differences and, therefore, both constituting and reflecting political relations that are defined through difference—we confront the open-textured quality of power. My use of the term "open-textured" points to the relational status of meaning. In other words, a thing is both what it is and what it is *not*, and what a thing is *not* is endless. A woman is not a man, but she is also not a multitude of other things. What she *is* is thus endless as well, because meaning is expressed through the relation of "is" and "is not." The problem here is not the relational meaning of difference but the hierarchical notion of difference that defines woman by what she is not, representing her as lacking. Difference in this instance is set up as a duality: woman is different from man, and this difference is seen as a deficiency because she *is not* man. This construction of difference homogenizes all women as different in the same way, the way they are different from all men, and establishes the duality man/woman. Instead we need to dislodge this opposition and recognize the ground in between. Difference must mean diversity, not homogeneous duality, if we are going to rethink the meaning of sex and gender.

Language represents gender at the same time that it is already a system of differences; it "makes the world intelligible by differentiating between concepts."[3] Language constructs these differences:

3. Catherine Belsey, *Critical Practice* (London: Methuen, 1980), p. 38; all further references to this work, abbreviated as *CP,* will be included in the text.

"Signs are defined by their difference from each other in the network of signs which is the signifying system" (*CP,* p. 40).[4] More directly, words have meaning in relation to other words through their difference: man/woman; reason/passion; fact/value; objective/subjective; real/ideal; white/black. Hierarchy is assumed *in* the difference, so these differences are defined in a relationship that privileges one of the "opposites." It is important to recognize that although one may, as I do, wish to reconstruct the hierarchy (and hence the difference), one cannot fully move outside the structure of dichotomy. The challenge to duality is still (historically) structured by duality. As a result, the space we occupy remains somewhere "in between."

My concern here is not with the nature of language itself but rather with how language partially constitutes political reality—how language constructs, interprets, and reflects political reality. Actually, I am not convinced that there is such a thing as the nature of language, because "words change their meaning from one discourse to another, and conflicting discourses develop even where there is a supposedly common language."[5] Discourses generate meaning rather than manifest preexisting meaning, although meanings often antedate the people who use the language. "A crucial argument concerning discourse is that meanings are to be found only in the concrete forms of differing social and institutional practices: there can be no meaning in 'language.'"[6]

Language is also not neutral. It is always embedded in dis-

And see Ferdinand de Saussure, *Course in General Linguistics,* ed. Charles Bally et al., trans. Wade Baskin (New York: McGraw-Hill, 1966).

4. For a discussion of language as a series of differences, see Jacques Derrida, *Writing and Difference,* trans. Alan Bass (Chicago: Univ. of Chicago Press, 1978); *Dissemination,* trans. Barbara Johnson (Chicago: Univ. of Chicago Press, 1981); and *Of Grammatology,* trans. Gayatri Chakravorty Spivak (Baltimore: Johns Hopkins Univ. Press, 1974).

5. Diane Macdonell, *Theories of Discourse: An Introduction* (London: Blackwell, 1986), p. 45.

6. Ibid., p. 12. And see Shoshana Felman, ed., *Literature and Psychoanalysis—The Question of Reading: Otherwise* (Baltimore: Johns Hopkins Univ. Press, 1982); Elizabeth Flynn and Patrocinio Schweickart, eds., *Gender and Reading: Essays on Readers, Texts, and Contexts* (Baltimore: Johns Hopkins Univ. Press, 1986); and Sally McConnell-Ginet, Ruth Borker, and Nelly Furman, eds., *Women and Language in Literature and Society* (New York: Praeger, 1980).

course. It constructs meaning at the same time that it reflects meaning. It sets the limits for what we can see and in some sense think. It defines, as Michel Foucault notes, "the limits and the forms of expressibility: What is it possible to speak of? What has been constituted as the field of discourse?"[7] Which terms disappear, and which become part of ritual, pedagogy, and control? Any discourse puts into play a privileged set of viewpoints; it makes certain thoughts and ideas present, others absent.

The Significance of Discourse

I am very much indebted to Foucault for my use of the term "discourse," but my use is not meant to be an explication of his. His discussion of discourse is neither fully consistent nor all decipherable, and he probably would not accept a generalized theory of discourse to begin with. Nevertheless, I will clarify my use of the term with and against his. Through his decentering of the state, Foucault points us in the direction of a radical pluralist epistemology of power relations. But his theory of the dispersion of power is incomplete; he replaces the notion of concentrated centered power (as in a state theory) with one of heterogeneous and multiple power sites. He does not offer an analysis of the unities that exist or are established through the discourse(s) about power and the state. He does not recognize the significance of the unity or centrality of power as it exists in state formations or engendered forms of sex class; therefore, he leaves us with little understanding of the hierarchical relations that define dispersed sites of power. He gets lost in his own dispersion. But we need not do the same.

My use of the term "discourse" focuses on the politics of language and knowledge—the awareness that power is constructed in and through language, which crisscrosses the realm of "fact" (the real) and "interpretation" (the ideal). Language as discourse transects the splits between objective and subjective, empirical and normative, value free and biased. The process of naming facts destroys these neat dichotomies and uncovers the more complex relationship that Foucault terms "power/knowledge." Language em-

7. Michel Foucault, "History, Discourse, and Discontinuity," *Salmagundi* 20 (Summer–Fall 1972): 234; all further references to this work, abbreviated as "HDD," will be included in the text.

bodies a standpoint. As Catherine Belsey states, "A *discourse* is a domain of language-use, a particular way of talking (and writing and thinking). A discourse involves certain shared assumptions which appear in the formulations that characterize it" (*CP*, p. 5). Discourse focuses on the importance of context within meaning and the open-texturedness of reality. There can be multiple standpoints, multiple truths, multiple sites of power/knowledge. This multiplicity can lead to a radical theorization of power if we recognize the hierarchical relations of truths.

Foucault admits to several uses of the term "discourse," "treating it sometimes as the general domain of all statements, sometimes as an individualizable group of statements, and sometimes as a regulated practice that accounts for a certain number of statements." He continues: "In the most general, and vaguest way, it denoted a group of verbal performances; and by discourse, then, I meant that which was produced (perhaps all that was produced) by the groups of signs. But I also meant a group of acts of formulation, a series of sentences or propositions."[8] For Foucault, discourses are transparent; they do not need interpretation.[9] Their meaning is supposedly assigned; no one has to assign them meaning. They are "practices that systematically form the objects of which they speak" (*AK*, p. 49). In this sense, discourse cuts through the separations between speaking, thinking, acting. "Of course, discourses are composed of signs; but what they do is more than use these signs to designate things. It is this *more* that renders them irreducible to the language (*langue*) and to speech. It is this 'more' that we must reveal and describe" (*AK*, p. 49).

"Discourse" as a term focuses on the open-endedness of meaning; "a statement is always an event that neither the language (*langue*) nor the meaning can quite exhaust" (*AK*, p. 28). Discourse is something more than language—it moves into the realm of thinking and acting. This movement—"with its gaps, its discontinuities, its entanglements, its incompatibilities, its replacements,

8. Michel Foucault, *The Archaeology of Knowledge and the Discourse on Language*, trans. A. M. Sheridan Smith (New York: Pantheon, 1972), pp. 80, 107; all further references to this work, abbreviated as *AK*, will be included in the text.

9. "Truth and Power," interview with Alessandro Fontano and Pasquale Pasquino, in *Michel Foucault: Power, Truth, Strategy*, ed. Meaghan Morris and Paul Patton (Sydney: Feral Publications, 1979), p. 33.

and its substitutions" (*AK,* p. 72)—is what defines the realm of discourse. Sometimes a discourse *is* a form of power; sometimes it just expresses a form of power. Discourse is completely tied up with a notion of language, knowledge, and signs as part of the domain of power.[10] Separateness between these realms is replaced by a dialectic. None can be reduced to another. Each is constituted in relation to the others while helping to define them.

Through discourse, power comes to be dispersed and heterogeneous. Foucault acknowledges the contradictory aspects of this kind of positioning: "We must make allowance for the complex and unstable process whereby discourse can be both an instrument and an effect of power, but also a hindrance, a stumbling-block, a point of resistance and a starting point for an opposing strategy. Discourse transmits and produces power; it reinforces it, but also undermines and exposes it, renders it fragile and makes it possible to thwart it."[11]

Foucault does not sufficiently recognize that the dispersion of power through and in discourse operates within concentrated forms of power that discourses about "the" state establish. To recognize this context is not to centralize "the" state as the center of power but rather to acknowledge that liberal discourse which establishes the state as "the" center in part constructs it as such. As we shall see, although law(s) can reflect contradictory standpoints and therefore diversify the meanings of state power, law and laws also operate in a context formulated inside the discourses of the state. We need to elaborate further the relationship between dispersed and concentrated forms of power. In what sense does the state articulate discourses as aspects of power relations themselves? This is a particularly significant question today. One political analyst, noting the importance of imagery and rhetoric for the Reagan administration, has stated that ideas *themselves* have be-

10. See Alan Sheridan, *Michel Foucault: The Will to Truth* (London: Tavistock Publications, 1980), p. 186. See also Mark Cousins and Athar Hussain, *Michel Foucault* (New York: St. Martin's Press, 1984); and Hubert L. Dreyfus and Paul Rabinow, *Michel Foucault: Beyond Structuralism and Hermeneutics* (Chicago: Univ. of Chicago Press, 1982).

11. Michel Foucault, *The History of Sexuality, Volume 1: An Introduction,* trans. Robert Hurley (New York: Pantheon Books, 1978), p. 101. And see his *The Use of Pleasure,* Vol. 2 of *The History of Sexuality,* trans. Robert Hurley (New York: Pantheon Books, 1985).

come the salient form of contemporary American politics: "Image and ideology, style and substance are not opposites but complements. They are fused in Reagan."[12] Language *as* discourse defines a political fabric that can sometimes make the sign or symbol one and the same as the "real."

Ideology and the Problem of the "Real"

"Ideology" as a term presents problems when we attempt to deal with reality as a realm that intersects with the ideal. "Ideology," particularly in its classic Marxist meaning, presumes a notion of the real that is clearly differentiated from the ideal (meaning a false reality). Ideology supposedly inverts the real and represents it in an untrue form. It presents reality from the bourgeois standpoint; for example, alienated labor is seen as private property, stolen stored labor as capital, the ideological as the real.[13] The distinction between "true" (meaning "the" truth) and "false" gives the term "ideology" its meaning.

According to Foucault, the Marxist notion of ideology "always stands in virtual opposition to something else which is supposed to count as truth." He argues that, given this starting premise, the use of the term "ideology" poses a series of problems. Rather than assume that truth structures our being, Foucault wants to figure out how "effects of truth are produced within discourses which in themselves are neither true nor false." Further, he rejects the Marxist view that ideology "stands in a secondary position relative to something which functions as its infrastructure, as its material, economic determinant."[14] Foucault uses the term "discourse" as I

12. Sidney Blumenthal, *The Rise of the Counter-Establishment: From Conservative Ideology to Political Power* (New York: Times Books, 1986), p. 11, and see p. xiii.

13. See Karl Marx and Frederick Engels, *The German Ideology, Parts 1 and 3*, ed. R. Pascal (New York: International Publishers, 1947); and Karl Marx, "On the Jewish Question," in *Writings of the Young Marx on Philosophy and Society*, ed. and trans. Kurt Guddat and Lloyd Easton (Garden City, N.Y.: Doubleday, Anchor Books, 1967). See also Ernesto Laclau, *Politics and Ideology in Marxist Theory* (London: Verso Press, 1977).

14. Michel Foucault, "Truth and Power," in *Power/Knowledge: Selected Interviews and Other Writings, 1972–1977*, ed. Colin Gordon, trans. Colin Gordon et al. (New York: Pantheon Books, 1980), p. 118.

do, connoting a more plural set of relations within language that recognizes their material and ideal content but standing outside Marxist epistemology.

Louis Althusser works in a similar direction, but from a starting point: inside Marxist epistemology. We can locate Althusser's conception of ideology somewhere uneasily between Marx and Foucault. Althusser assumes the materiality of ideology, meaning its relative independence: "Ideology is an objective social reality."[15] According to Paul Hirst, Althusser's advance has been "to treat ideology *as social relations*" rather than treating (reducing) "ideology to a *representation in thought of social* relations."[16] In this reading, ideology is not reduced to an independent realm of consciousness or ideas, nor is it viewed as a distorted representation of reality.[17] Belsey agrees with Hirst that Althusser has moved beyond the oppositions characteristic of the classic Marxist notion of ideology. For Althusser, according to Belsey, ideology is both true and false, "real [true] in that it is the way in which people really live their relationship to the social relations which govern their conditions of existence, but imaginary [false] in that it discourages a full understanding of these conditions of existence and the ways in which people are socially constituted within them" (*CP,* p. 57).

Althusser's treatment of ideology as systems of meanings that define people within imaginary relations to their real relations[18] entails a clearer demarcation between real and ideal than Foucault wants to assume. Stephen Resnick and Richard Wolff acknowledge this problem in Marxist epistemology when they discuss these realms as "concrete-real" (meaning the material realm) and "thought-concrete" (meaning the ideological realm).

Thinking is a process of change: changes in both the concrete-real and in thought-concretes. Thinking cannot, therefore, be conceived as *either* the cause or essence of the concrete-real *or,* on the other hand, as its effect. Rather . . . thinking is both a creative, active constitutive part of

15. Louis Althusser, *For Marx,* trans. Ben Brewster (London: Penguin Press, 1965), p. 12.
16. Paul Hirst, *On Law and Ideology* (London: Macmillan, 1979), p. 13.
17. See ibid., p. 23.
18. See Althusser, *For Marx,* pp. 152–54.

the concrete-real *and* a process overdetermined in and by the concrete-real.[19]

Discourse, with its pluralist epistemology, better represents the multiple meanings of the "real," of power/knowledge. There is no truth, there are only partial truths, which are explored through absence, omissions, contradictions, and gaps. Barry Hindess and Paul Hirst argue a similar point. In their perspective, the "real" is never fully separate from discourse.

The relation between discourse and its "objects" need not be represented in terms of both a distinction and a correlation between a realm of discourse and an independently existing realm of objects. . . . The entities in discourse must be referred to solely in and through the forms of discourse, theoretical, political, etc., in which they are constituted. . . . The question of the "reality of the external world" is not the issue[;] . . . the entities discourse refers to are constituted in it and by it.[20]

To sum up: there is no moment "outside" discourse—whereas there *is* an "outside" to ideology. This is the significant difference between the two philosophic traditions encompassed in the terms "ideology" and "discourse." The latter has a pluralist epistemology regarding the status of truth and the relations between language and power. This plurality has significance for what I understand to be a radical pluralist's understanding of the dispersed power relations of the state.

My conception of dispersed power differs from the liberal pluralist's notion, which assumes that equality underlines power relations. It also differs from Foucault's pluralism because I think concentrations of power remain within the dispersion. Our com-

19. Stephen Resnick and Richard Wolff, "Marxist Epistemology: The Critique of Economic Determinism," *Social Text* 2 (1982): 44. For several other interesting discussions of the problem of ideology, see Anthony Giddens, *A Contemporary Critique of Historical Materialism* (Berkeley and Los Angeles: Univ. of California Press, 1981), and *Profiles and Critiques in Social Theory* (Berkeley and Los Angeles: Univ. of California Press, 1982); and Douglas Kellner, "Ideology, Marxism, and Advanced Capitalism," *Socialist Review* 8 (November–December 1978): 37–67, and "T.V. Ideology and Emancipatory Popular Culture," *Socialist Review* 9 (May–June 1977): 13–54.

20. Barry Hindess and Paul Hirst, *Mode of Production and Social Formation: An Auto-Critique of Pre-Capitalist Modes of Production* (London: Macmillan, 1977), p. 20.

monsense experience of "a" state belies his analysis of mini-centers of power. My radical pluralist vision recognizes inequality in the hierarchical dispersion of power; the state is both pluralist and unified in its activity and its structuring of power. It is to this issue that I now turn: the way power is both a totality and a series of specificities—universal *and* specific, homogeneous *and* heterogeneous, stable *and* unstable, centered *and* decentered, concentrated *and* dispersed.

The "Decentered" State

When I use the term "dispersed," I mean that power has many centers, that it is sometimes disorganized and contradictory, that there is no set location from which power emanates.[21] This is not to say that there is not a state in which power is concentrated or that all power sites are equally significant.[22] Power need not be seen as a unified whole to be recognized as having concentrated sites that formulate hierarchical privilege. Nor does the awareness of power as a positive force negate its repressive, oppressive characteristics. We need, though, to focus on how power is both concentrated in its dispersion—how its multiple sites articulate a unity—and dispersed in its concentration—how sites of power are heterogeneous and contradictory.

Foucault is not clear on this issue. Sometimes he seems to be revising an approach that addresses only one side of the issue. At other times he seems to be articulating a completely dispersed and positive notion of power in which decentering reduces power to a series of "micro-practices."[23] On the view of power as a negative force, he writes,

Now I believe that this is a wholly negative, narrow, skeletal conception, . . . one which has been curiously widespread. If power were never any-

21. See Mark Poster, *Foucault, Marxism, and History: Mode of Production versus Mode of Information* (Cambridge: Polity Press, 1984), p. 104.

22. Foucault focuses on discontinuity rather than continuity and erases the state while doing so. For critiques of Foucault's overemphasis on "micro-practices," see David Couzens Hoy, ed., *Foucault: A Critical Reader* (Oxford: Blackwell, 1986); and Barry Smart, *Foucault, Marxism, and Critique* (Boston: Routledge & Kegan Paul, 1983).

23. See Barry Smart, "The Politics of Truth and the Problem of Hegemony," in Hoy, *Foucault: A Critical Reader*, pp. 160–63.

thing but repressive, if it never did anything but to say no, do you really think one would be brought to obey it? What makes power hold good, what makes it accepted, is simply the fact that it doesn't only weigh on us as a force that says no, but that it traverses and produces things, it induces pleasure, forms knowledge, produces discourse. It needs to be considered as a productive network which runs through the whole social body, much more than as a negative instance whose function is repression.[24]

Power is everywhere for Foucault, "not because it embraces everything, but because it comes from everywhere. . . . Power is not an institution, and not a structure; . . . it is the name that one attributes to a complex strategical situation in a particular society."[25] He argues that "power isn't localised in the State apparatus and that nothing in society will be changed if the mechanisms of power that function outside, below and alongside the State apparatuses, on a much more minute and everyday level, are not also changed."[26] There are also "technologies of power,"[27] which establish themselves outside the state.

In Foucault's view, politics as the activity of power is not singular. The family, the body, sexuality all constitute the relations of power, and there is no center to power.

The family . . . isn't the simple reflection, the extension of state power; the family isn't the state representative in respect of children, just as the male isn't the state representative in respect of the woman. For the state to function as it does, it is necessary that there be between the man and woman or the adult and child quite specific relations of domination, which have their own configuration and relative autonomy.[28]

The state is a site like any other, and other sites of power, such as the body, technology, knowledge, and so forth, do not mirror or represent state power. State power in its decentered form becomes another localized micro-site. "Power is in play in small individual parts."[29]

24. "Truth and Power," p. 119.
25. Foucault, *The History of Sexuality, Volume 1: An Introduction*, p. 93.
26. Michel Foucault, "Body/Power," in *Power/Knowledge*, p. 60.
27. Poster, *Foucault, Marxism, and History*, p. 104.
28. As Foucault stated in an interview by Lucette Finas, in *Michel Foucault: Power, Truth, Strategy*, pp. 70–71.
29. Ibid., p. 60.

Because of Foucault's preoccupation with the notion of dispersed power, he identifies his own thinking with a pluralist view. "I am a pluralist: the problem which I have set myself is that of the *individualization* of discourses" ("HDD," p. 226). Discourses are individualized in the sense that "there is an individualized discursive formation every time one can define a similar set of rules" ("HDD," pp. 227–28). Foucault is also occupied with trying to understand "clusters of relationships" rather than a unitary view. "Nothing, you see, is more foreign to me than the quest for a constraining sovereign and unique form" ("HDD," p. 229). He is much more interested in *dis*continuity than in continuity. "My problem is to substitute the analysis of *different* types *of transformation* for the abstract general and wearisome form of 'change' in which one so willingly thinks in terms of succession" ("HDD," p. 229). Instead of focusing on what he terms "weak continuities," Foucault chooses to emphasize the "intensity of difference."

The problem with this emphasis on disparate sites of power is that it privileges diversity, discontinuity, and difference while it silences unity, continuity, and similarity. If one looks for difference, that is what one finds. If one looks for discontinuity, one does not see continuity. We need instead a method that focuses on the relation between similarity and difference, unity and specificity, coherence and incoherence. There may not be *a* system of power, but there are systems of power—or a system of powers. Put another way, power may not be centered in *a* state, but it may be concentrated in a state defined by the relations of power that are dispersed. To say that there is *a* state is not necessarily to accept that power is located only there, or even centered there, or always dispersed from there, but it is to say that the relations of power are sometimes concentrated there, even if in contradictory and conflictual ways.

Anyone looking at the Reagan administration has to recognize that power is neither unitary nor coherent, yet state power does exist, and its relations are differentiated and complex. A picture of state power that includes prisons, madhouses, hospitals, and such as sites that are not on the periphery allows us to view (state) power as a vast continuum. But having deconstructed the dispersions of the state and its power(s), we need to reconstruct the hierarchical relationships within power. After all, the male body takes its engendered privilege with it to particular sites; the privilege is not uniquely and independently constituted in each instance. There is an aspect of continuity through the locations.

I believe that Foucault's focus on micro-practices carries deconstruction too far. It leaves us with the disconnections of power, but there are connections between sites of power, even if no center exists. A reductionism that makes politics—as the activity of powers—equivalent to the state should not be replaced by a reductionism that substitutes the heterogeneity and differences of micro-practices for the unity or unities and continuity or continuities of power. I criticize Foucault not for decentering the state but for not reconnecting the dispersions he illuminates to the hierarchical system(s) of power(s) represented through the discourses of the state. Without some notion of unity and centrality, we cannot conceptualize hierarchy or the inequality of difference(s).

I disagree with Michael Walzer's statement that Foucault does not believe in a ruling class. Rather it seems to me that Foucault's method keeps us from seeing, or recognizing, what we might want to do with the state.[30] A more generous interpretation might be that Foucault rejects a "state conception of politics" and thereby improves existing discussions of power.[31] That interpretation is fine, but the unity or unities of power can be recognized without reducing power to a center.

This fuller notion of politics, which recognizes the extrastate dimensions of power, must, however, take the state into account. As I have written elsewhere, "The relations of the state reflect and construct the relations of power in society and yet the state does not fully uncover the entirety of power relations themselves. The state, rather, condenses the relations of power in society."[32] It does so largely through discourse. The state establishes a context in which the relations of power operate. In other words, power is located in and through multiple sites, but these sites exist *in relation to a state*, which helps to establish the multiple discourses

30. Michael Walzer, "The Politics of Michel Foucault," in Hoy, *Foucault: A Critical Reader,* p. 63.

31. Samuel Bowles and Herbert Gintis, *Democracy and Capitalism: Property, Community, and the Contradictions of Modern Social Thought* (New York: Basic Books, 1986), pp. 23–24.

32. Zillah Eisenstein, *Feminism and Sexual Equality: Crisis in Liberal America* (New York: Monthly Review Press, 1984), p. 90.

about power. Liberal and Marxist discourse are the most important concerning this point because they locate and center power in the state. On this level of discourse, if on no other, there is a relationship between the unity of state power and its dispersions.

To the extent that laws and the law operate as authorized discourses for the state, we must examine how powers within the state articulate differing and conflicting views of sex equality and sexual "difference." Focusing on law(s), we see a dispersed, heterogeneous expression of power relations that is related to state activity yet does not necessarily center power within the state. We see the multiplicity of expressions of power—plural views of a hierarchical system. Not only is there pluralism within the law but there are plural views of a hierarchical system that privileges the phallus in specifically classist and racist ways. Further, there are multiple interpretations of various hierarchical forms. Because of the unity in the hierarchy—in the privilege—it is not sufficient to examine only the specificity. Laws and the law operate in a heterogeneous viewing of engendered "difference"; the phallus expresses unity in its dispersion.

I therefore focus on the discourse of liberal law and the sexual discourses subsumed in it. How does law—as an authorized language of the state—manifest the (oppositional) differences that constitute and construct language: man/woman; nature/culture; rational/irrational; same/different? In what sense is law engendered through these constructions of "difference," which are considered to be one and the same as biological fact? The discourse regarding law—its objectivity, its neutrality, its fairness—is constructed through political discourses concerning sex and gender premised on the duality of man/woman. Therefore, the sexual politics of liberal law(s) is presented as though it were neutral, and thinking about the law as though it were objective and fair allows this presentation. The sexual discourses in law constitute and construct the problem of "difference" for a theory of sex equality because the phallus is privileged along with the patriarchal structure of meaning itself.

Let me clarify my terms. Patriarchy is the process of differentiating women from men while privileging men.[33] It is the process

33. See Zillah Eisenstein, *The Radical Future of Liberal Feminism*, North-

of transforming (biological) females into women and males into men. Sex "difference" becomes the engendered differentiation of sex. We are no longer in the realm of nature but somewhere between culture and nature. The term "patriarchy" connotes the social, historical, and economic relations of power in society that create and reflect gendered inequality. I differentiate patriarchal social relations from the rule of the phallus, or what is termed "phallocratic discourse,"[34] because I want to distinguish—though not sever—the realm of language, signs, and symbols from the structural and institutional meaning of engendered "difference." For my discussion, the phallus is the symbolic guarantor of significance, which privileges the male body. It pits the penis against the pregnant body. "Phallocratic" describes the male-oriented symbolization of biological difference. The phallus misrepresents the relationships between biology and culture and sex and gender. It constructs and represents the dominant discourse through a male viewing.

There is a problem with this discussion. The realm of phallocratic language (often assumed to constitute the "ideal" realm) is not separate from the political and economic structural relations of patriarchy (assumed to be the "real"). Patriarchal social relations are in part signs themselves; they are how we name them and know them. Nevertheless, the symbols (re)presenting power are not the same as the relations of power; they are only a partial expression of power, as the societal relations of power are only a partial (re)presentation of the politics of the phallus. By distinguishing between patriarchy and phallocratic discourse, I mean to recognize the incompleteness of each term; the problem is that I rest uneasily somewhere *in between* them.

Law occupies this in-between space. It constructs and mirrors patriarchal social relations through its phallocratic interpretations

---

eastern Series in Feminist Theory, vol. 3 (Boston: Northeastern Univ. Press, 1981), esp. ch. 2.

34. See Jacques Lacan and the *école freudienne, Feminine Sexuality,* ed. Juliet Mitchell and Jacqueline Rose, trans. Jacqueline Rose (New York: Pantheon Books, 1982); Jacques Lacan, *Speech and Language in Psychoanalysis,* trans. Anthony Wilden (Baltimore: Johns Hopkins Univ. Press, 1968); Elaine Marks and Isabelle de Courtivron, eds., *New French Feminisms: An Anthology* (Amherst: Univ. of Massachusetts Press, 1980).

of truth, but there is no one interpretation through the law. The law names reality at the same time that it mystifies reality; males and females are not biologically the same, yet they are not as different as the law assumes. Men and women are not the same, given nature and culture, yet they are not as different as the law makes them seem. Sex and gender are not as similar as the law assumes, yet they are connected.

Language and the "Real"

If my starting point is a vision of reality that is defined through language, then it challenges the conventional notion of an objective reality. This doesn't mean that my view of reality is "merely" subjective but rather that it is neither subjective nor objective. (Foucault might say that everything is already interpretation and that there are plural interpretations of any moment.) Belsey makes clear that this perspective does not necessarily consider subjectivity a problem. "In reality, we all participate in a range of discourses—political, literary, scientific, and so on—and these are 'subjective' only to the extent that they—and the contradictions and collisions between them—construct our world of meaning and experience" (*CP*, p. 54). Such a view dislocates notions of objective reality, truth, and falsity. It calls into question the idea that anyone can ever completely know what is true because we know only through the discourses we live. To focus on reality as a series of discourses is to recognize that meaning is open rather than closed, that truth may have multiple meanings and is often shifting in meaning, that there is probably no place outside discourse, and that the term "discourse" exists *within* a theory of knowledge and power that gives it its meaning *in* a particular discourse.

To say there is no truth, no objective reality, is to argue that there are truths; "truth is already itself power"[35] because it is an interpretation that has been accepted as true. We view truth not as objective but rather as a part of a discourse concerning power and specific historical relations. "The political question, in short, is not error, illusion, alienated consciousness or ideology; it is truth itself."[36] Hence, in this view truth is no longer self-justifying. Ac-

35. "Truth and Power," p. 47.
36. Ibid.

cording to Foucault, we need to detach "the power of truth from the forms of hegemony, social, economic and cultural, within which it operates at the present time."[37] He goes a step too far, though, when he argues: "The problem is not changing people's consciousness—or what's in their heads—but the political, economic, institutional regime of the production of truth."[38]

Without privileging truth, or reality, as self-justificatory (because of their objective status), we are left with making arguments in behalf of our interpretation. To do so, however, is not to slide into pure subjectivity or "the conundrum of 'relativism.'"[39] Once objectivity loses its privileged status, the critic's criticism finds new open space. As Mary Jacobus states, we can have more confidence in the critic's statements than in the statements being criticized. The feminist critic's "criticism remains imbricated within the forms of intelligibility . . . against which it pushes. . . . But surely, the direction from which that criticism comes—the elsewhere that it invokes, the putting in question of our social organization of gender" is a better place.[40] Or as Linda Gordon puts it,

It is wrong to conclude, as some have, that because there may be no objective truth possible, there are no objective lies. There may be no objective canons of historiography, but there are degrees of accuracy; there are better and worse pieces of history. The challenge is precisely to maintain this tension between accuracy and mythic power.[41]

It is only within a standpoint that privileges objectivity and absolutes that relativism and pluralism present a problem. Plurality does not mean that all truths are equal; it merely uncovers the role of power in defining truth. Once truth has been defined, we are free to argue in behalf of our interpretation, but we cannot use the claim to truth itself as our defense. Although I assume that knowl-

37. Ibid.
38. Ibid. And see Foucault, *Discipline and Punish: The Birth of the Prison*, trans. Alan Sheridan (New York: Vintage Books, 1979).
39. See Roger Krohn, "Scientific Ideology and Scientific Process: The Natural History of a Conceptual Shift," in *The Social Production of Scientific Knowledge*, ed. E. Mendelsohn, P. Weingart, and R. Whitley (Boston: Reidel, 1977), p. 75.
40. Mary Jacobus, "Feminist Readings," in Mary Jacobus, *Reading Woman: Essays in Feminist Criticism* (New York: Columbia Univ. Press, 1986), p. 66.
41. Linda Gordon, "What's New in Women's History?" in *Feminist Studies, Critical Studies*, ed. Teresa de Lauretis (Bloomington: Indiana Univ. Press, 1986), p. 22.

edge (and truth) is plural, I do not allow this assumption to keep
me from arguing that society must be organized around a notion of
sex equality that recognizes the specificity of the pregnant body
from a standpoint of radical pluralism. The assumption of plurality
does, though, keep me from bringing closure to the meaning of the
pregnant body in terms of the meaning of sameness or difference
or equality. We must leave meanings open at the same time that
we act on them.

I recognize that no theory is complete. As Thomas Kuhn has
argued, "Any description must be partial." This incompleteness of
knowledge underlines my discussion of sex equality. "To be accepted as a paradigm, a theory must seem better than its competi-
tors, but it need not, and in fact never does, explain all the facts
with which it can be confronted."[42] Once again, this awareness
need not leave us paralyzed, as some critics of deconstruction and
the Critical Legal Studies movement would have it. The critics ask,
"If we not only don't know how to get there from here, but also
don't know where 'there' is[,] doesn't it follow that we should stay
here until more information comes along?"[43] Not necessarily.

If we recognize the changing nature of knowledge, discourse,
and politics, we operate politically but self-critically. Deconstruction in this sense can lay the basis for a radical democratic and
feminist politics based in the open-texturedness of new under-
standings of power. It recognizes that knowledge does not always
bring closure—and knowledge includes science, because even science is not fixed or complete. I write "even" science, because science is used to represent the very conception of objectivity that
defines the realm of the real and the natural in all aspects of social
life.

Subjectivity, Knowledge,
and Science

Not just the scientist but science itself is subjective—and objectivity gives subjectivity its meaning. To challenge one is to question

42. Thomas S. Kuhn, *The Structure of Scientific Revolutions* (Chicago: Univ.
of Chicago Press, 1962), pp. 16, 17–18; all further references to this work, abbreviated as *SSR*, will be included in the text. See also the enlarged second edition,
1970.

43. Phillip E. Johnson, "Do You Sincerely Want to Be Radical?" *Stanford Law
Review: Critical Legal Studies Symposium* 36 (January 1984): 282.

the other. According to Ruth Bleier, science is a "system of cognitive production"[44] that constitutes a plurality of socially constructed ways of comprehending natural and social phenomena. In other words, "Science is a cultural institution."[45] Everett Mendelsohn writes,

Science is an activity of human beings acting and interacting, thus a social activity. Its knowledge, its statements, its techniques, have been created by human beings and developed, nurtured and shared among groups of human beings. Scientific knowledge is therefore fundamentally social knowledge. As a social activity, science is clearly a product of a history and of processes which occurred in time and place and involved human actors.[46]

In this meaning, science is *not* about the study of objective reality comprising finite facts; it is constituted in and through visions of knowledge. Donna Haraway emphasizes this point. For her, there are no facts, no raw data. "All facts are laden with theory and thus with value and history."[47] All facts involve theory, all theories involve values, and all values reflect a history.

A great deal stands or falls with this conception of the social, historical, and theoretical notion of science, because if *science* is not objective and cannot establish givens as truth, what can? For the most part, in present society science "is the most respectable legitimator of new realities."[48] Science helps establish how people think about what is real, what they consider fact, what is knowable.

44. Ruth Bleier, "Biology and Women's Policy: A View from the Biological Sciences," in *Women, Biology, and Public Policy*, ed. Virginia Sapiro (Beverly Hills, Calif.: Sage Publications, 1985), pp. 19–20.

45. Ruth Bleier, "Social and Political Bias in Science: An Examination of Animal Studies and Their Generalizations to Human Behavior and Evolution," in *Genes and Gender II: Pitfalls in Research on Sex and Gender,* ed. Ruth Hubbard and Marian Lowe (New York: Gordian Press, 1979), p. 49.

46. Everett Mendelsohn, "The Social Construction of Scientific Knowledge," in Mendelsohn, Weingart, and Whitley, *The Social Production of Scientific Knowledge,* p. 4.

47. Donna Haraway, "In the Beginning Was the Word: The Genesis of Biological Theory," *Signs: Journal of Women in Culture and Society* 6 (Spring 1981): 477; all further references to this work, abbreviated as "IBWW," will be included in the text. See also her "Animal Sociology and a Natural Economy of the Body Politic, Part I: A Political Physiology of Dominance," and "Animal Sociology and a Natural Economy of the Body Politic, Part II: The Past Is the Contested Zone: Human Nature and Theories of Production and Reproduction in Primate Behavior Studies," *Signs* 4 (Autumn 1978): 21–36, 37–60.

48. Hubbard, "Have Only Men Evolved?" p. 9.

And we shall see that the articulation of law as a whole assumes the "scientific" stance of objectivity or knowable "reality" when legislating issues are tied to the so-called biology of gender "difference."

Kuhn's writings have cracked the image of scientific objectivity. He argues that normal science is by and large conservative and protective of established paradigms of thought, that it often operates to suppress "fundamental novelties because they are necessarily subversive of its basic commitments." Not only are new kinds of phenomena often greeted with hostility but they are often simply not seen—silenced altogether (*SSR*, p. 5; and see p. 24). Not until the theoretical and subjective aspects of science are recognized can we hope to create a more balanced view of reality: theory and empirical data need to be carefully explored together. "Thus all science is dialectical and positive, both a process of argument in counter-concepts and images, and one of purposive experience and observation. The dialectic by itself is a recipe for persistent error, and empiricism by itself is directionless and a-theoretical."[49]

The process by which science represents and produces meaning is translated and transmitted through language; science's vision of reality is partially constituted through and in language. "Scientific knowledge, like language, is intrinsically the common property of a group or else nothing at all" (*SSR* [1970], p. 210). Language is embedded in reality and reality in language. There is no objective science as such—only discourses that create science and scientific methods. "Language *generates* reality in the inescapable context of power; it does not *stand for* or *point to* a knowable world hiding somewhere outside the ever-receding boundaries of particular social-historical inquiries" ("IBWW," p. 479).

We need a rethinking of objectivity and subjectivity and what they might mean in the context that discourse partially constitutes the "real." As long as objectivity remains a privileged standpoint, subjectivity will continue as a suspect category for science, for law, for the social sciences.[50] Subjectivity *lacks* objectivity—as women supposedly *lack* the rationality of men—therefore, subjectivity is seen as a problem.[51] Do we therefore need to move outside the

---

49. Krohn, "Scientific Ideology and Scientific Process," p. 96.
50. See Sandra Harding, *The Science Question in Feminism* (Ithaca, N.Y.: Cornell Univ. Press, 1986), p. 249.
51. See Margrit Eichler, *The Double Standard: A Feminist Critique of Femi-*

existing epistemological assumptions about an objective reality and its subjective opposition? Donna Haraway poses the question for feminists clearly.

> Would a feminist epistemology informing scientific inquiry be a family member to existing theories of representation and philosophical realism? Or should feminists adopt a radical form of epistemology that denies the possibility of access to a real world and an objective standpoint? Would feminist standards of knowledge genuinely end the dilemma of the cleavage between subject and object or between non-invasive knowing and prediction and control?
>
> ("IBWW," p. 470)

I think we need to reject a notion of objectivity that privileges itself and makes subjectivity a problem. We need a method that can elucidate the relation between these realms and reconstitute their meaning while challenging their oppositional definition.

Science and its methods present a vision of reality that is already "structured by expressions of gender."[52] Science exists in discourses that are differentiated by sex. Anne Fausto-Sterling makes this point nicely. "Scientists who deny their politics—who claim to be objective and unemotional about gender while living in a world where even boats and automobiles are identified by sex—are fooling both themselves and the public at large." She argues that our sense of self as male or female is one of the more personally significant ways we understand our identity. Therefore, scientists should articulate how "they *feel* deep down in their guts about the complex of personal and social issues that relate to their area of research." Then the reader can view scientific research data in the context in which the scientist has articulated it and can look for any undetected blind spots. The problem, however, is that the scientific method belies such a standpoint. "To be scientific is to be

nist Social Science (New York: St. Martin's Press, 1980); and Sandra Harding and Merill B. Hintikka, eds., *Discovering Reality: Feminist Perspectives on Epistemology, Metaphysics, Methodology, and Philosophy of Science* (London: Reidel, 1983).

52. Harding, *The Science Question in Feminism,* p. 57. And see Elizabeth Fee, "Women's Nature and Scientific Objectivity," in *Woman's Nature: Rationalizations of Inequality,* ed. Marian Lowe and Ruth Hubbard (New York: Pergamon Press, 1983), pp. 9–28; and Evelyn Fox Keller, "Feminism and Science," *Signs* 7 (Spring 1982): 589–602.

unsentimental, rational, straight thinking, correct, rigorous, exact."[53] Gut feelings and blind spots supposedly stand outside the methods of science and its presentation of the "real."

The realm of science, the realm of the "real," is supposed to depict—to make sense—of nature. Once again, however, the problem is that the depiction of nature is already engendered: nature is seen as feminine. The woman represents nature; she is unruly and needs to be controlled and ordered. Reason, which is represented in and through man, must be established through the scientific method, or by law, as I will argue later. Further, nature is seen as a mother: Mother Nature. The supposedly unruly sexuality of woman is transformed into the guise of nurturing mother, and then woman and nature are both tamed.[54]

The scientific revolution and the *law* of nature, depicted as reason, triumph. The phallus triumphs as well because science and reason are engendered: they are seen as masculine. In the discourses of Western political philosophy, for Aristotle or Rousseau, for instance, the man of reason is male.[55] The rational soul is male,

53. Anne Fausto-Sterling, *Myths of Gender: Biological Theories about Men and Women* (New York: Basic Books, 1985), pp. 12, 10, 8; all further references to this work, abbreviated as *MG*, will be included in the text. I believe this skepticism in viewing science and the recognition of knowledge/reality as continuous, organic, and fluid are themselves a specific discourse, which arises under particular conditions. An important question, which lies beyond the scope of this discussion, is why and how a discursive rupture happens when it does. See Harding and Hintikka, *Discovering Reality,* for some beginning thoughts on this point.

54. For discussions of the issue of women and "nature," see Genevieve Lloyd, *The Man of Reason: "Male" and "Female" in Western Philosophy* (Minneapolis: Univ. of Minnesota Press, 1984); Carol McMillan, *Women, Reason, and Nature* (Princeton, N.J.: Princeton Univ. Press, 1982); Carolyn Merchant, *The Death of Nature: Women, Ecology, and the Scientific Revolution* (New York: Harper & Row, 1980); Martha Lee Osbourne, ed., *Woman in Western Thought* (New York: Random House, 1979); Susan Moller Okin, *Women in Western Political Thought* (Princeton, N.J.: Princeton Univ. Press, 1979); Julia Sherman and Evelyn Torton Beck, eds., *The Prism of Sex: Essays in the Sociology of Knowledge* (Madison: Univ. of Wisconsin Press, 1979); and Mary Vetterling-Braggin, Frederick Elliston, and Jane English, eds., *Feminism and Philosophy* (Totowa, N.J.: Rowman & Littlefield, 1981).

55. See Lloyd, *The Man of Reason,* p. ix. See also Jean Bethke Elshtain, *Meditations on Modern Political Thought: Masculine/Feminine Themes from Luther to Arendt* (New York: Praeger, 1986); Alison M. Jaggar, *Feminist Politics and Human Nature* (Sussex: Harvester Press, 1983); and Arlene Saxonhouse, *Women in the History of Political Thought: Ancient Greece to Machiavelli* (New York: Praeger, 1985).

and the follies of the body are female; the mind needs to dominate the body. The language of political philosophy assumes a sexual politics that privileges man.[56] Its starting point is nature itself, seen as a text authored by men (see "IBWW," p. 471). It is also therefore discourse constructed in and through the relations of power.

The scientific method with its standpoint of objectivity establishes the study of biology as the science of *the* body. According to it, the only thing more natural than nature is the body. The body connotes a definite, concrete, finite thing. Its meaning and contours are given and static. The body stands outside society, history, and language. The problem here, however, is that there is no such place as outside, even for the body. According to Thomas Laqueur, there is no "natural" way of representing the body. Although the body is treated as an objective thing, "cultural concerns have free license here, however embedded they may be in the language of science."[57]

A viewing of the body as a capacity rather than a static entity is key to the argument of this book. For now, though, I want to keep these questions about the body unresolved: To what extent is there such a thing as *the* body, or more specifically, the pregnant body? If there is no place *outside* discourse, how can one establish its meaning? Is the body completely a construction *in* discourse, with no *outside*? Is the body sexed? Gendered? A mix? The problem with the scientific method is that it rarely allows these kinds of questions to be formulated. If the objective standpoint is taken as a given, then there is no problem to be understood, because the body is treated as an established fact, disconnected from discourse.

According to Fausto-Sterling, it is impossible to answer, even in theory, the question of what aspect of biology is socially based. "Unanswerable questions drop out of the realm of science altogether" (*MG*, p. 8). Nevertheless, the question has been asked. We still want to know what the reconstituted contours of the "real"

56. See Elizabeth Spelman, "Aristotle and the Politicization of the Soul," in Harding and Hintikka, *Discovering Reality*, pp. 17–30. See also Jean Bethke Elshtain, *Public Man, Private Woman: Women in Social and Political Thought* (Princeton, N.J.: Princeton Univ. Press, 1981).

57. Thomas Laqueur, "Orgasm, Generation, and the Politics of Reproductive Biology," *Representations* no. 14 (Spring 1986), p. 35. And see Susan Rubin Suleiman, ed., *The Female Body in Western Culture: Contemporary Perspectives* (Cambridge, Mass.: Harvard Univ. Press, 1986).

might be as we come to recognize the politics of a gendered discourse. "It is difficult to resist the urge to ask, 'But what, *underneath it all*, really *are* the differences between men and women.' *What we must begin to give voice to as scientists and feminists is that there is no such thing, or place, as underneath it all.*"[58] If the body or its correlate notion of sex "difference" is unknowable from an objective standpoint, then the epistemological foundation of science and knowledge shifts to a place where knowledge is open-textured and not closed, where the pregnant body is constituted in and through the language of gender.

A number of scientists have tried to locate this realm.[59] Kuhn helps to do so, although he never specifies the issue of gender, when he states, "There is, I think, no theory-independent way to reconstruct phrases like 'really there'; the notion of a match between the ontology of a theory and its 'real' counterpart in nature now seems to me illusive in principle" (*SRR* [1970], p. 206). Stephen Jay Gould makes the related point of the openness of the "real" in his discussion of the issue of personhood in relation to Siamese twins.

We inhabit a complex world. Some boundaries are sharp and permit clean and definite distinctions. But nature also includes continua that cannot be neatly parceled into two piles of unambiguous yeses and noes. Biologists have rejected, as fatally flawed in principle, all attempts by anti abortionists to define an unambiguous "beginning of life," because we know so well that the sequence from ovulation or spermatogenesis to birth is an unbreakable continuum—and surely no one will define masturbation as murder. . . . Ritta and Christina [the Siamese twins] lay in the middle of another unbreakable continuum. They are in part two and in part one.[60]

58. Susan Leigh Star, "Sex Differences and the Dichotomization of the Brain: Methods, Limits, and Problems in Research on Consciousness," in *Genes and Gender*, p. 116.

59. See, especially, Lynda Birke, *Women, Feminism, and Biology* (New York: Methuen, 1986); Ruth Bleier, *Science and Gender: A Critique of Biology and Its Theories on Women* (New York: Pergamon Press, 1984); Henifin and Fried, *Women Look at Biology Looking at Women;* Evelyn Fox Keller, *Reflections on Gender and Science* (New Haven, Conn.: Yale Univ. Press, 1985); Marian Lowe and Ruth Hubbard, eds., *Woman's Nature: Rationalizations of Inequality* (New York: Pergamon Press, 1983); and Fausto-Sterling, *Myths of Gender.*

60. Stephen Jay Gould, *The Flamingo's Smile: Reflections in Natural History* (New York: Norton, 1985), p. 76; all further references to this work, abbreviated

Instead of viewing what is knowable as divisible into dichotomous or containable parts, Gould constructs a continuum that does not necessarily bring closure. Likewise, Alfred Kinsey, who was a tax-onomist of wasps before he became a sex researcher, focuses on the primacy of variation and diversity. "It is a fundamental of taxonomy that nature rarely deals with discrete categories. Only the human mind invents categories and tries to force facts into separate pigeon-holes. The living world is a continuum in each and every one of its aspects" (qtd. in *FS*, p. 164).

What is important about Kinsey's statement is that he not only sees the diversity of the "natural" realm but recognizes that categories are created by the human mind. The categories become "real" to the extent that we confront diversity through divisions that presume unity. I think, therefore, that we must recognize both the unity—the concept of the "body"—and the diversity—actual bodies—as they exist. Of course, it is necessary not to over-state either the differences or the unity. For example, we must recognize simultaneously both the category of engendered sex "dif-ference" as it exists between men and women and differences among women and among men. "Difference" rooted in duality that is the homogenizing of women *as* different from men exists as a dominant discourse and is therefore both true and false. "True," in this instance, is quite different from "a truth." Males and females are a mix of differences and similarities, and not all differences apply to each individual. In this case, difference means plurality and heterogeneity.

A Methodology of Difference(s)

We need to recognize that differences exist within and between the sexes. There are a variety of kinds of female bodies: thin, fat, small-breasted, large-breasted, muscular, flabby, and so forth. These differences exist within other differences as well: sexual

---

as *FS*, will be included in the text. There is a necessary tension in this statement between the idea of a continuum and possible "clear" and "sharp" points on or in the continuum. See Gould, *The Panda's Thumb: More Reflections in Natural History* (New York: Norton, 1980), and *Hen's Teeth and Horse's Toes: Further Reflections in Natural History* (New York: Norton, 1983).

preference, economic class, race, age, and so on. Age has a specifically gendered meaning, given women's life cycle and its relation to pregnancy. Individuated experiences are a part of women's lives. Recognizing the multiple and diverse meanings of difference in these instances is quite distinct from recognizing engendered "difference" per se. The first viewing focuses on differences as diversity, acknowledging the differences among women and between women and men. The second focuses on "difference" as homogeneity, meaning women are different, all in the same way, from men. Focusing on the mix of differences that establish individuals' lives allows us to celebrate difference rather than view it as a problem because it makes one *not* the same as something else.

We can focus on "difference" as an institution, as is done in research on sex "difference." This viewing flattens out the meaning of individual diversity. Ruth Hubbard has argued that if one sets out in research to find sex "difference," one will find it. Hubbard and Marian Lowe state that "it is a central methodological question whether *any* valid results can come of work that sets about deliberately to look for sex differences." They argue that it is dangerous to "try to prove the existence of differences by looking for them."[61] The focus on differences distorts the reality of similarity. Men and women are much more similar than they are different.

Luce Irigaray argues that the concern with sex "difference" leads to an unconcern about the specificity of differences. Women are treated as like men—or not like men—but not specifically as women. She argues that it makes no sense to ask the question What is woman? Instead, we need to see how "the feminine finds itself defined as lack, deficiency or as imitation and negative image of the subject."[62] Men are privileged by presenting themselves as nondifferent. Women are generalized in terms of their "difference" and therefore lose their individual specificity. "And . . . it is worthy of respect because it is the gender of the *general* and to be masculine is to be both general and specific at the same time (the dream of all those who are only 'specific' and remain so)."[63] Women are

61. Ruth Hubbard and Marian Lowe, Introduction to *Genes and Gender*, pp. 28, 29.

62. Luce Irigaray, *This Sex Which Is Not One*, trans. Catherine Porter, with Carolyn Burke (Ithaca, N.Y.: Cornell Univ. Press, 1985), p. 78.

63. Colette Guillaumin, "The Masculine: Denotations/Connotations," *Feminist Issues* 5 (Spring 1985): 65.

abnormal as in menopause or menstruation. Men are normal—as defined by the male body.

This problem of the male standard is not inherent, either in the method or in the concept of differences. Foucault and Gould, albeit in very dissimilar ways, focus on differences to understand better reality and its relations of power. But they concentrate on explicating the multiple views of variety and diversity—on developing a radical pluralism. This viewing of difference challenges a silent referent. Differences are positive. They are only a problem when a particular standard that denies the pluralism is privileged. Evelyn Fox Keller believes that the focus on difference per se is what enriched the work of scientist Barbara McClintock.

Making difference understandable does not mean making it disappear . . . an understanding of nature can come to rest with difference. 'Exceptions' are not there to 'prove the rule'; they have meaning in and of themselves. In this respect, difference constitutes a principle of ordering the world radically unlike the principle of division, of dichotomization (subject-object, mind-matter, feeling-reason, disorder-law). . . . Respect for difference remains content with multiplicity as end in itself.

If one's method and focus assume that diversity is part of nature, then one can recognize variety rather than separateness through difference as the basis for order. One's vision of the world is then not falsely ordered, but it is also not chaotic. "In this world of difference, division is relinquished without generating chaos."[64]

Lowe and Hubbard further specify this method for the sciences. "We need to understand more about the different capacities of different people in different environments, rather than about the averaged, abstracted capacities of groups of people in some imaginary homogenized reconstruction of contemporary [W]estern societies."[65] Elaine Showalter articulates this method of viewing difference(s) for the literary critic. Feminist critics imagined a space

in which gender would lose its power in which all texts would be sexless and equal, like angels. But the more precisely we understand the specificity of women's writing not as a transient by-product of sexism but as a fundamental and continually determining reality, the more clearly we realize that we have misperceived our destination. We may never reach the

64. Keller, *Reflections on Gender and Science*, pp. 163, 165.
65. Ruth Hubbard and Marian Lowe, Conclusion to *Genes and Gender*, p. 151.

promised land at all; for when feminist critics see our task as the study of women's writing, we realize that the land promised to us is not the serenely undifferentiated universality of texts but the tumultuous and intriguing wilderness of difference itself.[66]

Instead of undifferentiated universality, the feminist critic will encounter the richness of multiple differences in the text. The meanings of our difference(s) are open, and we need to be careful not to homogenize or essentialize them. The essentialist definition demands an underlying similar essence,[67] whereas our diversity does not.

There is an uneasy tension between diversity and similarity that should not be denied. To understand differences, we must utilize a method that will allow a variety of meanings. We must look for the "multiple blurrings" of sex lines, not in order to deny that difference exists but rather "to redraw and mix up the lines of difference."[68] Anyone who believes in the genetic uniqueness of the individual cannot believe that any two individuals are the same or *different in the same way.* If each person's brain has at least no less, if not more, physical individuality than a person's fingerprints, then differences of the brain cannot be considered a metaphor for the "difference" of sex (see *MG*, p. 60).

Questioning and even rejecting the homogenized notion of sex differences is quite different from rejecting the significance of differences in its individualized and uninstitutionalized meaning. As Mary Jacobus has argued, we need to put "the institution of difference in question without erasing the question of difference itself." Instead of seeing gender identity in terms of some fixed meaning, we must see "femininity" as "disclosing" and "discomposing" its own meaning, "endlessly displacing the fixity of gender identity by the play of difference and division which simultaneously creates and uncreates gender, identity, and meaning."[69]

The problem remains that although the pluralist method of viewing differences appreciates diversity, interconnections, and

66. Elaine Showalter, "Feminist Criticism in the Wilderness," in Showalter, *The New Feminist Criticism,* pp. 266–67.

67. See Ernst Mayr, *The Growth of Biological Thought: Diversity, Evolution, and Inheritance* (Cambridge, Mass.: Harvard Univ. Press, 1982), p. 256.

68. Susan Rubin Suleiman, Introduction to *The Female Body in Western Culture,* p. 4.

69. Mary Jacobus, "Reading Woman (Reading)," in Jacobus, *Reading Woman,* p. 24.

continua, it operates alongside, and sometimes within, the more privileged scientific and legal discourses that posit the notion of "difference" from a standpoint of opposition and dichotomy.[70] "Difference" framed as a duality attempts to make things clear-cut, much as the determinations in a court of law are supposed to be, as we shall see. Subtlety, ambiguity, and relatedness are denied, and in the process differences become inequalities.

A methodology of difference(s) focusing on diversity views differences as positive. I have used this radical pluralist methodology to critique the dualistic standpoint of engendered "difference," which denies variety and applauds homogeneity. It is important, however, not to overstate the heterogeneity of differences to the point of silencing the similarities and unities that exist. By being focused on the diversity of differences, we can easily overlook continuity. We must therefore seek the unities as well as the diversity in difference(s). We need to examine and understand "different similarities" and "similar differences."

Sex and gender differences exist, but their significance must remain open-textured while we try to sort through a meaningful notion of equality that does not preclude differences and is not simply based in sameness. We need to work from a position on differences that presumes a radical pluralism while it recognizes the power of discourse that establishes (already) engendered unities. Women differ among themselves, and they are also similarly different.

Let us turn to this one last issue of method—unity, or continuity. It is often assumed that those who adopt a deconstructionist mode of interpretation are left, much as Foucault is, with a focus on difference, discontinuity, and specificity. I have argued that Foucault's refocusing to (re)direct us to a concern with difference allows for a radical rethinking of power. I have cautioned, though, against a new reductionism to the "micro" level. We must recognize the importance of continuity for developing a theory of pluralism and difference. This is very much true of the issue of sex class.[71]

---

70. See Sander Gilman, *Difference and Pathology: Stereotypes of Sexuality, Race, and Madness* (Ithaca, N.Y.: Cornell Univ. Press, 1985). See also Stephen Jay Gould, "Cardboard Darwinism," *New York Review of Books* 33 (25 September 1986): 50–51.

71. My definition of sex class moves beyond the original radical feminist conception as developed by Shulamith Firestone, *The Dialectic of Sex* (New York: Bantam Books, 1970). See Eisenstein, *Feminism and Sexual Equality*, esp. ch. 6.

First, sex class focuses on the relations of power in society in a nonreductionist fashion. The sex-class structure is found both inside and at multiple sites outside the state; it is a theory of power that does not center the state. In the more popular and feminist phrasing, this view recognizes that the personal is the political. The sex-class structure of society cannot, however, be understood outside its relation to its state formulation(s). Second, sex class focuses on the reality that all women constitute a class, differentiated from men; at the same time, it recognizes that the "universalized" woman of the construct "sex class" must be specified in terms of her particularity, whether that be her color, her economic class, her sexual preference, or her individuality.

Sex Class as a Heterogeneous Unity

The importance of a method that makes difference (meaning diversity) rather than similarity (unity) its starting point is that it allows for a radical pluralism. It permits us to examine difference or individuality or uniqueness rather than similarity to some silent standard that privileges those closest to itself. The problem here, though, is that a focus on difference can also silence important similarities and connections. I therefore argue for a method that takes *both* specificity and unity (meaning homogeneity) as its starting point. By specifying any particular site of power, we can check ourselves against some silent abstract universalism—such as the white man—and instead try to develop a more specified universality—such as black women. As Ann Scales has said, "Concrete universalism takes differences to be constitutive of the universal itself."[72] This mix of concrete and universal dislocates the abstract standard. Instead we have to attempt to diversify the unity while rejecting a homogeneous viewing.

We must be committed to exploring the relationship between unity and specificity, coherence and heterogeneity, sameness and difference. The difficulty is that these concerns can be contradictory; it is hard not to overstate unity and to recognize particularity while looking for similarity. Nevertheless, I think we have to focus in between the poles in the hope of eventually creating a fuller

72. Ann Scales, "The Emergence of Feminist Jurisprudence: An Essay," *Yale Law Journal* 95 (June 1986): 1388.

conception of power. As Roger Krohn says, science necessitates both anarchy—giving up the *search* for coherence—and coherence itself.[73] This double-focused method is of particular importance in discussing relations of power that challenge the dominant hierarchy.

In discussions of patriarchy or sex class, the connection *between* difference and unity is essential. I have argued that we cannot understand patriarchy as a system of sexual hierarchy privileging men without seeing it in its continuous historical framework. "The universality of patriarchy in Western society is expressed in the sexual assignment of private and public life, to woman and man, respectively. Although the meaning of 'public' and 'private' changes in concrete ways, the assignment of public space to men and private space to women is continuous in Western history."[74] Further, the specifics of the meaning of public and private have to be elucidated if we are to understand the specified universality of patriarchy. To focus only on the continuity of patriarchal history gives us an abstracted notion of the unity; to focus only on the specific ways patriarchy exists at any moment disconnects patriarchy from its continuity.

On a somewhat different but related plane is the issue of the sex-class structure of patriarchal social relations. This structure reflects the engendered relations of men and women; women's "sexual-class identity is initially defined in terms of their being female but is fully revealed in the identification of females as women, that is, as nurturers, mothers, secondary wage-earners, and so on."[75] This conception remains too abstract; it needs further specificity in terms of the mix and continua of differences. Sex class identifies all females as women, but the process through which this is done differs among women, very much in accordance with their color or economic class, or sexual preference. These differences are silenced when sex class and individual women are treated as a homogeneous category. The recognition of women as a sex class—treatment "like a woman"—and the continuity it assumes about women's experience is both necessary to a feminist critique and in part an inaccurate accounting of the diversity of women's lives. The

---

73. Krohn, "Scientific Ideology and Scientific Process," p. 95.
74. Eisenstein, *The Radical Future of Liberal Feminism*, p. 22.
75. Eisenstein, *Feminism and Sexual Equality*, p. 146.

crisscross between unity and diversity is therefore not easy to articulate.

This effort is not made any easier because the viewing of women
as a unified group, the same as each other, has most often been
used to establish woman's (homogeneous) "difference" from man
and thus ignore her unique identity as an individual. In this case,
women are treated as a sex class to deny feminist claims. Irigaray
criticizes Freud for this viewpoint of women: "All Freud's statements describing feminine sexuality overlook the fact that the female sex might possibly have its own 'specificity.'"[76] She argues
that to recognize a specific female sexuality, we would have to
"challenge the monopoly on value held by the masculine sex alone,
in the final analysis by the father."[77] Irigaray's argument still treats
woman's sexuality as a unity. She develops an essentialist stance,
although this is not the only way she could have reasoned. If we
follow Gould, we can reject essentialism for its overstated unities.
"Although species may be discrete, they have no immutable essence. Variation is the raw material of evolutionary change. It represents the fundamental reality of nature, not an accident about a
created norm. *Variation is primary; essences are illusory*" (*FS*, p.
160; emphasis mine).[78] The problem with essentialism is that it
"establishes criteria for judgment and worth: individual objects
that lie close to their essence are good; those that depart are bad,
if not unreal" (*FS*, p. 161). Essentialism, much as abstract statements regarding unity, does not recognize variety and difference as
part of what is expected. Rather than seeing continua with variety,
essentialism imposes dichotomy—such as homo- and heterosexual, man and woman. Instead of seeing males and females as having similarities and differences, essentialism sees them as opposites—man and woman.

Anti-essentialist thinking forces us to "accept shadings and con-

---

76. Luce Irigaray, *This Sex Which Is Not One*, p. 69. And see her *Speculum of the Other Woman*, trans. Gillian Gill (Ithaca, N.Y.: Cornell Univ. Press, 1985).
See also Sigmund Freud, *Sexuality and the Psychology of Love*, ed. Phillip Reiff
(New York: Collier Books, 1963).

77. Irigaray, *This Sex Which Is Not One*, p. 73. And see Jane Gallop, *The
Daughter's Seduction: Feminism and Psychoanalysis* (Ithaca, N.Y.: Cornell Univ.
Press, 1982).

78. See Ernst Mayr, *The Growth of Biological Thought*, esp. chs. 2, 3, and 6.

tinua as fundamental. We lose criteria for judgment by comparison to some ideal" (*FS*, p. 161). Variation and diversity become the norm. Such a focus on difference(s) (meaning diversity) allows us more fully to understand the relations of power and knowledge. This use of the term "difference(s)" allows for a radical pluralist epistemology and politics, a resolution of multiplicity and recombination of meanings through differences.

Third World feminists have challenged the essentialism and universalism of the concept of sex class.[79] They have demanded the recognition of "common differences"[80] among women to remedy this abstractness. The phrase "common differences" requires acknowledgment that our similarities are similarly different and differently similar—specificity has to define the unity. In order not to be left only with the differences between ourselves, as Foucault might have it, we must also look for the specified unities. Instead of unity we will find multiple forms of unity and difference, which allow us to see the hierarchy in difference(s) between men and all women as well as between women themselves.

Chandra Mohanty, while trying to diversify the perspective of a "Third World woman," is critical of a universalization of sex class that does not focus on specificity and only recognizes the homogeneity of women, "which in turn produces the image of an 'average Third World woman.'"

By women as a category of analysis, I am referring to the critical assumption that all of us of the same gender, across classes and cultures, are somehow socially constituted as a homogeneous group identified prior to the process of analysis. . . . Thus the discursively consensual homogeneity of "women" as a group is mistaken for the historically specific material

79. For a sampling of this criticism, see Bell Hooks, *Ain't I a Woman: Black Women and Feminism* (Boston: South End Press, 1981), and her *Feminist Theory: From Margin to Center* (Boston: South End Press, 1984); Gloria T. Hull, Patricia Bell Scott, and Barbara Smith, eds., *All the Women Are White, All the Blacks Are Men, but Some of Us Are Brave* (New York: Feminist Press, 1982); Gloria I. Joseph and Jill Lewis, *Common Differences: Conflicts in Black and White Feminist Perspectives* (Boston: South End Press, 1981; New York: Doubleday, 1986); Audre Lorde, *Sister Outsider* (Trumansburg, N.Y.: Crossing Press, 1984); and Cherrie Moraga and Gloria Anzaldua, eds., *This Bridge Called My Back* (Watertown, Mass.: Persephone Press, 1981).

80. See Joseph and Lewis, *Common Differences*, for a full explication of their meaning of this term.

reality of groups of women. This results in an assumption of women as an always-already constituted group.[81]

She argues that in order to preclude a false sense of commonality, we must place discussions of women's lives locally and contextually.[82] I agree, but I do not think the analysis can be left here. Women are "already [a] constituted group." The discourse of engendered sex "difference" makes them so; it also establishes the construct of the "Third World woman." Therefore, the challenge is to specify the unity and not to deny it. The tension between diversity and unity must become the focus. The construct of the "Third World woman" must remind us of unity while making unity a suspect category.

As we have seen, the theoretical construct "sex class" wrongly universalizes all women as sharing a common place without recognizing their specified unity. Part of understanding the meaning of sex class is understanding how *a* female becomes *a* woman, specifically, how a black female becomes a black woman, a Chicana female a Chicana woman, an Indian female an Indian woman. Phallocratic discourse makes them all woman. But each is also black, Chicana, Indian. *All* are lacking, or are different, or are absent— but in specifically different ways. The phallocratic standard in Western industrial societies is the white, middle-class male. The types black, Chicana, Indian woman differ from this standard differently from each other and differently from white woman. A white woman is "less than"; she is *not* a man. A black woman is "less than"; she is *not* white, and she is *not* a man. In relation to the black man, a black woman is *not* a man. In relation to a black man, a white woman is *not* a man, but she is white. A black woman shares her blackness with black men, but as a woman, and shares her womanhood with white women, but as black. A black woman's claim to her difference and her specificity invokes her unity with black men. And her unity with white women invokes her difference from black men. We need to specify these distinctions as a

81. Chandra Talpade Mohanty, "Under Western Eyes: Feminist Scholarship and Colonial Discourses," *boundary 2: A Journal of Post Modern Literature and Culture* 12–13 (1984): 337, 337–38.

82. See ibid., p. 348. See also Maxine Molyneux, "Mobilization without Emancipation? Women's Interests, the State, and Revolution in Nicaragua," *Feminist Studies* 11 (Summer 1985): 227–54.

hierarchy of differences, and in doing so we need to challenge the opposition between *the* white woman and the category "women of color."

Phallocratic discourses treat women as a unity, although they have diverse ways of doing so. To the extent that discourse criss-crosses the "real" and the "ideal" and establishes someplace in between, the oneness of woman is a partial truth. Phallocratic discourses construct the "reality" that women constitute a sex class; by doing so they define all women as the same. But women are affected differently because power is dispersed and is not a unity. This constellation of power means that phallocentrism is multi-centered, that it takes diverse historical, cultural forms. The dispersion and discontinuity of discourse have to turn back on the phallus, and on feminism as well. They also need to underlie our understanding of law in its construction and reflection of the relations of power.

Chapter Two

The Engendered Discourse(s)
of Liberal Law(s)

In this chapter a discussion of law(s) will lead us to more direct exploration of the problem of sex equality. Clearly, legal equality is not the same thing as sex equality. Legal equality is only part of the issue of sex equality, because laws are only a partial expression of the relations of power that shape sex equality. The extralegal dimensions of the question, such as who actually bears the child, must also be acknowledged.

By distinguishing between legal and sexual equality, I am not taking the Marxist position, which reduces laws to the realm of ideology—the unreal, the nonconcrete, the false interpretation of the real. I see law as discourse(s) rather than ideology. Law is both real and ideal; it is both determined and determining.[1] Law is a collection of symbols and signs that structure and effect choices, options, consequences. It operates in the continua between the real (concrete facts) and the ideal (nonconcrete interpretation) and constructs there a dispersed and contradictory realm of hierarchical power.

In this chapter I argue that because law is engendered, that is, *structured through the multiple oppositional layerings embedded in the dualism of man/woman*, it is not able to move beyond the male referent as the standard for sex equality. Thus, difference, particularly sex "difference," is constructed through and as a part of

1. See Zillah Eisenstein, *Feminism and Sexual Equality: Crisis in Liberal America* (New York: Monthly Review Press, 1984), p. 97.

42

a hierarchical and dualistic relation. This epistemological stance—"difference," which is *already* in opposition to sameness—establishes men and women as opposites while privileging men. We shall see that the legal notion of sex equality resulting from this stance is contradictory. It is progressive to the degree that it assumes men and women to be the same, and reactionary to the extent that its notion of what is "the same" derives from the phallus. It is progressive to the degree that it recognizes sex difference(s) as potentially creative and productive, and reactionary to the extent that it differentiates women according to their gender. What complicates this problem, as I noted earlier, is the fact that sex and gender are not clearly distinguishable given the politics of language and knowledge. Further, the language of law usually collapses the distinction between sex and gender.

Law as Legal Discourse

Recognizing law as a discourse calls attention to how law establishes regulations, thoughts, and behavior and institutes expectations of what is legitimate and illegitimate behavior, what is acceptable and unacceptable, what is criminal and legal, what is rational and irrational, what is natural and unnatural. Therefore, the study of law *as* a discourse is not limited to specific laws or to the activity of litigation or litigators; rather it is the study of these laws as they operate as symbols for what is legal, honorable, natural, objective, and so on. In this sense the symbolization of law is more than its specific language.

My discussion of law focuses on the courts, judges, lawyers, and law professors as they help to establish law as a discourse. Judges and law professors formulate the discourse by interpreting law and thereby establishing its symbolic meaning. Their interpretation of law(s) is constrained by law itself; but law has no meaning without interpretation—no law can be applied or adjudicated without interpretation. As we shall see, this is the way the engendered structure of law—which extends to the oppositional dualities true/false, right/wrong, fact/value, and so on—comes to have its specificity defined. To understand fully the engendered meanings of laws, we must see how they are structured into law at their particular sites of interpretation. That is why, even though the problem of engendered law cannot be reduced to the fact that most judges are men, that fact is not irrelevant or unimportant. Even to the extent that women judges operate within the gendered formulations of society, they will not automatically interpret differently than men do, although they are often likely to do so because as women they are affected differently by the male standard.

The dominant discourse of law describes the legal system's adjudication process as fair and neutral. This discourse is a series of representations of the state as rational and objective. This view gives law its authority and its power *as* a discourse—as a way of thinking that has an effect on practices—and as a practice this view affects thinking.[2] This authorization breaks open the boundaries of law and establishes it as something more than specific regulations and sanctions. The discourse about law—the symbolization of law as a neutral and objective arbiter—yields discourses within law on the rule of the father (phallus) as though this rule were established in nature. The "idea" of the neutrality of law is viewed as one and the same as the law itself, and the phallus is misrepresented as the objectivity of nature.

Law, or ideas about law, are at the source of our thinking about order and disorder, virtue and vice, reasonableness and craziness, and, as Robert Gordon states, at the source "of some of the most commonplace aspects of social reality that ordinary people carry around with them and use in ordering their lives." He further argues that the power of law is not rooted in fear on the part of the violators but rather "in [law's] capacity to persuade people that the world described in its images and categories is the only attainable world in which a sane person would want to live."[3] In the process of symbolization law establishes its own authority as a theory about power, masquerading as nature, reason, and objectivity. "One never has more power than when one has so successfully appropriated the symbols of authority that one's actions are not seen as exercises of power at all, but simply as expressions of sound pragmatic common sense."[4]

2. See Judith Shklar, *Legalism* (Cambridge, Mass.: Harvard Univ. Press, 1964), p. 34.

3. Robert Gordon, "Critical Legal Histories," *Stanford Law Review* 36 (January 1984): 109.

4. Ibid., p. 112. And see his "Historicism in Legal Scholarship," *Yale Law Journal* 90 (1981): 1017–59.

Law operates as a "great reservoir of emotionally important social symbols"[5] that are intimately tied up with people's thoughts regarding the place of truth and reason in their lives. "Routinely, the justificatory language of law parades as the unquestionable embodiment of Reason and Universal Truth."[6] It is the nature of law to identify "truth conditions" for justification of its (legal) propositions.[7] The organization of law itself—its categories, its reasoning, its rhetoric—sets many of the limits in which people think and imagine their daily lives. "Our desires and plans tend to be shaped out of the limited stock of forms available to us: the forms thus condition not just our power to get what we want but what we want (or think we can get) itself."[8]

The prevailing discourse about law privileges the so-called objectivity of the scientific method, views nature as definitive, and assumes the superiority of rationality.[9] It does so while establishing a system of classification characterized by the "ideas" of similarity and difference within oppositions.[10] However varied the theories concerning law are—be they legal positivism, formalism, or realism—they do not exist outside this dominant discourse.[11] Gordon

5. Allan Hutchinson and Patrick Monahan, "Law, Politics, and the Critical Legal Scholars: The Unfolding Drama of American Legal Thought," *Stanford Law Review* 36 (January 1984): 214.

6. Elizabeth Mensch, "The History of Mainstream Legal Thought," in *The Politics of Law: A Progressive Critique,* ed. David Kairys (New York: Pantheon Books, 1982), p. 18. And see Franz Leopold Neumann, *The Democratic and the Authoritarian State: Essays in Political and Legal Theory,* ed. Herbert Marcuse (Glencoe, Ill.: Free Press, 1957); and the little-known work by the Austrian socialist Karl Renner, *The Institutions of Private Law and Their Social Functions,* ed. O. Kahn-Freund (London: Routledge & Kegan Paul, 1949).

7. Lewis A. Kornhauser, "The Great Image of Authority," *Stanford Law Review* 36 (January 1984): 351.

8. Gordon, "Critical Legal Histories," p. 111.

9. This is not to argue that law is the dominant discourse for defining norms in all societies, but it is in present Western industrial societies.

10. Ann Scales, "The Emergence of Feminist Jurisprudence: An Essay," *Yale Law Journal* 95 (June 1986): 1386. And see her "Towards a Feminist Jurisprudence," *Indiana Law Journal* 56 (Spring 1981): 375–444.

11. While legal positivism asserts the objectivity of truth within law as well as the distinctness of law and morality, natural law theorists recognize the importance of moral reasoning for law. Although positivists and natural law theorists assume contradictory stances on one level, they work from a standard that assumes the rationality of law, the idea of objectivity as a desired standpoint, and silent assumptions about the place of nature (as it pertains to woman) as a justificatory basis for law. See Craig Ducat, *Modes of Constitutional Interpretation* (St. Paul, Minn.: West Publishing, 1978); Lon Fuller, "Positivism and Fidelity to Law:

points out that mainstream legal scholarship's primary "aim is that of rationalizing the real, of showing that the law-making and law-applying activities that go on in our society make sense and may be rationally related to some coherent conceptual ordering scheme."[12] But I must insert a word of caution. I do not mean to adopt a simplistic instrumentalist view, that the law is a mere instrument of patriarchal and phallocratic social relations. This view would relegate the realm of law as discourse to what Gordon terms "rationalizing the real" when law constitutes the real as well.[13]

I wish to emphasize that law as discourse occupies a space between the "real" and "ideal" that is a continuum. Law reflects and impacts on the world. It is constitutive of *and* derivative of social and political change. Law operates as a political language because it establishes and curtails choices and action. The world is different when the law changes, and laws change because the world is different. Legalizing homosexual marriage would make the world different, even if not completely so. Sodomy laws exist, and even though people do not necessarily follow them, the world would be different if those laws did not exist. Recent changes in divorce and custody law both reflect and instigate "real" changes, even though the changes are insufficient and sometimes wrongheaded.

The changes in divorce and custody law assume a stance of sexual equality that does not recognize the societal disadvantage and inequality of women as they "really" exist. In this instance, law

A Reply to Prof. Hart," *Harvard Law Review* 71 (1958): 630–72; J. W. Harris, *Law and Legal Science: An Inquiry into the Concepts Legal Rule and Legal System* (Oxford: Clarendon Press, 1979); H. L. A. Hart, *The Concept of Law* (Oxford: Clarendon Press, 1961), and "Positivism and the Separation of Law and Morals," *Harvard Law Review* 71 (1958): 593–629; David Lyons, *Ethics and the Rule of Law* (Cambridge: Cambridge Univ. Press, 1984); J. C. Smith and David Weisstub, *The Western Idea of Law* (London: Butterworth, 1983); and Max Weber, *Economy and Society,* ed. Guenther Roth and Claus Wittich, 3 vols. (New York: Bedminister Press, 1968).

12. Gordon, "Historicism in Legal Scholarship," p. 1018.

13. For an interesting discussion of the relative autonomy of law, see Isaac Balbus, "Commodity Form and Legal Form: An Essay on the Relative Autonomy of the Law," *Law and Society Review* 2 (Winter 1977): 571–88, and *The Dialectics of Legal Repression: Black Rebels before the American Criminal Courts* (New York: Russell Sage Foundation, 1973; 2d ed., Edison, N.J.: Transaction Books, 1976); and David Trubek, "Complexity and Contradiction in the Legal Order: Balbus and the Challenge of Critical Social Thought about Law," *Law and Society Review* 2 (Winter 1977): 529–69.

articulates the "idea" of equality without necessarily creating equality in "real" terms. And although the idea of equality is not one and the same with real equality, the idea uncovers the absence of real equality. Each is incomplete; each is necessary to define a legal theory of equality that is truly real. The problem, however, is that the laws of the liberal patriarchal state do not recognize a conception of equality that moves beyond the liberal (and liberal feminist) doctrine of the oppositional stance—about sameness and difference—of law itself.

Neutrality, Objectivity, and the "Nature" of Law

Law, as the text or the word, is supposed to be disinterested. And the lawmaker is supposed to adjudicate impartially, to balance interests in a neutral and fair-minded way. Law authorizes what is meant by right and wrong, truth and falsity, fact and value from this stance. It presents power as rational and just and even neutral. Catharine MacKinnon has termed this presentation "the point-of-viewlessness" of law: "Objectivist epistemology is the law of law. It ensures that the law will most reinforce existing distributions of power when it most closely adheres to its own highest ideal of fairness."[14]

Ronald Dworkin, from a different vantage point, recognizes the power of law to determine right and wrong. In discussing the issue of right and wrong as it applies to deciding the "hard cases" in law, he argues that the "idea" that there is always a right and wrong way of doing something is "real" within law because people believe it to be so.

Surely it *cannot* be that in a genuinely hard case one side is simply right and the other simply wrong. But why not? It may be that the supposition that one side may be right and the other wrong is cemented into our habits of thought at a level so deep that we cannot coherently deny that supposition no matter how skeptical or hard-headed we wish to be in such matters. . . . The "myth" that there is one right answer in a hard case is

14. Catharine MacKinnon, "Feminism, Marxism, Method, and the State: Toward Feminist Jurisprudence," *Signs* 8 (Summer 1983): 645.

both recalcitrant and successful. Its recalcitrance and success count as arguments that it is no myth.[15]

In a related observation, Judith Shklar notes that analytical positivism "allow[s] judges to believe that there always is a rule somewhere for them to follow."[16]

This objectivist standpoint sets up a series of oppositions: true/false, right/wrong, and so on. My point is not that there are not times when things are true or false or right or wrong but rather that these oppositions can be clearly distinguished less often than legal positivists assume and that the distinctions are not based on an objective truth. The objectivist standpoint makes clear-cut demarcations rather than continua the basis of its epistemology. Law recognizes duality rather than diversity. Ann Scales argues that diversity "is obscured by the myth of objectivity[,] which opens up law's destructive potential."[17] Instead of being able to recognize complexity *within* the relationships between true and false, right and wrong, law constructs dichotomous oppositions that deny the complexity. In the courtroom, subtleties do not count: winning and losing do. The adversarial format makes winning more important than uncovering the possibility of multiple truths.

There is, however, a problem with this critique. It does not take into account that although the masquerade of neutrality often disguises and misrepresents power, it also does something else. The discourse of law, which establishes the idea that law is neutral and fair, simultaneously fosters the expectation that law *should* be neutral even if it is not. And this "idea" does not remain an idea; it has become part of legal discourse. This is what legal equality for the sexes means: law should be neutral in terms of sex. We shall see that there are serious problems with this conception, given the already engendered discourse(s) of law(s), but the idea that law should be sex neutral can be used to decenter the phallus along with its objectivist, dualistic standpoint.

The importance of the discourse of legal neutrality becomes

---

15. Ronald Dworkin, *Taking Rights Seriously* (Cambridge, Mass.: Harvard Univ. Press, 1977), p. 290. And see his *A Matter of Principle* (Cambridge, Mass.: Harvard Univ. Press, 1985), *Law's Empire* (Cambridge, Mass.: Harvard Univ. Press, 1986), and *The Philosophy of Law* (New York: Oxford Univ. Press, 1977).

16. Shklar, *Legalism*, p. 12.

17. Scales, "The Emergence of Feminist Jurisprudence," p. 1387.

clear when we compare it with the openly political vantage point of someone like Attorney General Edwin Meese. He made it clear that his legal agenda was President Reagan's political agenda; he made no pretense of being disinterested or neutral. He uncovered his politics of law as he attempted to shift the discourse away from a notion of judges as a balance wheel and away from the liberal democratic commitment to fairness, due process, and individual rights before the law. Although liberal democracy is not often in fact fair, neutral, or equal, it promises to be so—and on that level it gains the potential to be so, as its own best critic. Neutrality and objectivity, although similar in meaning, are not one and the same in my mind. Whereas neutrality connotes a place in between the opposition of man and woman, objectivity is a binary opposite; it loses its meaning when the phallus is decentered.

The supposed objectivity of law is often established in and through the "law(s) of nature." Natural law is presumed to be necessitated by nature itself. Natural rights, which are derivative from natural "man," stand as abstract givens in this view. The privileging of nature authorizes natural law, natural rights, natural "man." It is the power of the meaning of "natural"—its supposedly a priori status—that gives law its authority *within* society. Nature is both disorderly and tempestuous, and harmonious and rational. In the first instance, law makes sense of the disorder of nature and tames "her." In the second instance, nature is extended to society through law. In both instances, natural law is the law of reason; law is therefore reason itself. Rationality and the laws of nature are encoded as part of the objectivist standpoint. Evelyn Fox Keller criticizes this viewing of laws of nature as though they exist outside of or "beyond the relativity of language" and society. The notion of nature and the laws of nature is treated inappropriately as though the laws of nature were objective necessities. Keller further states that "the very concept of 'laws of nature' is, in contemporary usage both a product and an expression of the absence of reflectivity[,] . . . but nonetheless, laws of nature, like laws of the state, are historically imposed from above and obeyed from below."[18] Nature is named by the laws of nature, which are named by the "father."

18. Evelyn Fox Keller, *Reflections on Gender and Science* (New Haven, Conn.: Yale Univ. Press, 1985), pp. 130, 131.

Law as a politics is made invisible by the inevitability of nature. The rule of law through nature masks the hierarchy it seeks to protect.[19] Hierarchy is presented as the differences *in* nature, and natural law is in part the reasonable way to interpret these differences. In other words, "natural law [is] what reason discovers, and natural law was discovered by reason."[20] Reason establishes its own universality. Reason is not partial like passion is; reason is impartial, fair-minded, and just.

Plato criticized the inadequacies of the law existing in his day from this vantage point. In his view, law was supposed to dispense reason. The authority of the state was to be justified by the deification of law, and the state was to embody the divinity of reason.[21] The legislation Plato proposed in the *Republic* was seen as practicable because it was in accordance with nature.[22] This is the case for his discussion in the *Laws* as well: "Everything that takes place in the state, if it participates in order and law, confers all kinds of blessings" (1.487). Law can therefore be used to enforce men's and women's roles in procreation, if they are not otherwise persuaded to procreate (see 1.497). The law enforces nature while it is justified in light of nature. Weber, Montesquieu, and Blackstone also assumed the rationality of law and its role as a neutral arbiter. "The whole universe, on this view, is governed by laws which exhibit rationality."[23]

Critical Legal Studies (CLS) scholars critique the image of the inevitability and stasis of law as natural or as one with nature. They reject the way law is made to appear inevitable. "Inspired by a vision of the contingent nature of all social worlds, the CLS project is to identify the role played by law and legal reasoning in the process through which social structures acquire the appearance of inevitability."[24] The legal (re)presentation of reality suppresses the

19. See Hutchinson and Monahan, "Law, Politics, and the Critical Legal Scholars," p. 210.

20. *Encyclopedia of Philosophy*, s.v. "natural law."

21. See Plato, *Laws*, vol. 10, ed. R. G. Bury (London: Heinemann, 1926): xiv; all further references to this work will be included in the text.

22. See Plato, *Republic*, ed. Paul Shorey (Cambridge, Mass.: Harvard Univ. Press, 1930), p. 449.

23. *Encyclopedia of Philosophy*, s.v. "natural law."

24. Hutchinson and Monahan, "Law, Politics, and the Critical Legal Scholars," p. 217. For other work by Critical Legal Studies scholars, see Duncan Ken-

plurality and fluidity of meaning. Legal reasoning is supposedly the (re)presentation of reason as "a" truth. Scholars in CLS argue that we must "relate theory to practice and expose the dysfunction between reason and reality."[25] There is no one truth, there is only complexity.

The CLS critique focuses attention on the economic class politics of legal discourse: its premise is that law operates in defense of economic class interests. The critique, however, needs to be carried further—to uncover how law masks both the economic class hierarchy of capitalism, with its commodity forms, and the way sex and its relation to gender are misrepresented. "The" law is bourgeois *and* patriarchal, liberal *and* phallocratic. The engendered dualities of woman/man, nature/culture, subjective/objective, irrational/rational structure law itself.

The Engendered Form of Phallocratic Law(s)

Liberal democratic law helps to structure patriarchy in the way it differentiates woman from man; law embodies the relations of patriarchy through the differentiation, by sex, of gender. Woman is part of nature; man, like law, must sometimes tame and control her. The *reason* of man suppresses the passion of woman.[26] Diane Polan recognizes this aspect in law. "The whole structure of law— its hierarchical organization; its combative, adversarial format; and its undeviating bias in favor of rationality over all other values— defines it as a fundamentally patriarchal institution." She also argues that "it is not so much that laws must be changed; it is patriarchy that must be changed."[27] Polan herself, however, ac-

---

nedy, "Form and Substance in Private Law Adjudication," *Harvard Law Review* 89 (1976): 1685–1778; *Stanford Law Review* 36; and Roberto Unger, *Knowledge and Politics* (New York: Free Press, 1975), and "The Critical Legal Studies Movement," *Harvard Law Review* 96 (1983): 561–675.

25. Hutchinson and Monahan, "Law, Politics, and the Critical Legal Scholars," p. 213.

26. The dualism of man as rational and woman as passionate should not be overgeneralized; this distinction takes many different historical forms, and in some periods defines woman as passionless, although not necessarily rational.

27. Diane Polan, "Toward a Theory of Law and Patriarchy," in Kairys, *The Politics of Law*, p. 301.

knowledges that the structure of law is patriarchal. Why then separate these realms?[28]

Janet Rifkin argues that law is powerful as both a symbol and a vehicle of male authority because "it serves to mystify social reality and block social change."[29] I agree with this assessment but also believe, as I have stated earlier, that law as a discourse not only mystifies reality but constructs the "real" *while* (re)presenting it. So although the engendered nature of law—expressed in the competitive relations of winning and losing along lines of right and wrong, not guilty and guilty, truth and deceit—defines part of the problem, this is an incomplete viewing. Likewise, although law operates as a series of mystifications of gender differentiation, this is also an incomplete description of the problem. Not just the practice of law but also the institutionalization of engendered meanings into its structure presents the problem of gender *in law.* The problem is epistemological and political. Not only are most of the judges and a majority of lawyers men, although this is *a* problem, but their interpretations of law(s) are not external to law. Legal theory is already engendered; its stance centers the phallus while establishing the dualistic viewpoint of positivism: man is to woman as fact is to value. Interpretations mirror and reconstruct the gendered bias of law(s). And legal practice is rooted in law's engendered epistemology.

The practice of mainstream law reflects, as well as defines, this bias. This phallocratic stance is documented in the 1986 New York State Task Force/Report *Women in the Courts.* The report found a consistent bias against women in New York in all aspects of litigation—as judges, lawyers, clients, defendants, and jurors. Gender bias was defined from the outset by Chief Judge Lawrence H. Cooke as decisions made or "actions taken because of weight given to preconceived notions of sexual roles rather than upon a fair and unswayed appraisal of merit as to each person or situation."[30] The

28. See Eisenstein, *Feminism and Sexual Equality,* p. 97.

29. Janet Rifkin, "Toward a Theory of Law and Patriarchy," in *Marxism and Law,* ed. Piers Beirne and Richard Quinney (New York: Wiley, 1982), p. 295. For other discussions of the gender bias of law, see Leo Kanowitz, *Sexism and the Law: Male Beliefs and Legal Bias* (New York: Free Press, 1978).

30. *Report of the New York Task Force on "Women in the Courts,"* March 1986, p. 2; all further references to this work, abbreviated as *NY,* will be included in the text. And see *Report of the Committee to Implement Recommendations of*

study found that "cultural stereotypes of women's role in marriage and in society daily distort the courts' application of substantive law"; women face "a judiciary underinformed about matters integral to many women's welfare" (*NY*, pp. 50, 24).

Gender bias affects women as litigants and litigators.[31] It also affects the way issues specifically tied to women's needs (for example, domestic violence, rape, spousal and child support, custody, pregnancy and parental leave) are conceptualized and/or silenced. The way these issues are—or are not—thought about is tied up with the gender-biased practice of law. The task force found that "in each of these areas, cultural myths about women's role in the family and in society and expectations about appropriate modes of behavior at times obscure considerations that are highly relevant to the decision-making process" (*NY*, p. 24).

These problems of legal practice have roots deep within the engendered "nature" of law. "Law privileges objectivity, individualism, and rights over their binary opposites, subjectivity, collectivity, and responsibility, and this privilege is identified with the more general male privilege over females."[32] Law does not exist alongside the privilege but inside it. It establishes a gendered series of hierarchical differences.

In constructing social law on the basis of natural law, man has made much of the difference between male and female. . . . This definition assigns moral, practical, and psychological meanings to neutral biological differences. This has resulted in sexuality being the first and foremost classification of persons and in females being defined as unequal to males within that classification system.[33]

---

the New York Task Force on Women in the Courts, Unified Court System Office of Court Administration, State of New York, April 1987.

31. As litigants, women are often blamed for the problem. This is particularly true in matters pertaining to domestic violence. As litigators, women are often discriminated against. The task force received many complaints that women attorneys were disproportionately denied judicial appointments as counsel in the more lucrative and complex cases and that impediments existed to their appointments to judgeships.

32. David Cole, "Strategies of Difference: Litigating for Women's Rights in a Man's World," *Law and Inequality: Journal of Theory and Practice* 2 (February 1984): 45.

33. Barbara Brown, Ann Freedman, Harriet Katz, Alice Price, and Hazel Greenberg, *Women's Rights and the Law* (New York: Praeger, 1977), p. 7.

In the name of nature, and in the process of its naming, "genes are thought to affect everything from our emotions to our legal system."[34] And the genes have been engendered, in the name of nature, within law.

The language of law silences woman. Luce Irigaray argues that the presence of woman seems impossible to imagine within law as it is presently formed. "That would not fail to challenge the discourse that lays down the law today, that legislates on everything, including sexual difference, to such an extent that the existence of another sex, of an other, that would be woman, still seems, in its terms, unimaginable." She believes that the only way to create space for women is to develop a new language, one which no longer assumes that men are "everything"—"that [the masculine] could no longer, all by itself, define, circumvent, circumscribe, the properties of any thing and everything."[35] We need a starting place other than Jefferson's "All men are created equal," because it leaves us with a vision that equality can be articulated through a homogeneous standard: man.

This is not *just* a problem of language, because language is always more than it seems/means. This is a problem of how language operates as discourse, as symbolization of a gendered notion of nature, of human(ity). "As male is the implicit reference for human, maleness will be the measure of equality."[36] Men are the norm, so women *are* different (from men). But for women to be treated as equal, they must be treated *as* men, *like* men, because equality is premised on men. If one is treated as different *from* men, one is not treated as equal. "Women are permitted to compete with men under the same rules and within the same institutions, but those institutions were designed in accordance with normative male values, priorities and characteristics."[37] Requirements and standards are designed with men in mind.[38]

---

34. Anne Fausto-Sterling, *Myths of Gender: Biological Theories about Men and Women* (New York: Basic Books, 1985), p. 72.

35. Luce Irigaray, *This Sex Which Is Not One*, trans. Catherine Porter, with Carolyn Burke (Ithaca, N.Y.: Cornell Univ. Press, 1985), pp. 85, 80.

36. MacKinnon, "Feminism, Marxism, Method, and the State," p. 644.

37. Linda Krieger and Patricia Cooney, "The Miller-Wohl Controversy: Equal Treatment, Positive Action, and the Meaning of Women's Equality," *Golden Gate University Law Review* 13 (1983): 545.

38. See Monique Wittig, "The Mark of Gender," *Feminist Issues* 5 (Fall 1985): 3–12.

Gendered law is constructed through the differentiation of woman *from* man, and this differentiation takes several forms. Some law explicitly treats women as different from men—for example, in the denial of the rights to tend bar, administer an estate, or engage in combat. Before 1971 these kinds of prohibition were not seen as problematic in U.S. constitutional law. They were rather seen as necessitated by the "real" differences of women (from men). Today there is much less closure on this issue, as is reflected in the very idea of sex discrimination. After all, sex discrimination as a legal concept makes the treatment of someone in terms of sex (difference) or classification by sex problematic.

We need to recognize that much of the gendered nature of law masquerades subtly. The differentiation by sex is not explicit but implied through a silencing of difference in a supposedly neutral language, such as the notions of "veteran" or "worker" or "individual." There are also laws in which the term "men" supposedly applies to women as well, but the male standard is expressed explicitly in these cases.[39]

To conclude, within law, women are treated in four ways: as a sex class, as different from men—reproducers and gendered mothers; as the same as men, like men, and therefore not women; as absent but as a class different from men; and as absent but as a class the same as men. The phallus is centered in all these conceptualizations but in different formations.

Catharine MacKinnon makes a similar point. "The gender question is a question of difference. There are two options under it. The first option I call the 'male standard': Women can be the *same* as men. In law, it is called gender neutrality. The other option I call the 'female standard': You can be *different* from men. In law, it is called special protection." Either way, men articulate the standard of assessment. "You can be the same as men, and *then* you will be equal, or you can be different from men, and then you will be *women*."[40]

The engendered nature of law privileges man as the referent by

39. See Ray Stilwell, "Sexism in the Statutes: Identifying and Solving the Problem of Ambiguous Gender Bias in Legal Writing," *Buffalo Law Review* 32 (Spring 1983): 559–87.

40. Catharine MacKinnon, in Ellen Dubois, Mary Dunlap, Carol Gilligan, Catharine MacKinnon, and Carrie Menkel-Meadow, "Feminist Discourse, Moral Values, and the Law: A Conversation," *Buffalo Law Review* 34 (Winter 1985): 20, 21.

making woman "the" different "other," and thereby it homogenizes the differences among women. Woman's "difference" is assumed to be a part of the preferred order of things. Given this view, which treats the sex (biological nature) and gender (cultural mediation) of woman as one and the same, "classification by sex" is not viewed as problematic. As Justice Joseph Bradley stated in his concurring opinion in *Bradwell* v. *State,*

On the contrary, the civil law, as well as nature herself, has always recognized a wide difference in the respective spheres and destinies of man and woman. Man is, or should be, woman's protector and defender. The natural and proper timidity and delicacy which belongs to the female sex evidently unfits it for many of the occupations of civil life. The constitution of the family organization, which is founded in the divine ordinance, as well as in the nature of things, indicates the domestic sphere as that which properly belongs to the domain and functions of womanhood.[41]

Although few would argue today, as Bradley did in 1873, that *the* "difference" of sex requires separate spheres for men and women, differentiation by sex still underlies law.

So far, this discussion has treated engendered law as a unity; the phallus is centered in and by law. Now we need to examine further how this unity of patriarchal privilege establishes a coherence of hierarchical relations in law while presenting an often incoherent, dispersed, and contradictory view of the phallus. Law is both unified and contradictory: the symbolization of the phallus underlines multiple and sometimes incoherent interpretations of gender.

There is little clarity or consistency of legal thought about the meaning of *the* "difference" of sex—the difference of woman *from* man—and with it sex discrimination. Biology, according to MacKinnon, "is used to define both the grounds on which different treatment may be recognized as discriminatory and the grounds on which different treatment may be recognized as a consequence of 'real' sex differences; hence, reasonably based and not discriminatory."[42] In other words, if what is considered a "real" sex difference exists, one cannot argue categorically that differential treatment of "classification by sex" is discriminatory; instead, the specific treat-

41. 83 U.S. (16 Wall) 130, 141 (1873).
42. Catharine MacKinnon, *Sexual Harassment of Working Women* (New Haven, Conn.: Yale Univ. Press, 1979), p. 110; all further references to this work, abbreviated as *SHWW*, will be included in the text.

ment must be seen as warranted by *the* "difference." The problem here is the meaning of "real" in the phrase "real sex difference." What does "real" mean if we view reality as continua rather than as a construct in the dualism of truth/falsity? What if there are multiple differences of sex that are complexly related to differences of gender rather than *a* "difference" of sex established in nature that differentiates all women from all men? The problem is that the meaning of "real" cannot be established from *inside* the engendered meanings of "classification by sex" within law.

The engendered nature of law limits the possibility of recognizing sex discrimination. According to the Fourteenth Amendment, individuals deserve equal (similar) protection if they are similarly situated.[43] Women, however, are often not similarly situated to men. The pregnant female is not similarly situated to the non-pregnant male. MacKinnon writes that "similarly situated" should mean "that people who are the same should be treated the same"—that persons in relevantly similar circumstances should be treated relevantly similarly (*SHWW*, p. 107). But what is relevant similarity? And who is the standard?

Equal protection doctrine masks its male referent in the guise of neutrality. "Current equal protection doctrine fails to look beyond the appearance of neutrality and refuses to recognize that actions based on sexually unique physical characteristics such as pregnancy are sex based."[44] Under the equal protection clause, all persons are entitled to equal protection, unless some legitimate state purpose justifies differentiation by sex. Then treatment according

43. Section 1 of the Fourteenth Amendment reads: "All persons born or naturalized in the United States, and subject to the jurisdiction thereof, are citizens of the U.S. and of the state wherein they reside. No state shall make or enforce any law which shall abridge the privileges or immunities of citizens of the U.S., nor shall any state deprive any person of life, liberty, or property, without due process of law; nor deny to any person within its jurisdiction the equal protection of the laws."

44. Phyllis Segal, "Sexual Equality, the Equal Protection Clause, and the ERA," *Buffalo Law Review* 33 (Winter 1984): 129. And see Drew Alan Campbell, "Equal Protection and Gender Based Discrimination," *Villanova Law Review* 27 (November 1981): 182–97; Roxanne Barton Conlin, "Equal Protection vs. Equal Rights Amendment—Where Are We Now?" *Drake Law Review* 24 (Winter 1975): 259–335; and Earl Maltz, "Sex Discrimination on the Supreme Court: A Comment on Sex Equality, Sex Difference, and the Supreme Court," *Duke Law Journal* (February 1985): 177–94.

to sex is legal as long as the classification of sex is not unreasonable or arbitrary. So women can be treated as women—that is, as different from men—if they are not similarly situated (to men) and if the reasoning is not arbitrary. The phallus is privileged here—through men and/or the state.

The "legitimate state purpose" and "compelling reasons" qualifications to equal protection doctrine allow the state to interpret the "laws of nature" (qua biology) as it sees fit. Whether and to what purpose the state invokes the "name" of nature is utterly arbitrary. It does so when citing the immutable differences in nature and when recognizing the likeness of women and men. While doing both the state condenses and unifies varying and competing discourses about gender. Law has changed to permit the treatment of women and men as the same while preserving a notion of the "natural difference" of woman from man. Even though law has shifted to accommodate a notion of similarity between the sexes, it operates as if there is one objective reality, which establishes "real" sex difference. Interestingly enough, although nature and its derivative—"real" sex difference—are treated as givens in phallocratic discourse, law shifts and continues to renegotiate their meaning. Let us turn to this issue of the meaning(s) of sex "difference" in law(s), the dispersed and contradictory versions of the phallus.

Sex "Difference" and Classifications by Sex

This discussion will examine selected Supreme Court cases that document the shifting and contradictory views of woman's difference from man in legal discourse. I have chosen Supreme Court cases because of their particularly symbolic resonance as the highest law of the land. Before clarifying the problem of sex "difference" in the law—what it means and how I believe it differs from gender difference—let us see how the law treats "classifications by sex" under the guise of equal protection doctrine.

In common law there was no problem of sex difference. Women had no independent status, hence no difference. The husband and wife were one, and that one was the husband. This view was clearly articulated by William Blackstone: "By marriage, the husband and wife are one person in law: that is, the very being or legal existence of the woman is suspended during the marriage, or at least is in-corporated and consolidated into that of the husband; under whose wing, protection, and *cover,* she performs everything."[45] By the middle of the nineteenth century, this view was replaced by the separate spheres doctrine as defined in *Bradwell* v. *State* (1873). Both these views deny women's autonomous status to contract as an independent being. In 1873 Myra Bradwell applied for a license to practice law and was denied because "as a married woman [she] would be bound neither by her express contracts nor by those im-plied contracts which it is the policy of the law to create between attorney and client." Further, "God designed the sexes to occupy different spheres of action, and that it belonged to men to make, apply and execute the laws, was regarded as an almost axiomatic truth."[46]

The sexes were viewed as "different," occupying different spheres, and this viewing was seen as almost an axiomatic truth. Variations on this theme dominated most court decisions until 1971. Women were excluded from activities that appeared to con-flict with their roles as wives and mothers, such as tending bar unless one was the wife or daughter of the owner, or serving as a juror. Justice Frankfurter, in *Goesart* v. *Cleary* (1948), stated: "The fact that women may now have achieved the virtues that men have long claimed as their prerogatives and now indulge in vices that men have long practiced, does not preclude the state from drawing a sharp line between the sexes, certainly in such matters as the regulation of the liquor traffic."[47] He also argued that "nature made men and women different. . . . The law must accommodate itself to the immutable difference of Nature."[48] The Court made no dis-tinction between sex and gender. They are treated as one and the same.

Nature defines woman *by* her sex difference. And nature is

45. William Blackstone, qtd. in Wendy Williams, "The Equality Crisis: Some Reflections on Culture, Courts, and Feminism," *Women's Rights Law Reporter* 7 (Spring 1982): 176. And see Blackstone, *Commentaries on the Laws of England* [1765], vol. 1 (Chicago: Univ. of Chicago Press, 1979).

46. 83 U.S. (16 Wall) 130, 131, 132 (1873).

47. 335 U.S. 464, 466 (1948).

48. Felix Frankfurter, qtd. in William Chafe, *The American Woman: Her Changing Social, Economic, and Political Roles, 1920–1970* (Oxford: Oxford Univ. Press, 1972), pp. 125–26. And see David Kirp, Mark Yudof, and Marlene Strong Franks, *Gender Justice* (Chicago: Univ. of Chicago Press, 1986), p. 40.

taken as fact. This view lays the basis for the decision in *Muller* v. *Oregon* (1908), in which the Court upheld the constitutionality of an Oregon statute restricting to ten the daily working hours of women in laundries, factories, or mechanical establishments because of the limitations of their bodily strength.

The two sexes differ in structure of body, in the functions to be performed by each, in the amount of physical strength, in the capacity for long-continued labor, particularly when done standing, the influence of vigorous health upon the future well-being of the race, the self-reliance which enables one to assert full rights, and in the capacity, to maintain the struggle for subsistence. *This difference justifies a difference in legislation* and upholds that which is designed to compensate for some of the burdens which rest upon her.[49]

The Court found woman disadvantaged by her physical makeup and her maternal function; therefore, "the regulation of her hours of labor falls within the police power of the state, and a statute directed exclusively to such regulation does not conflict with the due process or equal protection clauses of the 14th amendment."[50] The limitation of working hours for women, when there is no such limitation for men, would only be a violation of a woman's right to equal treatment if women were similarly situated to men, and given the Court's interpretation they are not.

The differentiation of woman from man in its various articulations in law is acceptable as long as such treatment is justified by a legitimate state purpose and is not arbitrary. If, however, categorization by sex were viewed as suspect within the law, such classifications would have to be justified by "compelling" reasons. Although sex has yet to become a suspect category, the standards for establishing "legitimate government objectives" that justify classifications by sex have become more rigorous. In *Reed* v. *Reed* (1971), the Court decided unanimously to overrule an Idaho statute that gave men preference over women in appointments as administrators of deceased persons' estates.[51] After the *Reed* deci-

49. 208 U.S. 412, 422–23 (1908).
50. Ibid., p. 412.
51. See Ruth Bader Ginsburg, "Sexual Equality under the Fourteenth and Equal Rights Amendments," *Washington University Law Quarterly*, no. 1 (Winter 1979): 164; all further references to this work, abbreviated as "SE," will be included in the text. And see her "From No Rights, to Half Rights, to Confusing Rights," *Human Rights* 7 (May 1978): 12–47, "Gender and the Constitution," *Uni-*

sion, the Court insisted that the government would have to offer substantial justification for treating men and women differently, otherwise the practice would be in violation of the equal protection clause of the Fourteenth Amendment. "By providing dissimilar treatment for men and women who are thus similarly situated, the challenged section violates the Equal Protection Clause."[52]

The Supreme Court reached a similar decision in *Frontiero* v. *Richardson* (1973), which struck down a ruling that made it harder for servicewomen than for servicemen to get dependents' benefits for their families. The Court decided that married women in the uniformed services have the right to the same fringe benefits as married men ("SE," p. 165). The Court's language was stronger in this case than in *Reed*. Stricter criteria were to be used for warranting different treatment of the sexes. In a plurality decision, the justices argued that the statutes clarifying eligibility were suspect because of their classifications based on sex: dependents were defined as "his" spouse or his "wife," rather than in gender-neutral terms. The decision argued that "sex, like classifications based upon race, alienage, and national origin is inherently suspect and must therefore be subjected to close judicial scrutiny. We agree and, indeed, find at least implicit support for such an approach in our unanimous decision only last term in *Reed* v. *Reed*."[53]

The decision in the *Frontiero* case was one of the more progressive relating to classifications by sex. Justice Brennan, writing for the plurality, stated: "There can be no doubt that our nation has had a long and unfortunate history of sex discrimination. Traditionally, such discrimination was rationalized by an attitude of 'romantic paternalism' which in practical effect, put women, not on a pedestal, but in a cage" (411, p. 684). Four of the other justices also criticized the use of statutory distinctions that categorically relegate women to a secondary status.

And what differentiates sex from such nonsuspect statuses as intelligence or physical disability, and aligns it with the recognized suspect criteria, is

---

versity of Cincinnati Law Review 44 (1975): 1–42, and "Some Thoughts on the 1980's Debate over Special versus Equal Treatment for Women," *Law and Inequality* 4 (1986): 143–52.

52. 404 U.S. 71, 77 (1971).

53. 411 U.S. 677, 682 (1973); all further references to this work, abbreviated as 411, will be included in the text.

that the sex characteristic frequently bears no relation to ability to perform or contribute to society. As a result, statutory distinctions between the sexes often have the effect of invidiously relegating the entire class of females to inferior legal status without regard to the actual capabilities of its individual members.

(411, pp. 686–87)

In the *Frontiero* case, the differentiation of women from men as a sex class was found to be arbitrary and therefore unconstitutional. Even though this was the decision in *Frontiero,* the Court would still not treat sex as a suspect category. In *Craig* v. *Boren* (1976), the so-called intermediate standard of review was articulated as the way the Court would evaluate sex discrimination cases under the equal protection clause. Here the question was whether Oklahoma law could outlaw the sale of 3.2 percent (nonintoxicating) beer to males under age twenty-one while allowing females of the same age to purchase it. The Court found the law unconstitutional under the equal protection clause. Such "classifications by gender must serve *important* government objectives and must be *substantially related* to achievement of those objectives."[54]

The Court's decisions on this point, particularly through the 1970s, have been neither consistent nor of one voice (see "SE," p. 171). A series of unclear judgments—such as *Kahn* v. *Shevin* (1974), *Schlesinger* v. *Ballard* (1975), and *Califano* v. *Webster* (1977)[55]—has upheld different aspects of sex-based law. In *Rostker, Director of Selective Service* v. *Goldberg et al.* (1981), the Military Selective Service Act, which authorized the president to require registration of males, but not females, for possible military service was upheld. The Court stated that "the decision to exempt women from registration was not the 'accidental by product of a traditional way of thinking about females'"; rather "the existence of the combat restrictions clearly indicates the basis for Congress' decision to exempt women from registration."[56] The Court argued that the purpose of the draft is to prepare troops for combat. "Men and women, because of the combat restrictions on women[,] are simply not similarly situated for purposes of a draft or registration for a

----

54. 429 U.S. 190, 197 (1976).
55. See 416 U.S. 351 (1974), 419 U.S. 498 (1975), and 430 U.S. 703 (1977).
56. 453 U.S. 74, 77 (1981); all further references to this work, abbreviated as 453, will be included in the text.

draft" (453, p. 78). Quoting from *Schlesinger* v. *Ballard*, the Court further argued that "the gender classification is not invidious but rather realistically reflects the fact that the sexes are not similarly situated" and that "the constitution requires that Congress treat similarly situated persons similarly, not that it engage in gestures of superficial equality" (453, p. 79).

From the engendered standpoint of the law, men and women will very seldom be similarly situated; indeed, standards are articulated from the male point of view, which defines combat as man's territory to begin with. This male viewing assumes a series of starting points that really aren't starting points at all but rather points within an engendered discourse. But in order not to overstate the unity of the Court, I should point out that many of its decisions have been sharply divided. For example, in the dissenting opinion of Justices White, Marshall, and Brennan in *Rostker* v. *Goldberg*, Marshall wrote, "The court today places its imprimatur on one of the most potent remaining public expressions of 'ancient canards about the proper role of women'. . . . It upholds a statute that requires males but not females to register for the draft, and which thereby categorically excludes women from a fundamental civic obligation."[57] The standard for equality, even in this dissenting opinion, is still defined by being similarly situated to the male—women are to be treated as like men in order to be equal to them; thus, they should be drafted, as men are.

Let us examine one last case that further focuses on this problem of engendered sex "difference" in the law. *Michael M*. v. *Superior Court* (1981) challenged the California statutory rape law on the ground that it violated the equal protection clause. The Supreme Court affirmed the California law, which defined sexual intercourse with a female minor (under age eighteen) by a male as unlawful and made men alone criminally liable for this violation. Justice Rehnquist (with Justices Burger, Stewart, and Powell) concluded that the statute did not violate the equal protection clause because "the clause does not require that a statute apply equally to all persons . . . nor does it require that the law treat things which are different similarly."[58] Men and women and boys and girls are differ-

57. 453 U.S. 74, 78 (1981).
58. 450 U.S. 464, 469 (1981); all further references to this work, abbreviated as 450, will be included in the text.

ently situated; it is an "immutable physiological fact that it is the female exclusively who can become pregnant" (450, p. 467).

The decision in the *Michael M.* case does not label gender-based classification as suspect. Gender distinctions are acceptable as long as they have a "fair and substantial relationship" to legitimate state ends and/or a "substantial relation to important government objectives" (450, p. 469). Justice Rehnquist argued that the state's legitimate aim in this law was to deter males from sexual intercourse with a female minor. "The risk of pregnancy itself constitutes a substantial deterrence to young females. No similar natural sanctions deter males. A criminal sanction imposed solely on males thus serves to roughly 'equalize' the deterrents on the sexes" (450, p. 473). Justice Stewart, in his concurring opinion, stated that the gender-based classification in this law was based not on administrative convenience or on archaic assumptions about the proper role of the sexes. "But we have recognized that in certain narrow circumstances men and women are *not* similarly situated; in these circumstances a gender classification based on clear differences between the sexes is not invidious and a legislative classification realistically based upon those differences is not unconstitutional" (450, p. 478). By this reasoning, discrimination in and of itself is only illegal or unconstitutional when the classes being compared are similarly situated. Once again we find that the different situations of males and females justify their different treatment in law. In order to be treated similarly, the two would first have to be similarly situated.

The engendered discourse of law is *already* a series of gender classifications based on what are considered "real" differences between the sexes. One cannot recognize discrimination if one believes that the different treatment of the sexes is required by the "real" differences of woman from man as established in nature, or biology. When differentiation of the sexes according to their engendered meaning(s) is said to be constitutional, the politics of sex inequality masquerades in law as legal.

Although Justice Stewart said that there are "narrow" circumstances when men and women are *not* similarly situated and seems to have assumed that these instances are defined by *the* biological "difference" of women from men in terms of their childbearing capacity—pregnancy—the gendered bias of law is not limited to these instances, nor is pregnancy as a basis for classification by sex/ gender used with any consistency. Sometimes it is used to define women as a class, but sometimes, such as when women are being treated as "like" men, it is ignored as an issue. Justices Rehnquist and Stewart argued in the *Michael M.* case that the key question was "whether women and men are 'different in fact' in the context of the law at issue" (450, p. 469).[59] They determined that sex-based laws and disproportionately burdensome neutral rules are not harmful because they reflect "natural" differences between men and women; "the 'real' differences between the sexes have necessary—and not undesirable—social consequences" ("SESD," p. 918).

Ann Freedman calls this the "real differences" standard; if differences are found to be "real," based in "fact," then differential treatment is acceptable. She notes that the initial notion of "difference in fact" comes from the case *Tigner* v. *Texas* (1940).[60] Justice Frankfurter used this reference while upholding the exclusion of women from tending bar in *Goesart* v. *Cleary* (see "SESD," p. 929). The interpretation of "difference in fact" is supposed to apply to the distinctive reproductive and sexual characteristics that define the membership of a sex. The standard's meaning, however, is much more varied. The Court seldom agrees about how to interpret this "fact" of "real difference."

Justices Brennan and Marshall have often been joined by Justice White, and more recently Justice O'Connor, in arguing that alleged differences of nature do not in themselves justify sex classifications. "All rules based on sex, whether or not the underlying differences between women and men can be characterized as biological, must be tested against the same standard of social justification: Is the sex-based classification 'substantially related' to an 'important' governmental goal?" ("SESD," p. 949). Justice O'Connor similarly held the position in *Mississippi University for Women* v. *Hogan* (1982) that classifications based on sex "must be applied free of fixed notions concerning the roles and abilities of males and

---

59. See Ann Freedman, "Sex Equality, Sex Differences, and the Supreme Court," *Yale Law Journal* 92 (May 1983): 913–68, for a discussion of the "real difference" argument. All further references to this work, abbreviated as "SESD," will be included in the text.

60. 310 U.S. 141, 147 (1940).

females" and that the statutory objective itself must not reflect stereotypic and anachronistic notions about woman's role.[61] Although there is disagreement within the Court about the justificatory status of sex-based classification, the justificatory status of governmental goals in and of themselves stands outside the critique. The (patriarchal) state is privileged within law; its needs can justify sex discrimination and make it constitutional.

"Similarly Situated" and (Not) Pregnant

Pregnancy defines women as not similarly situated to men and therefore different from men. On this basis, differential treatment is acceptable—it is not a problem. In much the same way, classifications based on pregnancy have not been viewed as sexually discriminatory; rather they have been treated as neutral. Several cases deal with the issue of pregnancy in this light: *Geduldig* v. *Aiello* (1974), *General Electric Co.* v. *Gilbert* (1976), and *Nashville Gas Co.* v. *Satty* (1977).[62]

In *Geduldig* v. *Aiello*, a California district court held that the exclusion of four pregnant women from a disability insurance system violated the equal protection clause. The Supreme Court reversed this decision, claiming that the insurance company did not discriminate "against any definable group or class in terms of the aggregate risk protection derived by that group or class from the program" (417, p. 496). They found that not gender but rather a physical condition (pregnancy) was at issue in this exclusion. "While it is true that only women can become pregnant, it does not follow that every legislative classification concerning pregnancy is a sex-based classification" (417, p. 496, n. 20). Pregnancy is *not* a category of sex because *non*pregnant persons are both men and women. "The program divides potential recipients into two groups—pregnant women and nonpregnant persons. While the first group is exclusively female, the second includes members of both sexes" (417, p. 497).

The standard of evaluation here is the phallus. In other words,

---

61. 458 U.S. 718, 724–25 (1982).

62. See 417 U.S. 484 (1974)—all further references to this work, abbreviated as 417, will be included in the text; 429 U.S. 125 (1976); and 434 U.S. 136 (1977).

the male, as nonpregnant, is made the subject. The engendered nature of the law privileges nonpregnant persons. It is this category—which includes *all* men and *some* women—that is used to deny the sex-class status of pregnancy—which applies to no men but a majority of women. The interpretation of pregnancy is what is at issue here. It can be used both to differentiate women from men by institutionalizing *the* "difference" of the female body and to assume that men and women are the same if not pregnant: either way, the phallus rules.

This kind of thinking—which claims the male standard as a neutral standpoint—reappeared in *Personnel Administrator of Massachusetts et al.* v. *Feeney* (1979). In this case, granting preference to veterans when hiring was challenged as discriminatory against women and in violation of equal protection doctrine. The Court found the statutory classification to be neutral—that is, not gender based. Significant numbers of *non*veterans are men—and all *non*veterans (men and women) are at a similar disadvantage.[63] The Court's classification scheme once again advantages the male standard. The privileged category is men through the category *non*veteran. Because veterans are men and because nonveterans are also men, women are not discriminated against as a class as nonveteran.

The Court argued that "the distinction between veterans and non-veterans . . . is not a pretext for gender discrimination." Although the Court also acknowledged that few women benefit from veteran preference, it said "the non-veteran class is not substantially all female. . . . Too many men are affected by [the statute of preference] to permit the inference that the statute is but a pretext for preferring men over women" (442, p. 275). The distinction is between veterans and nonveterans, not between men and women. This is how an engendered discourse defines neutral law; it erases the presence of sex class at the same time it constructs it. Woman is made absent by the presence of the male standard, in this case through the category of the nonveteran, which is supposedly sex neutral. Men and women—as in *non*veteran—are similarly situated and treated as alike. This line of argument is used to erase the sexually discriminatory aspects of the classification "veteran."

63. 442 U.S. 256, 257 (1979); all further references to this work, abbreviated as 442, will be included in the text.

This kind of thinking makes it very difficult to recognize sex discrimination as problematic, especially when the issue is pregnancy. Here due process has proved to be a more progressive approach than equal protection. In *Cleveland Board of Education et al.* v. *La Fleur* (1974), pregnant public school teachers challenged the constitutionality of mandatory maternity leave rules and won on the basis of due process. The Court decided that terminating women's employment during pregnancy for the school's convenience was insufficient reason to infringe on women's basic constitutional liberty. The regulations "imply irrebuttable presumptions that unduly penalize a female teacher for deciding to bear a child."[64] More specifically, the Court argued that "freedom of personal choice in matters of marriage and family life is one of the liberties protected by the due process clause" (414, p. 639). The choice of how long to work during pregnancy is an individual matter that must be protected.

Justice Rehnquist dissented from this opinion, arguing that lawmaking requires presumptions that may appear arbitrary.

All legislation involves the drawing of lines. . . . The court's disenchantment with "irrebuttable presumptions," and its preference for "individualized determination" is in the last analysis nothing less than an attack upon the very notion of lawmaking itself. . . . If legislative bodies are to be permitted to draw a general line anywhere short of the delivery room, I can find no judicial standard of measurement which says the ones drawn here were invalid.

(414, p. 660)

Equal protection doctrine silently assumes a stance of sexual homogeneity through its criterion of "similarly situated." It is not always clear on what basis women are *not* seen as similarly situated, but most often the basis is their capacity to bear children and their obligation to rear them. The other side of this coin—how pregnancy and veteran status are seen as neutral rather than as sex-specific categories—further highlights the engendered basis of law. It makes clear that the standards, in terms of either how they are defined or how they are applied, are explicated through a phallo-

64. 414 U.S. 632, 648 (1974); all further references to this work, abbreviated as 414, will be included in the text.

cratic discourse that either marginalizes woman (as in *non*veteran status) or makes her completely absent (as in pregnant person). The engendered discourse of law treats women as "different," as in less than men, or treats them as equal, as in the same as men. The problem is that women are neither simply one or the other in terms of their sex or gender.

Contradiction in Engendered Law: Divorce and Custody

Because the law treats women differently from men, and as more different from men than they are, it exposes its own gendered partiality. The positioning of sex-neutral law is contradictory. To treat women as the same as men challenges the phallocratic structure of law from inside but also upholds the core of meaning that makes law's normative standard the "rational man." It both reflects and instigates the crisis of liberalism in the 1980s—the role of law in creating equality between the sexes.

The impact of changes in law that presumably create a greater equality between the sexes reflects this contradictory position. Further, many changes in law(s) presume the "sameness" standard, while society continues to treat men and women differently. This is very much the case for women in divorce and custody proceedings. On the one hand, no-fault divorce, equitable distribution of property, and the accompanying shifts in legal discourse that these developments encompass provide significant room for improving women's situation. On the other hand, there is a problem with treating men and women as the same in divorce when the social expectations that have defined their life in marriage have not done so. This is most true in the case of the homemaker. Law as a discourse about equality reflects the way equality is thought about in society and instigates new ways to think about equality even though it does not completely change the way we think or the way society operates. But legal discourse as well as society can also remain static, anachronistic, and resistant to change. This is why it is so difficult to assess exactly the impact of the shifts in the discourse of engendered law(s) and what they "really" mean.

Divorce Law

Historically, marriage was considered a lifelong union. The husband and wife became one, and the husband represented both. In traditional patriarchal marriage, the husband was viewed as the head of household, responsible for its support, and the wife was seen as responsible for domestic services, child care, and care of the husband. This model appears at least in part outdated. Today a majority of mothers are in the labor force. As early as 1977, this entry of mothers into the labor force was becoming apparent in people's changing attitudes toward marriage. A *New York Times/* CBS News nationwide survey conducted at that time found that "Americans today are more likely to believe that marriages in which partners share the tasks of breadwinner and homemaker are a more 'satisfying way of life' than the traditional marriage in which the husband is exclusively a provider and the wife exclusively a homemaker and mother."[65]

Changes in divorce law have been one way in which these changes in marriage and family life have been accommodated. The legalization of divorce itself reflects the changing nature of marriage. After all, divorce does not imply the end of the institution of marriage but rather puts closure on a specific marriage and allows an individual to enter another. "Divorce was not invented to destroy marriage since divorce is only necessary if marriage continues to exist."[66] The changes in divorce law that I will discuss began in California in the early 1960s and addressed issues of alimony (spousal support), child support and child custody, and the distribution of marital property. Although there is enormous variation in divorce laws between states, and in terms of the way the laws are applied within states, I will discuss these changes as symbolic of recent shifts in legal discourse about married life and divorce.

New California divorce law, according to Lenore Weitzman, dates from 1970 and reflects a move away from the notion of marriage as a partnership to the notion of individualism within mar-

65. Qtd. in Lenore Weitzman, *The Marriage Contract: A Guide to Living with Lovers and Spouses* (New York: Free Press, 1981), p. 175.

66. Christine Delphy, *Close to Home: A Materialist Analysis of Women's Oppression,* trans. Diana Leonard (Amherst: Univ. of Massachusetts Press, 1984), p. 94.

riage. "Implicit in the new laws . . . are incentives for investing in oneself, maintaining one's separate identity, and being self-sufficient."[67] Individualism as a legal discourse supposedly replaces the idea of marriage as a partnership. The changes in California law assume the liberal individualist stance in divorce but not necessarily in marriage or society in general. Although California divorce law moves to the point of treating women as like men—as independent individuals—it does so within the context of a marriage and labor-market system that treats women as unequal—in wages, job opportunity, and so on. Woman begins to be treated as an equal (to man) in divorce law, but this change is not the same as being treated as an equal. Legal equality is part of, but not the same as, sexual equality, which involves extralegal relations of power. Nor is sexual equality the same as economic equality. They do, however, relate to and affect one another. That is why legal equality between the sexes can create such contradictory results.

No-fault divorce dislodges the notion of blame in justifying marital dissolution. Divorce is now possible upon "one party's assertion that 'irreconcilable differences' have caused the irremediable breakdown of the marriage" (*DR*, p. 15). No grounds based on fault are needed; one spouse can decide unilaterally to get a divorce; financial awards are not tied to fault; and new standards for spousal support and property awards "treat men and women equally—rejecting sex based assumptions of traditional law" (*DR*, p. 16). These changes deny the relevance of the gendered division between woman as domestic and man as income earner.

Equal division of property between husband and wife has been a part of the no-fault package in California. Weitzman asks whether this rule has brought about more equitable results in divorce for women. She answers that in fact under the equal division rule there is often greater inequality. Equal division means that the husband gets half and the wife *and* the children get the other half. And when spousal and child support are taken into account, "divorced women and the minor children in their households experi-

67. Lenore Weitzman, *The Divorce Revolution: The Unexpected Social and Economic Consequences for Women and Children in America* (New York: Free Press, 1985), p. 374; all further references to this work, abbreviated as *DR*, will be included in the text.

ence a 73 percent decline in their standard of living in the first year after divorce. Their former husbands, in contrast, experience a 42 percent rise in their standard of living" (*DR*, p. xii).

Treating women as *like* men in divorce does not necessarily create more economic equality for women because many women's situations are not the same as men's. Many older wives have not participated in the labor force. Women in the labor market earn disproportionately less than their (former) husbands. And whether or not these women are wage earners, most of them are the custodial parents of their children. The engendered circumstances of divorced women's lives make equal treatment contradictory at best. Yet an equal division of property may be preferable to an equitable division because it gives women at least half the property.

Weitzman is hesitant to make this judgment because she is particularly concerned with full-time homemakers of long duration. "They should be awarded a larger share of the property to achieve the goal of 'equality of results,' i.e., equality in the post-divorce standards of living of the two spouses" (*DR*, p. 105). Gender-neutral rules are therefore troublesome at best. "Rules designed to treat men and women 'equally' have in practice served to deprive divorced women (especially older homemakers and mothers of young children) of the legal and financial protections that the old law provided" (*DR*, p. xi). The economic inequality of marriage has to change before divorce law that treats the wife as economically self-sufficient can make sense. Given present society and child-rearing practices, "we cannot treat men and women as 'equals,' in divorce settlement. We must find ways to safeguard and protect women, not only to achieve fairness and equity, but also to encourage and reward those who invest in and care for our children and ultimately, to foster true equality for succeeding generations" (*DR*, pp. 365–66). The problem is how to treat women fairly without reengendering their lives.

More recent changes in New York State divorce law seem to have had similar contradictory results. Equitable distribution became a part of New York divorce law in 1980. Previously property was awarded to the titleholder. Under the new law, marriage is viewed as an economic partnership, a view that recognizes the non-wage-earning spouse's contribution when dividing property and awarding maintenance. "The function of equitable distribution is to recognize that when a marriage ends each of the spouses . . . has a stake in and right to a share of the marital assets accumulated while it endured . . . because those assets represent the capital product of what was essentially a partnership" (*NY*, p. 96).

In the 1986 *Report of the New York Task Force on Women in the Courts* discussed earlier, equitable distribution was overwhelmingly viewed as creating "unfairness and undue hardship on women." The report found that women suffered from short-term maintenance after long-term marriage; they were given *de minimis* shares of business and professional practices and terminable and modifiable maintenance in lieu of indefeasible and equitable distribution (see *NY*, p. 116). Rather than recognize marriage as an economic partnership, some judges want to ensure that the EDL (Equitable Distribution Law) doesn't "make reluctant Santa Clauses out of ex-husbands" (*NY*, p. 100). Property divisions were found to continue to place an insufficient value on the homemaker's services and her lost earning capacity. Judges continue to think in terms of *his* business, *his* house, *his* pension when deciding settlements. The supposedly gender-neutral law is biased. The supposedly objective interpreters of the law are biased as well.

The resulting picture is complex. Although equitable distribution treats men and women similarly, it does not make them similar. It does, however, begin to shift the discourse. Although there still are inequities "in fact," equality between the sexes becomes the dominant idea, and this conflict can be used progressively. Today there is a disjuncture between full-time homemakers, who make up a small portion of the female population, and the majority of women, who are in the labor force. Divorce focuses attention on the difficulty of the full-time homemaker; it completely challenges her way of life. Given the majority of women's lives, equal or equitable distribution does not necessarily create *more* inequality, but it does highlight the precarious position of women in the economy and the family. This revelation is not all bad: it reflects the fact that women are caught between the real and the ideal, between the meaning of gender neutrality as a legal discourse and its meaning as a societal practice.

Child Custody

The disjuncture between legal discourse and social practice appears even more starkly in the area of child custody. Historically, the mother was viewed preferentially as the custodial parent. Recently, though, the "tender years" doctrine, which assumes that young children need to live with their mother, has been replaced with the sex-neutral phrases "best interests of the child" and "joint custody." By 1985 more than thirty states had adopted some form of joint custody law, to allow—and possibly encourage—fathers' involvement in postdivorce parenting (*NY*, p. 216). This is an instance, however, in which law has shifted more than the practices of men have. On the whole, women remain the childrearers both in marriage and after divorce.

One realm in which changed custody law seems to have had an impact, and not necessarily to women's advantage, is contested custody. Whereas women remain the custodians of children in uncontested custody cases, men very often win custody in contested cases with the help of "the best interests of the child" as the revised legal standard. The preference for mothers in these cases is replaced by sex-neutral determinations. Although the "best interests of the child" standard appears "to be sex neutral, it is increasingly being undermined by the development of criteria that discriminate against women."[68] The courts are minimizing the value of past day-to-day care and instead are emphasizing the parent's economic resources and life-style. Thus, women "are faced not with sex neutral custody standards applied appropriately to whoever does the primary caretaking, but rather with standards that ignore or devalue primary parenting and are sex discriminatory."[69]

Joint custody opened doors for fathers who wanted custody. "In this regard, the passage of the no-fault divorce law coincided with the first stages of the father's rights movement and reflected, in part, men's increased interest in parenting both during marriage and after divorce" (*DR*, p. 225).[70] Nevertheless, the number of fa-

68. Carol Lefcourt, *Women and the Law* (New York: Boardman, 1984), ch. 6, p. 3.
69. Ibid.
70. See Nancy Polikoff, "Gender and Child-Custody Determinations: Exploding the Myths," in *Families, Politics, and Public Policy: A Feminist Dialogue on*

thers asking for custody is small. Of those who do seek custody, a disproportionate number receive it. The New York Task Force found that "there is substantial evidence that when fathers do litigate custody, they win at least as often as mothers do" (*NY*, p. 161).

A further problem with the "best interests of the child" standard is that if and when custody is contested, the mother, particularly if she is a wage earner, is very often viewed by a judge as not like a woman, a good parent, because a mother who works in the labor force doesn't have time to be a good mother. A father who works— as men are expected to do—is seen as able to be a good father and still hold a job.

This kind of thinking does not characterize all judges. As frequently as not, judges are still swayed by the "tender years" doctrine, but there are problems either way. Although maternal preference may seem like a way to protect women's interests within the family structure as it presently exists, "the stereotype of a mother on which it is based has negative consequences for the custody-seeking woman who does not conform to an image which is both sexist and out of touch with reality" (*NY*, p. 166). This is more and more the case, because a majority of women with children work in the labor force.

Whatever the problems with joint custody as a doctrine having disproportionate and unfair impact on women, it represents a shift in the gendered discourse of law. It recognizes both mothers and fathers as parents and thus stands ahead of much-needed change in the actual societal relations of parenting. We are still, however, left with the question: How can we take the differential effects of gender-neutral law into account without reestablishing engendered law as acceptable? The issue of the Equal Rights Amendment touches on this problem.

Engendered Sex Neutrality

The Equal Rights Amendment (ERA) states that "equality of rights under the law shall not be denied or abridged by the U.S. or by

Women and the State, ed. Irene Diamond (New York: Longman, 1983), pp. 183–202.

any state on account of sex." Originally introduced in 1923 and reintroduced in 1970, the amendment calls for equal protection of the law for women, meaning same treatment, except for unique physical characteristics, which might require different treatment.[71] The essential intent of the amendment is to create similar treatment for women and to make the categories "women" and "sex classification" themselves suspect within law. Under the ERA, the state would have to do more than justify "sex classification" on the basis of the state's rational interests; it would have to show compelling reasons for differential classifications by sex.

The ERA points out the insufficiency for women of the Fifth and Fourteenth amendments, which state the principle of equal protection under law. The ERA would establish sex classification as suspect within law primarily in economic terms. It would not help to clarify the specific sex characteristic of pregnancy in relation to a notion of sex equality. Nor would it clarify the place of difference(s) in a theory of equality. The ERA is premised in a vision of equality that assumes that women are the same as men, and to the degree that they are, there is no problem. However, both sex and gender differences *and* sex and gender similarities pose a dilemma for equal rights legislation because such legislation is formulated within an engendered discourse. The dilemma is this: there is no such thing as gender-neutral law. Gender already presumes "institutionalized" sex differences.

To the extent that the ERA attempts to create gender-neutral law, it is caught in this contradiction of (liberal) phallocratic law: equality between men and women is an engendered equality. The phallus still needs to be decentered, even though the jurisdiction of the ERA is limited to protect one's right to privacy in performing bodily functions without intrusion of the opposite sex. (In other words, the ERA does not require unisex toilets.) The phallus remains centered even though laws based on characteristics unique

71. See Barbara Allen Babcock, Ann Freedman, Eleanor Holmes Norton, and Susan Ross, *Sex Discrimination and the Law* (Boston: Little, Brown, 1975); Barbara Brown, Ann Freedman, Harriet Katz, and Alice Price, *Women's Rights and the Law* (New York: Praeger, 1977); Karen De Crow, *Sexist Justice* (New York: Random House, 1974); Cynthia Fuch Epstein, *Women in Law* (New York: Basic Books, 1981); and Equal Rights Amendment Project (Anita Miller, project director), *Impact ERA: Limitations and Possibilities* (Millbrae, Calif.: Les Femmes Publishing, 1976).

to one sex can still be used as a basis for sex classification. Pregnancy leave would be allowed.

When Alice Paul of the National Women's party first introduced the ERA to Congress, she argued that it would not endanger the protective legislation affecting wage-earning women. In 1923 she and her party argued that protective legislation was a form of reverse discrimination, that it was harmful and limiting for women. I will discuss this issue fully in Chapter 6. At this point I will just note that the issue of equality, as it is formulated in the ERA, is premised in a notion of woman's sameness to man, which makes "difference" as well as special legislation problematic. Protective legislation and/or pregnancy-related issues highlight the inadequacy of the male standard.

The engendered aspects of law reflect the differences that culture has defined as differences, although law very often presents these as natural and biological, in other words, sexual. Law therefore articulates gender differentiation that both reproduces and protects this system of sex classification. It also articulates a sameness standard between men and women that reproduces and protects this system. These visions in law rest uneasily with each other while the standards of equality, meaning sameness and neutrality, conflict with the differentiation of woman from man.

The discourse of liberalism, which espouses a commitment to equality for all individuals, articulates an important and necessary view regarding the treatment of women. The fact that liberalism has always privileged the phallus and the social relations of patriarchal society explains why the tension between women's similarity (to) and difference (from men) is embodied *within* liberal law. As a gendered discourse, liberal law ends up exposing the phallus, because in its view men and women are supposedly homogeneous individuals and not sex classes. Liberalism thus establishes the expectation that women will be treated as individuals, not as women, classified by their sex.

The problem with the notion of liberal individualism in this instance is that the individual is a man, in a male body. On the one hand, to differentiate women's rights delegitimizes the liberal discourse of law. On the other hand, when law posits the sameness of women to men, it highlights the inconsistencies between law and patriarchal social relations. Although woman is often reduced to her body and its sex "difference," to gain equality in the law she must be like a man. Further, although equal treatment will often be sufficient for women, it will not always be. We are left with the problem of difference and the question of how the relationship between sex and gender constructs difference(s).

It would seem, as MacKinnon has argued, that "biologically different people are to be treated the same except when their biological differences are relevant" (*SHWW,* p. 111). But the issue of relevance here is no small matter. This issue becomes all the more problematic when we recognize the pregnant body. "Differential treatment by sex with respect to pregnancy is impossible because no pregnant men exist to whom we can be compared" (*SHWW,* p. 111). Additionally, as Sylvia Law notes, present constitutional equality doctrine confuses reproductive biology and its cultural expressions, thus denying the applicability of equality doctrine to laws governing reproductive biology. She argues that this problem could be partially remedied if law distinguished "between reproductive biological difference and cultural generalization that prohibits regulation of reproductive biology whenever it oppresses women or reinforces cultural sex-role stereotypes."[72] The problem, however, remains the same: distinguishing between biology and culture and between sex and gender.

Gender differences exist, although they are often exaggerated. A sex difference—defined as the pregnant body—exists as unique. It has no point of comparison to males. So we are left with the problem of sex equality. In order for the pregnant body not to be a problem, it must be used to reinvent the meaning of equality. The pregnant body is used to relocate the phallus in a series of multiple differences. Bodies are viewed plurally, as are differences. Multiplicity and diversity replace polarity and homogeneity. Opposition and hierarchy are challenged. Differences will be reconstructed as we pluralize the meaning of the body.[73]

72. Sylvia Law, "Rethinking Sex and the Constitution," *University of Pennsylvania Law Review* 132 (June 1984): 1033.
73. For an interesting discussion of "reinventing difference," see Cora Kaplan, *Sea Changes: Culture and Feminisms* (London: Verso Press, 1986); W. J. T. Mitchell, "Pluralism as Dogmatism," *Critical Inquiry* 12 (Spring 1986): 494–502; and Ellen Rooney, "Who's Left Out? A Rose by Any Other Name Is Still Red; or, The Politics of Pluralism," *Critical Inquiry* 12 (Spring 1986): 550–63. See also *Oxford Literary Review* 8, nos. 1–2 (1986).

Chapter Three

Sex "Difference"
and the Engendered Body

A woman's body is *not* a man's body. This becomes even more true when the body is pregnant. Man is never viewed as "*not* pregnant," so pregnancy must be constructed as woman's "difference" and not man's lacking. Part of the misrepresentation of the female body, as one and the same as the mother's body, is to define it *as "different."*

In this usage, being "different" is the same as being unequal. Although woman's body as a biological entity is engendered through a language that differentiates it from man's, woman's body is also unique and particular in terms of its capacity to reproduce sexually. This capacity should not be reduced to a problem of gender, yet gender plays an active part in defining the pregnant body. There is a politics to sex "difference" because there is a politics to the discourse that names it. I therefore want to explore how the pregnant body is used to establish woman as "different," and, equally important, how this use poses the dilemma of difference for a discourse premised in a notion of equality meaning sameness. The tension between dualism and diversity and how this tension is expressed through the privileging of the phallus will be the focus of this chapter.

The Engendered Body

Women are both biological sexual selves and selves engendered through their bodies.[1] Sex and gender play back on each other

1. See Zillah Eisenstein, *Feminism and Sexual Equality: Crisis in Liberal*

79

through a complicated process. The woman's body is particularized as female, but it is inevitably associated with the mother's body, which is more than female because it embodies institutionalized gender "difference." The woman's body is the mother's body in a different way than the man's body is *not* the father's body, because men do not get pregnant. A woman's "potentially" pregnant body is significant in defining her as a woman qua mother in patriarchal and phallocratic society. The meaning of her body does not exist outside this context, yet her body is more than this meaning because it contains the possibility of other meanings. The woman's body must be contextualized to be understood, yet it cannot be reduced to its contextual meaning. When all is said and done, there is still the "reality" of the body. However contextualized, it is also real. There is no innate body, but there are bodies. Mary Jacobus may not completely agree with me. She argues that the issue is the textuality of sex rather than the sexuality of the text: "Instead of asking 'Is there a woman in this text?' ask, 'Is there a text in this woman?'"[2] I believe we need to ask both questions.

My point is not that the body—as established in biological "fact"—determines its own meaning outside discourse or the relations of patriarchal society. There is no "outside" or biological "fact" as such. But we should not reduce the question of the body to its contextualized meaning within discourse if doing so results only in recognizing diversity—the difference(s) created in discourse—and silencing the unity of meaning in the body. Both the body as "fact" and the body as "interpretation" are real, even if we cannot clearly demarcate where one begins and the other ends.

These coexistent realities argue against drawing the distinction between sex and gender too starkly.[3] Gayle Rubin first distinguished these realms for feminist scholars.

Sex is sex, but what counts as sex is equally culturally determined and obtained. Every society also has a sex/gender system—a set of arrange-

America (New York: Monthly Review Press, 1984), for an earlier discussion of this issue.

   2. Mary Jacobus, "Women and Theory," in Mary Jacobus, *Reading Woman: Essays in Feminist Criticism* (New York: Columbia Univ. Press, 1986), p. 109.

   3. My use of the term "sex" is narrow. For the purposes of my argument, it applies to the idea of "the body" as only biologically sexed rather than gendered. "Sex" does not imply a more complex notion of sexuality per se.

ments by which the biological raw material of human sex and procreation is shaped by human social intervention and satisfied in a conventional manner, no matter how bizarre some of the conventions might be.[4]

Sex is the realm of biological raw material, and gender reflects human social intervention. But we need to recognize that even what is thought of as raw biology is socially constructed. This ambiguity makes it difficult to distinguish between the institutionalized notions of gender and their nongendered components because the two are never completely separate. This is true of the distinctions between woman's biological particularity and her sex "difference": between the pregnant body and woman's body and between the institution of motherhood and biological motherhood.[5] More recently Rubin has expressed a similar position. She writes, "I don't have any problem with thinking of sex and gender as relatively autonomous. I don't mean to make the separation quite so absolute as people seem to think. I think the systems are interconnected and interpenetrated, and the distinction I want to make is largely analytical, to sort out some of the issues and not keep reducing sex issues to gender ones, or deriving sex from gender."[6]

Even though it is not possible to answer the question What is this "thing" called the body? I keep asking it. To the extent that engendered discourse assumes some "thing" called the body, there is such a thing, because we act on this assumption as though it were real. This process becomes most true and most problematic when political discourses, such as law, assume the stance of the "real" biological (sex) "difference" of woman's body as fact. Instead of recognizing the part that cultural interpretation plays in the designation of woman as "different," these discourses make woman's body masquerade as scientific proof that she is, and is meant to be, "different": a mother. The potential of woman's body to exist outside phallocratic discourse is lost. And although it is impossible to exist completely outside this discourse, much is still to be lost if we give up trying to imagine the female body outside discourse.

4. Gayle Rubin, "The Traffic in Women: Notes on the 'Political Economy' of Sex," in *Toward an Anthropology of Women,* ed. Rayna Reiter (New York: Monthly Review Press, 1975), p. 165.

5. See Adrienne Rich, *Of Woman Born: Motherhood as Experience and Institution* (New York: Norton, 1976), for the explication of this distinction.

6. Gayle Rubin, personal correspondence, 20 May 1982.

The Discourse about
Sex "Difference"

The discussion of and theorization about sex "difference" shift and change historically, although they present a static, natural, objective standpoint of "the" body as their starting point.[7] This disjuncture between a changing discourse concerning the meaning of "difference" and an unchanging conception of the body, on which the "difference" is premised, directs us to my next point. Sex "difference" arises as a concern in political discourse most often during conservative eras, which react to the threatened boundary lines between the sexes. This clearly was the case for New Right and neoconservative politics in the United States in the 1980s, and it was also true of bourgeois radicalism in eighteenth-century England. Thomas Laqueur states that "representations of the body were more than simply ways of reestablishing hierarchy in an age when its metaphysical foundations were being rapidly effaced." Cultural, political, and economic upheavals in the eighteenth century "created the context in which the articulation of radical differences between the sexes became culturally imperative."[8]

The discussion and (re)articulation of the theme of sex "difference" arises most frequently when men's and women's lives appear to be becoming more similar. Notions of difference are reformulated to ensure that similarity between the sexes does not obliterate their "difference." When men's and women's lives are clearly differentiated, as in the case of a male wage earner and female homemaker, the demarcation of the sexes does not need (re)formulation. It does, however, need (re)articulation when the homemaker enters the work force *as* her husband did. She does not actually enter the labor force exactly the way her husband did, because she is a woman. She most likely enters a sexual ghetto in the market. Nevertheless, the clear demarcations between man and woman become blurred. This happened in the United States

7. Ancient formulations of sex "difference" were conceived in terms of the oppositions of mind/body, passion/reason; the masculine form was seen as moderate, the feminine immoderate. See Michel Foucault, *The Use of Pleasure*, vol. 2 of *The History of Sexuality*, trans. Robert Hurley (New York: Pantheon Books, 1985). See also Plato, *Republic*, ed. Paul Shorey (Cambridge, Mass.: Harvard Univ. Press, 1926), bks 1–5, and *Laws*, ed. R. G. Bury (London: Heinemann, 1926), bks. 1–2, as examples of how "difference" is encoded in the Western canon.

8. Thomas Laqueur, "Orgasm, Generation, and the Politics of Reproductive Biology," *Representations*, no. 14 (Spring 1986): 18–19, 35.

in the latter half of the nineteenth century. "Because the home no longer defined the limits of female activity and women were joining the men in the outside world, however marginally, many Americans believed that the need to draw a clear line between appropriately male and female activities had become acute."[9] This trend returned with renewed vigor again after World War II.

According to Peter Gay, until well into the nineteenth century, woman was viewed as a "vessel of lust." The segregation of the sexes, mirrored in their differential education and the separate spheres assigned them, was seen as a "prescription of nature." Gay quotes Max Planck, director of the Institute for Theoretical Physics at the University of Berlin, on the prevailing opinion on difference: "'One cannot emphasize enough that nature itself has prescribed to woman her vocation as mother and housewife' and that the laws of nature are ignored, or contravened, only at exorbitant cost."[10] Difference is assigned its sexual meaning by nature, in the name of nature. Charles Darwin established this as the dominant view in his *Descent of Man* in 1871. As a physician of the time asked, "Why spoil a good mother to make an ordinary grammarian?" (*BSS*, p. 8).

This viewing of women as mothers makes them their bodies. They are weaker and less intelligent than men; they are dominated by their reproductive function. This vision has given way to a more modern notion, which recognizes a certain independence of woman's body from her mind. In the United States by the early twentieth century, intelligence was not viewed as a secondary sex characteristic (*BSS*, p. 103). Scientist Leta Hollingsworth challenged the idea that menstruation inhibits the intellectual functioning of women; nothing in her tests "provided any evidence for the widespread belief that women suffer periodic incapacity in their physical and intellectual abilities . . . during menstruation" (*BSS*, p. 97). By the 1920s the link between the brain and "sex difference" was being dropped by American scientists and psychologists, but the idea that sex "difference" is genetically determined rather than socially constructed still held sway.

9. Rosalind Rosenberg, *Beyond Separate Spheres: Intellectual Roots of Modern Feminism* (New Haven, Conn.: Yale Univ. Press, 1982), p. xv; all further references to this work, abbreviated as *BSS*, will be included in the text.

10. Peter Gay, *The Education of the Senses*, vol. 1 of *The Bourgeois Experience* (New York: Oxford Univ. Press, 1984), p. 225.

Although we have moved away from the "separate spheres" doctrine—that women are completely different from men—toward the contemporary notion that recognizes similarity between women and men, our standpoint still privileges "difference" as a homogeneous standard that can be applied to women. On May 18, 1981, the cover story of *Newsweek* magazine was entitled "Just How the Sexes Differ." It is interesting that the article found that men and women differ less than "we might think they do." This point is key to understanding the discourse about sex "difference." Sex "difference" has been able to operate so effectively as a "discourse" because people believe the alleged "differences" are a *true* depiction of reality, of nature itself. Whether men have been "proved" to be more aggressive than women is only part of how difference is established as a "difference" of sex. The fact that people believe that men are more aggressive—and believe that this aggression has been objectively proved—both reflects and affects the discourse on sex "difference." Whether this belief is "really true" matters less. "The idea that male hormones make men more competitive, better at sports, go-getters in the business world, and ready to fight to defend their honor and family certainly captures the popular imagination."[11]

The force and impact of the discourse of sex "difference," rather than its biological justifications, are what is at issue. The view of sex "difference" operates politically to reinforce differentiations that very often are not based on biological differences at all. This actuality does not keep New Right spokesman George Gilder from arguing that women should not go into combat because the "hard evidence" has shown men to be more aggressive than women. Nor does it keep him from asserting that it is established fact that women do not commit themselves to the work force in the same spirit as men do.[12] The *discourse* of sex "difference"—not woman's body per se—establishes these supposed differences as "fact."

Eleanor Maccoby and Carol Jacklin, psychologists who study this issue, argue that men and women are not really all that differ-

11. Anne Fausto-Sterling, *Myths of Gender: Biological Theories about Women and Men* (New York: Basic Books, 1985), p. 126; all further references to this work, abbreviated as *MG*, will be included in the text.

12. See George Gilder, "Sexual Suicide and Marriage," *Conservative Digest* 12 (November 1986): 41. See also his *Sexual Suicide* (New York: Quadrangle/New York Times Book Co., 1973), and *Wealth and Poverty* (New York: Basic Books, 1981).

ent to begin with. More important, they argue that we do not know the truth about sex "difference."[13] "We have seen that the sexes are psychologically much alike in many respects. We have also seen that some of the ways in which they do differ probably have a biological basis, whereas others do not." Nevertheless, Maccoby and Jacklin feel that many differences which are considered to be sexual are not; rather, they are differences constructed in society. Besides, "a variety of social institutions are viable within the framework set by biology. It is up to human beings to select those that foster the lifestyles they most value."[14] Anne Fausto-Sterling argues similarly, that differences in cognition between men and women should not be assumed to be biological in origin (see *MG*, pp. 59–60). That premise has yet to be proved.

Although there is a good amount of contradictory evidence that analytically defines a sex "difference"—how it can be tested, what its origin is—the scientific discourse that surrounds sex "difference" continues to portray it as a unified representation of nature. Difference, as in sex "difference," is formulated as natural. This engendered view of sex "difference," set forth as one and the same as the "real" body, presents us with the seamless web of being female and being a woman. Sex "difference" is someplace between the real and the ideal because the body exists but always through its signs. There are differences between male and female bodies, but the "difference" of sex is not found just in the body. It is also in the discussion and language that interpret the body and the social arrangements surrounding it. "Difference" is therefore articulated and reproduced through the body as flesh and "sign": the language of sex "difference" may not be all *true*, but it is *real*.

This is a point that I am not sure feminists have always understood sufficiently. In the early 1970s many feminists—and I include myself among them—denied the importance of difference(s) for articulating a theory of women's liberation or sex equality. This was most true of liberal and socialist feminists: they thought that women are the same as men and should be treated as such.[15] Betty

13. See Eleanor Maccoby and Carol Jacklin, *The Psychology of Sex Differences* (Stanford, Calif.: Stanford Univ. Press, 1974), p. 355. And see Maccoby, *The Development of Sex Differences* (Stanford, Calif.: Stanford Univ. Press, 1966).

14. Maccoby and Jacklin, *The Psychology of Sex Differences*, pp. 373, 374.

15. Although socialist feminists made clear that equality did not mean being treated as "like" men, if likeness assumed the exploitative aspects of capitalist

Friedan, well-known liberal feminist in the 1960s, argued in *The Feminine Mystique* for a notion of equality that assumed the sameness of men and women. In the 1980s, in her book *The Second Stage*, she criticizes feminism for not recognizing the significance of difference.[16] Alison Jaggar, a socialist feminist, argued in the early 1970s "that the concept of sex is in no way essential to the concept of a person." She did not think that maleness or femaleness should underline the order of society. "If having a sex is *not* one of the defining characteristics of a person[,] . . . then we can draw no justification from the concept of a person for arguing that our ideal society requires a social distinction between persons of different sexes." Because she denied difference and bodily identity, Jaggar could argue that "the rights of women can be protected quite adequately in a society which recognizes basic human rights."[17]

Noted socialist feminist author Juliet Mitchell took this same stance in the mid-1970s when she wrote, "Biological differences between men and women obviously exist but it is not these that are the concern of feminism."[18] Since then, however, developments in feminism have pushed it beyond its earlier notions. Today, as a result of more than a decade of feminist gains in the realms of affirmative action and reproductive rights, women occupy a place more similar to men's than ever before. From this position— whether in the labor force or in the bedroom—feminists can more easily rethink the question of difference(s). And although "similar" does not always mean more equal, it does make equality a greater possibility.

---

class relations, they otherwise accepted the idea of sameness of treatment. Woman's body posed no particular problem for equality, or "liberation," which was the term usually preferred by socialist feminists.

16. See Eisenstein, *Feminism and Sexual Equality*, esp. ch. 8, for a discussion of Friedan as a neoconservative feminist.

17. Alison Jaggar, "On Sexual Equality," *Ethics* 84 (July 1974): 279, 280, 285. This feminist stance dates back to liberal feminists such as Mary Wollstonecraft and Elizabeth Cady Stanton. See Mary Wollstonecraft, *A Vindication of the Rights of Woman*, ed. Charles Hagelman, Jr. (New York: Norton, 1967); and Elizabeth Cady Stanton, Susan B. Anthony, and Matilda Joslyn Gage, eds., *History of Woman Suffrage* (New York: Source Book Press, 1970).

18. Juliet Mitchell, "Women and Equality," in *The Rights and Wrongs of Women*, ed. Juliet Mitchell and Ann Oakley (Harmondsworth: Penguin Books, 1976), p. 379. And see Juliet Mitchell, *Woman's Estate* (New York: Pantheon Books, 1971).

Developments outside feminism have also had their impact. The New Right and neoconservative preoccupation with the "difference" of the sexes has forced feminists to take the issue into greater account, and often not on their own terms. The feminist examination of the issue of sex difference(s) and its relation to women's equality is often put on the defensive by the conservatives' interpretation of sex "difference" as natural, necessary, and even God given.

Given the right wing's denial of equality on the basis of the equation between sex "difference" and the mother's body, feminists remain fearful of the notion of difference, and rightly so. Instead of being able to focus on the open-textured meanings of woman's body and its capacity to express difference(s), feminists must explore difference while trying to put careful closure on its meaning. My concern with clarifying the meaning(s) of sex "difference" reflects these developments: progressive moves *within* feminism toward equality, the cautious exploration by feminists of the meaning of "difference," *and* conservative concerns during the Reagan era. For this reason I move uneasily between openness and closure, sex and gender, difference(s) and sameness. This process is both necessary and suspect.

Gender, Biology, and Difference(s)

Biology supposedly sets up the constraints within which human experience occurs. But biology, as nature, is not static or inevitable. Evelyne Sullerot argues that "given the present state of science and civilization, it seems to me much easier to change natural than cultural facts. It was much easier to relieve women from obligatory breastfeeding than to make fathers give babies their bottles. . . . It is inertia built into cultural phenomena that seems to slow down our control over natural phenomena."[19] Ruth Bleier also argues that "rather than a biology acting to constrain and limit our potentialities[,] . . . [we] have produced *cultures* that constrain and limit those possibilities."[20] The meaning of "natural" is

19. Evelyne Sullerot, "The Feminine (Matter of) Fact," trans. Yvonne Rochette-Ozzello, in *New French Feminisms: An Anthology,* ed. Elaine Marks and Isabelle de Courtivron (Amherst: Univ. of Massachusetts Press, 1980), p. 158.

20. Ruth Bleier, *Science and Gender: A Critique of Biology and Its Theories on Women* (New York: Pergamon Press, 1984), p. 7.

not all that clear to begin with. Ruth Hubbard, Mary Sue Henefin, and Barbara Fried state, "Women's biology not only is not destiny, but is often not even biology."[21] Gender is socially constructed, but so is biology; the language of sex "difference" operates in the realms of both sex and gender.

Simone de Beauvoir, although ambivalent when depicting a woman's body, asserts that cultural determinants have more to do with defining woman than does biology. "Biology is not enough to give an answer to the question that is before us: Why is woman the Other?" According to her, history intervenes to define humanity. "Human society is never abandoned wholly to nature." This understanding leads to de Beauvoir's now famous statement "One is not born, but rather becomes a woman. No biological, psychological, or economic fate determines the figure that the human female presents in society: it is civilization as a whole that produces this creature intermediate between male and eunuch."[22] Yet de Beauvoir distinguishes between women and the proletariat because women have *always* been subordinated to men; hence their dependency is not the result of a historical event or a social change.[23] For de Beauvoir, one is born a female and becomes a woman; one undergoes a biological *and* a historical process.

If biology plays a part in defining how gender is constructed and gender plays a part in constructing what biology means, then biology erects the confines within which human choices are made. Fausto-Sterling clarifies this point. "No matter how our ideas about male and female physique evolve in the coming years, one thing remains certain: our cultural conceptions will change the way our bodies grow, and how our bodies grow will change the way our culture views them" (*MG,* p. 220). The constraints operate more in the realm of culture than in that of biology because the discourse of sex "difference" imposes greater limitations on the way we think about possibilities than the body itself does.

I do not deny Jeffrey Weeks his point that "the bodily differences

21. Ruth Hubbard, Mary Sue Henefin, and Barbara Fried, eds., *Women Look at Biology Looking at Women* (Cambridge, Mass.: Schenkman Publishing, 1979), p. xiii.

22. Simone de Beauvoir, *The Second Sex,* trans. and ed. H. M. Parshley (New York: Bantam Books, 1949), pp. 33, 456, 249.

23. See ibid., p. xviii.

are the irreducible sites for the inscription of sexual difference."[24] But the process of naming these sites reveals as much about phallocratic discourse as it does about the body. Patriarchal relations mystify the politics of sex in the name of biology; they inscribe the relations of gender while they do so. "Males are not dominant by *nature*, or they would *always* be dominant, in the way females *always* have the babies. In one sense, patriarchy is an attempt to make male dominance a 'natural' fact."[25] It is the unnaturalness of sex "difference" that requires its engendered form: the institutionalized hierarchical differentiation of woman from man.

Given this context, what does it mean to argue that women are "different" from men? The question itself privileges the phallus. Emmanuelle de Lesseps makes this point when she argues that "man is the reference, woman is the difference."[26] As such, woman becomes the "other," as asserted by Monique Wittig. "Men are not different, whites are not different, nor are the masters."[27] The notion of sex difference obscures more than it clarifies, because we are not necessarily as different as we are said to be or different in the ways in which we are described as being. "We are in fact different. But we are not as different FROM men (as false consciousness claims) as we are different FROM THAT WHICH men claim that we are."[28] The language of sex "difference," which already presumes a gendered vision of the body, makes nature more than biology. Nature is part culture—part of the political relations of the phallus—but it is also in part a physical body with a unique capacity for sexual reproduction. It is not culture or politics that defines this capacity; yet this capacity is always formulated through language, culture, and a politicized notion of nature.

The biological capacity that females have to bear children, which is only a small part of what constitutes their sexual identity, defines

24. Jeffrey Weeks, *Sexuality and Its Discontents: Meanings, Myths, and Modern Sexualities* (London: Routledge & Kegan Paul, 1985), p. 249.

25. Marilyn French, *Beyond Power: On Women, Men, and Morals* (New York: Ballantine Books, 1985), p. 65.

26. Emmanuelle de Lesseps, "Female Reality: Biology or Society?" *Feminist Issues* 1 (Winter 1981): 101.

27. Monique Wittig, "The Straight Mind," *Feminist Issues* 1 (Summer 1980): 109.

28. Colette Guillaumin, "The Question of Difference," *Feminist Issues* 2 (Spring 1982): 43.

female sexuality within the discourse of sex "difference." The basic problem is not that the capacity to become pregnant is unimportant to sexual identity but that it should not be all important, or more important than any other aspect of our sexual selves. A theory of sexuality should not be reduced to the pregnant body or its engendered form, the mother's body. It is the capacity partially to shape and define our sexual selves, as opposed to being wholly determined by them, that makes women creative and interesting. When the "difference" of childbearing homogenizes females as mothers, women are denied their individuality: all women become the same—mothers—which immediately classifies them as "different" from men. As de Lesseps asks, "Isn't the multiplicity of individual varieties richer than the ineluctability of two types?"[29] Female physicality that is engendered is not the most interesting thing about women; rather, the multiplicity of ways that femaleness can be expressed is. The distinctiveness of human existence lies in the differences between individuals as individuals not as sexual types. Personal distinction is silenced when the "difference" of sex is made dominant. The individuality of differences can *fully* develop only outside the engendered meaning of the body. Although aspects of female individuality exist, they do so in opposition to the phallus. This opposition distorts the meaning of diversity because it constrains the mix of differences.

As long as woman's body is viewed as "different," she will also be viewed as not human in that word's generalized meaning. This consequence makes the generalized theory of equality unacceptable, because it excludes the female body. There are two aspects to the problem. The body is homogenized as "different," *and* it has the capacity to express a plurality of individual differences.

The Body, the Phallus, and "Difference"

As we have seen, the body is most often the starting point for a discussion of sex "difference." But "no science or discipline can peel off layers of culture and learning and find an untouched core

29. De Lesseps, "Female Reality," p. 100.

of biological *nature.*"[30] The body is not a starting point, because it is *already* a constructed and particularized view of nature. "The cultural significance of the female body is not . . . that of a flesh-and-blood entity, but that of a *symbolic construct.* Everything we know about the body . . . exists for us in some form of discourse; and discourse . . . is never unmediated, never free of interpretation, never innocent."[31] The female body is presented as the mother's body, and this presentation obscures our understanding of women *and* men. "As a result of unconscious presuppositions about the sexes, there is almost never a symmetrical analysis of the status of man and woman and of father and mother, since they are in fact considered relevant to different levels of reality."[32] Femininity and biological motherhood are one and the same; masculinity and fatherhood have no similar biological relationship.

What does it mean to say that there is no such thing as the body, or the pregnant body, outside its contextual meaning? In part, it means that the body is a relation defined by its meaning(s). Ruth Hubbard and Marian Lowe use the term "social body" because they believe that biology is shaped by society. Lowe declares that "biology cannot be taken as something fixed and immutable."[33] Hubbard and Lowe argue that there is no way to isolate the contributions of biology and culture in defining the body. And in this discussion biology can be applied to both the study of the body and the body itself.

Our perception of the body changes, as does the body itself. Neither is static, and the two are not separate. Edward Shorter makes clear that the body operates in a societal and medical network that affects it in fundamental ways. "Maybe the actual structure of women's bodies doesn't change so much over the years, but what has happened to them—in terms of the misadventures of

30. Bleier, *Science and Gender,* p. 7.

31. Susan Rubin Suleiman, Introduction to *The Female Body in Western Culture: Contemporary Perspectives,* ed. Susan Rubin Suleiman (Cambridge, Mass.: Harvard Univ. Press, 1986), p. 2.

32. Nicole-Claude Mathieu, "Biological Paternity, Social Maternity," *Feminist Issues* 4 (Spring 1984): 70.

33. Marian Lowe, "The Dialectic between Biology and Culture," in *Woman's Nature: Rationalizations of Inequality,* ed. Marian Lowe and Ruth Hubbard (New York: Pergamon Press, 1983), p. 54.

childbirth, abortion, and various diseases—has changed dramatically."[34] According to his study, "women have become taller and heavier; they have overcome their traditional inequality in access to food; their pelvises are no longer misshapen by a disorder called 'rickets.'" Shorter argues that these changes toward physical and bodily equality laid the foundation for greater personal autonomy for women. "Before 1900, women were saddled with large numbers of unwanted children; they were dragged down by anemia, enervated by all kinds of diseases for which there is no male counterpart, and in every way imaginable denied the platform of physical equality which is the ultimate launching pad of personal autonomy."[35] Multiple examples demonstrate the kinds of change in bodies that have come about in the last century. There are women bodybuilders today. There are women professional runners, who have greatly increased their speed. There are numerous ways to alter pregnancy itself: artificial insemination, prenatal genetic testing, in vitro fertilization, frozen embryos, amniocentesis, surrogate motherhood. Science develops and changes, and bodies develop and change—with each other.

Bleier writes about the importance of contextualizing biology for understanding the human brain. According to her, the brain, like the rest of the body, has evolved genetically in constant interaction with its environment. "The capacity of the brain to be modified by environment and experience, to *learn,* to acquire language and to *invent* has freed human behaviors from stereotypical or predetermined responses to biological factors, though not, unfortunately, to cultural forces." She views biology as a potential and a capacity, not a static entity. "Biology itself is socially influenced and defined; it changes and develops in interaction with and response to our minds and environment, as our behaviors do."[36] Fausto-Sterling agrees. "The physical structure of the adult brain—its size, number of cells, and most importantly, its neuronal pathways—establishes itself in intimate interaction with the environment of the developing individual" (*MG,* p. 74). Nutrition, exercise, physical

34. Edward Shorter, *A History of Women's Bodies* (New York: Basic Books, 1982), p. xi.
35. Ibid., pp. 17, 285.
36. Bleier, *Science and Gender,* p. 52.

contact with others all play a part in the development of the brain and the body.

A contextualized view of the body raises the problem of gender. If the body is defined in and through its environment, it operates within the established engendered context. If the body is *already* engendered in this way, how can we claim our bodies without reproducing the inequities of the gender system? Or can we only claim our bodies while questioning and challenging their engendered meaning? The choices at hand are problematic at best. "Certainly, women's physiology has important meanings for women in various cultures, and it is essential for us to express those meanings rather than to submit to male definitions—that is, appropriations—of our sexuality. But the female body hardly seems the best site to launch an attack on the forces that have alienated us from what our sexuality might become."[37] It may not be the best site, but it is a site that must be reckoned with. What matters is how we locate that site.

The female body—as dynamic, in the process of change, rather than as a static or essentialist thing—need not be engendered with the meaning of the mother's body. We need not "consider the body as some absolute (milk, blood, breasts, clitoris) for no 'body' is unmediated. Not body but the 'body' of psychosocial fabrications of difference. Or again, of sameness. Or again, of their relation."[38] We must avoid using the body to "flatte[n] out the lived differences among women,"[39] although this is easier said than done. Many of the radical feminists who early in the 1970s dealt with the issue of women's bodies often did essentialize and overgeneralize it. And antifeminists have always done so. To find a way of speaking or writing about the body that does not reconstitute the institutionalization of gendered sex "difference" is not easy.

Adrienne Rich is one radical feminist who has tried to recognize the body but disassociate it from its engendered forms. Her dis-

37. Ann Rosalind Jones, "Writing the Body: Toward an Understanding of *l'Ecriture féminine*," in *The New Feminist Criticism: Essays on Women, Literature, and Theory*, ed. Elaine Showalter (New York: Pantheon Books, 1985), p. 368.

38. Rachel Blau DuPlessis, "For the Etruscans," in *The New Feminist Criticism*, p. 273.

39. Jones, "Writing the Body," p. 371.

tinction between biological motherhood—the bearing of a child—
and its institutionalized form—the rearing of children and the
maintenance of the household—is an example of this effort. In
1976 she wrote that "we have tended either to *become* our bodies—blindly, slavishly, in obedience to male theories about us—or
to try to exist in spite of them." The body has been so problematic
for women "that it has often seemed easier to shrug it off and travel
as a disembodied spirit." Rich argues that a feminist vision must
recognize "physicality as a resource, rather than a destiny."[40] The
problem here is that woman's physicality, or her capacity to bear
children, is never just *that*.

To have borne and reared a child is to have done that thing which patriarchy joins with physiology to render into the definition of femaleness. But
also, it can mean the experiencing of one's own body and emotions in a
powerful way. We experience not only physical, fleshy changes but the
feeling of a change in character. We learn, often through painful self-
discipline and self-cauterization those qualities which are supposed to be
"innate" in us: patience, self-sacrifice, the willingness to repeat endlessly
the small, routine chores of socializing a human being.[41]

The body and its engendered meaning are not easily separated,
yet we must distinguish between them. It becomes more important to do so today, when sociobiologists appear to be garnering
respectability for their view that one can "biologicize" human activity. Fausto-Sterling defines sociobiology as "the systematic study of
the biological basis of all social behavior" (*MG*, p. 158). This discipline posits the genetic component of human behavior and assumes the determining quality of biology *on* human behavior.

David Barash, one of the foremost sociobiologists, argues that
sex "difference" orders social life. "La différence is one of sociobiology's most important concerns."[42] In his now classic articulation of
the fundamental difference between men and women, he states,
"Sperm are cheap. Eggs are expensive. Accordingly, females have
a much greater stake in any one reproductive act" (*WW*, p. 48). He
clarifies his position thus:

40. Rich, *Of Woman Born*, pp. 285, 40, 39.
41. Ibid., p. 37.
42. David Barash, *The Whisperings Within* (New York: Harper & Row, 1979),
p. 46; all further references to this work, abbreviated as *WW*, will be included in
the text.

I will be telling many animal stories, providing, perhaps, a somewhat novel perspective on the birds and the bees—stories of rape in ducks, adultery in bluebirds, prostitution in hummingbirds, divorce and lesbian pairing in gulls, even homosexual rape in parasitic worms. . . . What I hope is that the animals you'll meet in the following pages will help you know yourself better.

(*WW*, p. 2)

Barash thinks that we can identify general principles for human social life from the behavior of animals. He does not differentiate sex and gender. To him they are the same thing, although it is not always clear how they are one: the gendered nature of animals or the biological nature of society.

Rape in humans is by no means as simple [as in animal life], influenced as it is by an extremely complex overlay of cultural attitudes. Nevertheless, mallard rape and bluebird adultery may have a degree of relevance to human behavior. Perhaps human rapists, in their own criminally misguided way, are doing the best they can to maximize their fitness.

(*WW*, p. 55)

For Barash, culture becomes a "biological adaptation." He writes, "In behaving culturally we are also behaving biologically. Our culture is natural to us, just as quills are natural to a porcupine" (*WW*, p. 221).

E. O. Wilson, another major exponent of sociobiology, also assumes that the "natural difference" between men and women defines their cultural adaptations. "In hunter-gatherer societies men hunt and women stay at home. This strong bias persists in most agricultural and industrial societies and on that ground alone, appears to have a genetic origin. . . . Even with identical education and equal access to all professions, men are likely to continue to play a disproportionate role in political life, business and science."[43] Wilson thinks that genes direct brain development, which in turn affects behavior, which in turn determines social structure. John MacKinnon, author of *The Ape within Us*, takes a similar view, specifically in terms of the effect of genes on gender struc-

43. E. O. Wilson, "Human Decency Is Animal," *New York Times Magazine*, 12 October 1975, p. 48. And see his *Sociobiology: The New Synthesis* (Cambridge, Mass.: Harvard Univ. Press, 1975), and *On Human Nature* (Cambridge, Mass.: Harvard Univ. Press, 1978).

ture. He states that the woman who works outside the home will
be less aggressive and more emotional than the woman who does
not because "her biological make-up has . . . designed her in ful-
filling quieter, less spectacular roles. . . . For all her opportunity
and capability, Ms. Average is going to end up in a supportive domestic role."[44]

Stephen Jay Gould criticizes sociobiology for its pure function-
alist approach, which "denies history and views organic structure
as neutral before a molding environment." He argues that what we
need instead is a "richer theory, a structural biology, that views
evolution as an interaction of outside and inside, of environment
and the structural rules for genetic and developmental architec-
ture—rules set by the contingencies of history and physiochemical
laws of the stuff itself."[45] Fausto-Sterling also argues that human
sociobiology defies proof because it is impossible to sort out which
essences are adaptations arising from natural selection and which
are part of natural selection itself. "Monkeys even have culture.
They invent things and pass on their discoveries by nongenetic
means" (*MG*, p. 200).

The demarcation of biology and culture and of sex and gender is
still what is at issue, and the question of biological potentiality versus biological determinism is implicated in these oppositions.[46] Determinism has always been used to justify societal arrangements as
biologically inevitable, or natural, and therefore as genetically necessary. But Gould argues that although the range of an individual's
potential behavior is circumscribed by biology, to say this is quite
different from saying that "our specific patterns of behavior and
social arrangements are in any way directly determined by our

44. John MacKinnon, *The Ape within Us* (New York: Holt, Rinehart & Win-
ston, 1978), p. 264.

45. Stephen Jay Gould, "Cardboard Darwinism," *New York Review of Books*
33 (25 September 1986): 54.

46. See Stephen Jay Gould, "Biological Potential vs. Biological Determinism,"
in *The Sociobiology Debate*, ed. Arthur Caplan (New York: Harper & Row, 1978),
p. 344; all further references to this work, abbreviated as "BPBD," will be included in the text. See also Bleier, *Science and Gender*, esp. ch. 2; Troy Duster
and Karen Garrett, eds., *Cultural Perspective on Biological Knowledge* (Nor-
wood, N.J.: Ablex, 1984); James Fetzer, ed., *Sociobiology and Epistemology* (Boston: Reidel, 1985); King's College Sociobiology Group, ed., *Current Problems in
Sociobiology* (Cambridge: Cambridge Univ. Press, 1982); and Marian Lowe,
"Viewpoint: Sociobiology and Sex Differences," *Signs* 4 (Autumn 1978): 118–25.

genes ("BPBD," p. 343). "Potential" and "determination" are different concepts, and they should be used to elucidate the way biology and culture interact. For Gould, flexibility and variability are a crucial part of our potential. "Our biological nature does not stand in the way of social reform. We are, as Simone de Beauvoir said, *l'être dont l'être est de n'être pas'*—the being whose essence lies in having no essence" ("BPBD," p. 351).

It is difficult to clarify the relationship between areas such as gender, biology, and culture. Similarly, it is hard to articulate fully the meaning of sex "difference" as it is defined from within these realms. Gender, biology, and culture presume patriarchal social relations at the same time that they constitute a challenge to them. The boundaries of the phallus's dominance are not clear-cut or easily discernible, so we become involved in explicating patriarchal relations without knowing where patriarchy begins and ends in the definition of a woman's or a mother's body. What aspect of the body constitutes a woman's potential capacities, and what part articulates her oppression? How can a woman express her physical capacity for pregnancy *and* enjoy equality when the phallus has already defined her pregnant body as the mother's body? There are no objective or true answers to these questions. The first question is problematic in and of itself: it remains embedded in a positivist vision of reality that is defined through discrete parts rather than continuous (even if conflictual) relationships. The second question reflects the problem of boundaries and may thus be wrongheaded. These are, however, the queries we must move through.

The body, which is defined through the methods of science, which are gendered, is defined by biology, which is engendered by sex, which is defined in law through the methods of objectivity. From this standpoint, sex "difference" sometimes means nothing more than the pregnant body. At other times it not only means biological motherhood but encompasses the cultural processes of mothering. Bearing and rearing children are then collapsed alongside the distinction between sex and gender; sex "difference" denies the diversity of differences. In the collapse, sex erases gender, and gender erases sex. Equality comes to mean sameness between men and women. The potential for biological specificity to redefine sex equality is lost. Individual differences become reduced to *the* "difference" of sex, and the politics of sex becomes a politics of inequality. Such a politics makes it very difficult indeed to utilize the epistemological standpoint that presumes heterogeneous variety as integral to a theory of equality.

I want to examine two instances in law that pose the dilemma of difference(s) for a theory of sex equality rooted in the idea of sameness. In the first instance, the pregnant body (as in sex) is at issue. In the second, the notion of woman's cultural "difference" (as in gender) is of concern. I will argue that the pregnant body is never just itself, and the cultural manifestations of the pregnant body pertain to more than culture. Law, instead of recognizing this complexity, treats "the" pregnant body and "the" woman as one and the same. In turn, women are treated as either equal to men or "different" from them. Legal discourse leaves little room for the subtle and complex relations of sex *and* gender—difference(s) *and* sameness.

The Pregnant Body and Equality

The pregnant body represents a dilemma for legal discourse. "The court has conceptual difficulty dealing with 'different' women seeking 'similar' treatment."[47] This difficulty poses a problem for women themselves, given the choices of law: should they be treated as equal to men, that is, as men are, or should they be treated differently from men, and therefore unequally? Should women reject the concept of equality because it is premised in this phallocratic dualism, or should they reconstruct the meaning of equality while recognizing the richness of differences? These are the questions facing feminist litigators today.

Chapter 2 discussed several of the constitutional cases dealing with pregnancy as a focal point of sex discrimination. We saw that pregnancy has been treated as a non-sex-specific category in a classification based on the distinction between pregnant and nonpregnant persons. The sexual specificity of the body was erased in *Geduldig* v. *Aiello* (1974) by using men as the standard.

In *Nashville Gas Co.* v. *Satty* (1977),[48] the Court used the stan-

47. David Cole, "Strategies of Difference: Litigating for Women's Rights in a Man's World," *Law and Inequality* 2 (February 1984): 37.
48. 434 U.S. 136 (1977).

dard established in *General Electric Co.* v. *Gilbert* (1976), which applied the *Geduldig* constitutional definition of discrimination to rule that the company's use of seniority policy to discriminate against pregnant women violated Title VII. The Court decided that women workers could not be deprived of accumulated seniority because they took maternity leave, even though the company's refusal of pay for that leave was not found to affect women workers disproportionately. Throughout the 1970s, the Court denied the sexual specificity of pregnancy at the same time that it would not allow arbitrary and enforced pregnancy leave to be used to differentiate pregnant workers from nonpregnant workers.

The Pregnancy Discrimination Act (PDA), passed in 1978, was Congress's response to the Supreme Court's treatment of pregnancy. Under the act, it is a violation of Title VII "for an employer to refuse to hire a pregnant woman, to terminate her employment or to compel her to take maternity leave."[49] An employer must treat pregnancy as like "any other temporary disability." A written or unwritten employment policy or practice that excludes employees or applicants for employment on the basis of pregnancy is in prima facie violation of Title VII. Pregnancy is defined in the guidelines of the Equal Employment Opportunity Commission as a temporary disability, which means that benefits that apply to other nonoccupational temporary disabilities also apply to pregnancy.[50] This "equal" treatment approach assumes that women who are affected by pregnancy or childbirth will be treated as the same as nonpregnant workers for all employment-related purposes in terms of their ability or inability to work.[51] Pregnancy is to be treated as the same as other nonoccupational disabilities, the same as men's and nonpregnant workers' disabilities.

To assure that women would not be discriminated against on the basis of pregnancy, the PDA denies the "difference" of pregnancy.

49. Claire Sherman Thomas, *Sex Discrimination* (St. Paul, Minn.: West Publishing, 1982), p. 217.

50. Jeanne M. Stellman, *Maternity and Pregnancy Provisions: U.S. and Abroad,* Trade Union Women's Studies series [New York State School of Industrial and Labor Relations, Cornell University] (January 1976): 6.

51. Wendy Williams, "Equality's Riddle: Pregnancy and the Equal Treatment/Special Treatment Debate," *New York University Review of Law and Social Change* 13 (1984–85): 325; all further references to this work, abbreviated as "ER," will be included in the text.

By doing so, the act assesses pregnancy within the phallocratic discourse of duality: difference equals inequality; sameness equals equality. These equations force us to treat pregnancy, as a biological occurrence, as we would treat any illness or disability. But pregnancy is not like any illness or disability. Pregnancy disability leave recognizes only a small part of what pregnancy presently involves, namely, that the pregnant body is at one and the same time the mother's body. As such, pregnancy marks the beginning of a state that lasts as long as motherhood does. Pregnancy leave recognizes only the fact that women bear children. The model of pregnancy as generic temporary disability does not meet the complex needs of women in an engendered society. Pregnant women are usually not just pregnant; they most often are also or will become mothers.

This issue of the legal definitions of pregnancy must be clarified because it is so fundamental to the way we think about equality. We can see the problem time and time again in the way the ERA is defended: "Nothing in the amendment itself nor in its legislative history mandates that the Supreme Court limit or refuse to apply the unique physical characteristics exception in a pregnancy disability/sick leave case."[52] Sex and gender are not easily differentiated, and neither are pregnancy and its relation to motherhood. Women are never just pregnant in the biological sense of the term, because biology, as well as their bodies, is engendered. This does not mean that pregnancy per se makes women "different" from men, but pregnancy as we know it does.

The issue of similar treatment of pregnancy-related disability cuts both ways. In *Miller-Wohl Co.* v. *Commissioner of Labor and Industry* (1981), Miller-Wohl defended its firing of Tamara Buley, a newly hired worker, because of illness related to pregnancy.[53] Miller-Wohl's policy allowed no leave during the first year of employment. Under the Montana Maternity Leave Act (MMLA), however, Buley should have been given a leave rather than fired, and the Supreme Court found Miller-Wohl guilty of sex discrimination. The employer argued that its policy on sick leave treated all disabilities (including those that were pregnancy related) alike

52. Ann Scales, "Towards a Feminist Jurisprudence," *Indiana Law Journal* 56 (Spring 1981): 419.

53. 515 F. Supp. 1264 (D. Mont. 1981), vacated, 685 F. 2d 1088 (9th Cir. 1982).

and therefore was not discriminatory.[54] Miller-Wohl argued as well that the MMLA was unconstitutional because it required special treatment of pregnant workers.

Let us examine this issue further in *California Federal Savings and Loan Association et al.* v. *Mark Guerra et al.* (1985). Cal Fed did not allow Lillian Garland, a receptionist/PBX operator, to return to work for seven months after she was ready to end her pregnancy leave. The employer requested that the Supreme Court absolve it of responsibility for compliance with the California Fair Employment and Housing Act, which requires that women temporarily incapacitated as a result of pregnancy receive up to four months unpaid leave time with job security. Cal Fed argued that this policy conflicts with Title VII, which requires that pregnant workers be treated like other employees.

The brief filed by the American Civil Liberties Union in this case argued that equality between the sexes has the best opportunity to be enacted when pregnancy is treated *like* any other disability. "Women will secure equality, equity and greater tangible benefits when legal distinctions based on sex and pregnancy are eliminated, and when the similarities in the rights and needs of both sexes are seen to override their differences."[55] According to the ACLU, the focus should be on the need for disability leave for all workers, not pregnant workers per se. Pregnancy is comparable to other temporary physical conditions that can affect any employee's ability to work ("ACLU," p. 7). Therefore, if other employees are not terminated for temporary disabilities, it is impermissible to discharge a woman for pregnancy. This is the plus side to equal treatment: being treated as like a man in this instance protects the pregnant woman's job. Equal treatment, however, is a "model which fits pregnancy into the category of temporary medical disability in order to make it comparable to a male experience."[56]

54. See Linda Krieger and Patricia Cooney, "The Miller-Wohl Controversy: Equal Treatment, Positive Action, and the Meaning of Women's Equality," *Golden Gate University Law Review* 13 (1983): 513–72.

55. Amici Curiae, Supreme Court of the United States, October term, 1985, no. 85–494, p. 6; all further references to this work, abbreviated as "ACLU," will be included in the text.

56. Wendy Chavkin, "Walking a Tightrope: Pregnancy, Parenting, and Work," in *Double Exposure: Women's Health Hazards on the Job and at Home*, ed. Wendy Chavkin (New York: Monthly Review Press, 1984), p. 208.

Pregnancy is defined by the phallus as *like, the same as,* nonpregnancy. There are two issues here: sameness as being like men and sameness as a privileged standard to begin with. Why not applaud variety? The fact that "difference" has been interpreted as an inequality doesn't mean that it has to remain so.

Nevertheless, the ACLU brief in this case argued against pregnancy as a special category. "Is pregnancy so different a disability as to negate the congressionally-mandated right to legal equality between the sexes in the workplace?" ("ACLU," p. 5). The authors of the brief believe that it is possible to recognize the needs of pregnant workers without giving way to stereotypes of difference that have been used to discriminate against pregnant workers as wage earners. The ACLU holds the position that legislative distinctions based on sex and pregnancy are *inherently* dangerous, even when they are supposed to be used for the advantage of women (see "ACLU," p. 10). The "inherent" danger derives from the privileged status of the phallus, which establishes the politics of "difference" as a politics of inequality.

The ACLU brief argued that the notion of the incomparability—biological difference—between men and women "can always then be turned to justify the denial of rights" ("ACLU," p. 23). This point is obviously true, but it moves the argument to the question of making strategic use of the issue of pregnancy rather than clarifying the status of pregnancy. I think we need to clarify the status of pregnancy, even if the courts give us little room to do so. The epistemological status of the meaning of "difference" and more particularly "pregnancy" should not be reduced to the politics of the courts, even though current standards of law will necessarily constrain the litigation involving issues of sex equality.[57]

Isabelle Katz Pinzler and Joan Bertin of the ACLU Women's Rights Project restate the ACLU's position.

It is precisely because we believe that pregnancy should not be treated worse than other potentially incapacitating conditions that we resist the urge (however tempting) to treat it better. Those who urge a preferential

---

57. This view of sex equality is not one and the same as a legal theory of equality, which works *within* the constraints of the dualistic standpoint of law. Because of these constraints, I think it important to carry on a critique of legal strategy committed to sex equality that, I hope, will help challenge the discourse that privileges the language of sameness.

approach for pregnancy based on its unique and incomparable qualities forget that the idea that pregnancy is unique does not always (or even usually) lead to its receiving preferred treatment.[58]

But why term the recognition of pregnancy as sex-specific preferential treatment? Why isn't the treatment of pregnancy as *non–sex specific* considered to be preferential treatment of the phallus?

This is not to say that I am in complete disagreement with the ACLU position. To the extent that equality is a compelling goal, the union's arguments are persuasive. Bertin explains,

One of the things that offends me is that laws like the California one persist in using sex as the primary characteristic dividing up the world. Obviously the workplace must accommodate pregnancy and the needs of parents but I believe the central issue is that people shouldn't be fired for absence from work because of any temporary disability whether it's pregnancy or a hernia. . . .

The notion that pregnancy is a special disability is a stereotype, and stereotypes hurt us. The only way to eradicate that is to put pregnancy in the context of the whole range of things that happen to people over a lifetime.[59]

In the ACLU brief, Bertin asked the Supreme Court to interpret the California law as providing up to four months unpaid leave for any disabled worker. In this way, Cal Fed could comply with both the California statute and Title VII—disability or short-term leave would not be specific to pregnancy, but leave for pregnancy would be considered legal.

We are still left, however, with the engendered question: Is pregnancy comparable to other physical conditions, or is it special? This framing of the question highlights "difference" as a problem for equality. Wendy Williams, a law professor at Georgetown University, supports the ACLU position on sameness. She believes that sex-unique physical characteristics are comparable to other distinguishing characteristics and that we must focus on this otherness. She denies that this perspective treats women as like men. "The goal of the feminist legal movement that began in the early

58. Isabelle Katz Pinzler and Joan Bertin, [letter to the editor], "Pregnancy in the Workplace," *New York Times Book Review,* 8 June 1986, p. 33.

59. Joan Bertin, qtd. in Tamar Lewin, "Pregnancy Leave Suit Has Divided Feminists," *New York Times,* 28 June 1986, p. D52.

seventies is not and never was the integration of women into a male world any more than it has been to build a separate but better place for women. Rather, the goal has been to break down the legal barriers that restricted each sex to its predefined role and created a hierarchy based on gender" ("ER," p. 331). In Williams's mind, the equal treatment approach to pregnancy works toward this goal because it reduces the structural barriers to women's full participation in the work force.

The problem with this line of reasoning is that pregnancy—and its counterpart, motherhood—given engendered social relations, is a structural barrier to begin with. Williams thinks that the equal treatment approach addresses this problem, that it is part of "a larger strategy to get the law out of the business of reinforcing traditional sex-based family roles and to alter the workplace so as to keep it in step with the increased participation by women" ("ER," p. 352). The equal treatment model is supposed "to discourage employers and the state from creating or maintaining rules that force people to structure their family relationships upon traditional sex-based lines and from refusing to respond to pregnancy as within the normal range of events which temporarily affect workers" ("ER," p. 354).

Williams does not argue that pregnancy is the same as other physical events or disabilities, but she thinks that "the position of the pregnant worker [is] analogous to the position of other workers" ("ER," p. 363). By reasoning in this vein, she believes that we shift from the idea of the worker as male to the concept of the worker as either male or female. We thereby begin to change the workplace for women through equal treatment doctrine, which is different from making special accommodations for women in a workplace defined as male. The special treatment approach supposedly adopts the male model and seeks special provisions for women to the extent that they are not like men. Because Williams views regulations concerning pregnancy as "singularly burdensome and unfair" to women, she thinks that special treatment legislation sells equality short ("ER," p. 380).

Others in the feminist legal community criticize the "equality" view and instead opt for a position that recognizes the specificity of pregnancy. Linda Krieger and Patricia Cooney argue that, given the heterogeneity of sex, we must face the limitations of equal treatment. They contend that we need to recognize difference "but face the potential dangers and uncertainties such an endeavor will entail." They believe that the liberal view of equality assumes homogeneity while it establishes hierarchy. It "fails to focus on the effect of the very *real* sex difference of pregnancy, on the relative positions of men and women in society and on the goal of assuring equality of opportunity and effect within a heterogeneous 'society of equals.'"[60]

Sylvia Law takes a somewhat similar position. She thinks that law must take into account the particularity of reproductive biology without rearticulating its cultural manifestations.

Recognizing that men and women are different in relation to reproductive biology does not necessarily mean that the law can assume that we are different in relation to capacity to think, to lead, or to nurture. . . . Confronting the myth and reality of biological differences may enable us to create a stronger equality concept in relation both to laws premised on cultural stereotypes and to laws that regulate reproductive biology.[61]

With a somewhat different emphasis, Betty Friedan argues a similar point. In responding to the Cal Fed case, she also emphasizes the importance of recognizing the "difference" of pregnancy within a new doctrine of equality. "I think the time has come to acknowledge that women are different from men, and that there has to be a concept of equality that takes into account that women are the ones who have the babies. We shouldn't be stuck with always using a male model, trying to twist pregnancy into something that's like a hernia."[62]

The Equal Rights Advocates, a San Francisco–based public interest law firm specializing in issues of sex-based discrimination,

60. Krieger and Cooney, "The Miller-Wohl Controversy," pp. 572, 541–42.

61. Sylvia Law, "Rethinking Sex and the Constitution," *University of Pennsylvania Law Review* 132 (June 1984): 1033.

62. Betty Friedan, qtd. in Lewin, "Pregnancy Leave Suit Has Divided Feminists," p. 52. It is troublesome that Friedan takes no responsibility for having articulated the male liberal model for feminists; she acts as though she had nothing to do with this conception of equality in its early formulations for the Women's Liberation movement, even though her book *The Feminine Mystique* (1963) articulated this notion. Now she criticizes feminists for developing such a wrongheaded vision of equality. While she rejects the sameness model, she also attempts to deny the radical impetus of feminism that it entails. See Eisenstein, *Feminism and Sexual Equality*, ch. 8, for a fuller discussion of this point.

filed a brief in the Cal Fed case taking the special treatment/equal opportunity approach. It argued that California law, as well as federal law, "implicitly recognize[s] the *real differences* in the procreative roles of men and women. These biological reproductive sex differences must be taken into account if the goal of equal employment opportunity for pregnant women is to be attained."[63] The firm uses the standard of "real differences" to differentiate pregnancy-related law from other forms of protective legislation. "Protective legislation is based on false stereotypical notions of female roles, while the state statute is based on a recognition of the real biological sex differences accompanying reproductive roles."[64]

The Equal Rights Advocates take the position that pregnancy is episodic and should be dealt with as such. According to Herma Hill Kay, this approach means treating pregnancy as relevant for legal purposes only while its discrete episodes are occurring.

During those episodes, measured roughly from the sexual union of sperm and egg that initiates conception through the changes that are characteristic of pregnancy and culminating in the termination of pregnancy through childbirth, miscarriage, or abortion, women and men function differently. Before and after these reproductive episodes, however, men and women are capable of functioning alike. . . . Thus childbearing leave can be restricted to women, but childrearing leave must be available to fathers as well as mothers.[65]

The episodic approach assumes that pregnancy is only sometimes, in fact seldom, relevant to women's treatment by law. The problem with this approach is much the same problem we had earlier. How do we delineate the lines of relevance, of "real difference," of sex and gender? My point is not that we cannot draw legal lines but that we must be critical of them as we use them. The incapacity of law, at least at present, to recognize the complex relations between the pregnant body and the mother's body is the very reason we cannot depend on it to formulate an adequate

63. Amici Curiae, Supreme Court of the United States, October term, 1985, no. 85–494, p. 2; emphasis mine.

64. Ibid., p. 3.

65. Herma Hill Kay, "Equality and Difference: A Perspective on No-Fault Divorce and Its Aftermath," *University of Cincinnati Law Review* 56 (1987): 17. And see her "An Appraisal of California's No-Fault Divorce Law," *California Law Review* 75 (January 1987): 291–319.

theory of sex equality. Yet law sets up the constraints within which feminist litigators work, so we must keep the meanings of "difference(s)" open-textured. I would add that while the meanings of sex "difference(s)" remain open, the burden of proof lies with those who seek to define woman's capacity in terms of her "difference" rather than in terms of her sameness.

To recognize the particularity and specificity of woman's body need not be to define her as "different." Rather this recognition is meant to reconceptualize equality in light of variety. Females are more like males than they are unlike them, but I do not want to represent women's specificity as either a difference or a sameness. Differences must be reformulated so that diversity between the sexes is not incongruous with equality between them. The ruling in the Cal Fed case, upholding the disputed California law (which gives pregnant workers with up to four months unpaid pregnancy disability leave the right to return to the same or a similar job), begins this reformulation. Different treatment for pregnant workers is not unequal treatment in this instance. Justice Marshall, writing for the Supreme Court, specified that any use of the decision to limit the opportunities of pregnant workers would be seen as a violation of federal law.[66]

Concerns with similarity and with difference both have validity for a notion of equality, because males and females and men and women are similar and different, individually and collectively. Neither concern when taken alone is completely valid, because neither when taken alone is simply true. Because neither approach can resolve the tension between sameness and difference, we need to explore the relations between both.

The sameness model, given law's phallocratic standard, is radical, even if insufficiently so. It posits that women are the same as men—or should be treated as the same—in an engendered society that treats women as different (as unequal). Given that patriarchal relations are expressed through the differentiation of woman from man in a politics that interprets this "difference" as an inequality, the attempt to treat men and women similarly is a progressive move toward equality. Yet differences do exist and must be taken into account as we reconstruct equality. The danger is in rearticu-

66. 107 S. Ct. 683 (1987).

lating woman's particularity as a gendered "difference." Because there is no intellectual tradition on which to draw—no established vision of equality that recognizes the specificity of the pregnant body—and because there is a political tradition that has used the pregnant body against women, the focus on difference(s) can appear highly suspect. And it is, but so is the treatment of women as the same as men.

We need a more encompassing vision of "person" that recognizes pregnant bodies within a framework that allows plurality and diversity to be valued. The pregnant worker has a range of needs in terms of the workplace, home, family, and so on and therefore must be recognized within the continuum of individual difference(s). But the pregnant worker should not become a new standard: in other words, should not be used to impose a view of the male worker as like the female worker, the hernia as like pregnancy, the man as like the woman. Such thinking only posits the dualism of engendered sex "difference" from a different vantage point; it continues to privilege dualism over diversity, so homosexuality or nonpregnancy would continue to be devalued.

We are a long way from seeing the pregnant body or sex "difference" as continua of individual differences. And we are just as far from recognizing sex "difference" as a cultural construction. Instead, sex and gender are collapsed, and woman's gender "difference" is presented as natural and in conflict with her entitlement to equality. Woman's "difference" from man—derived by circuitous logic from the "mother's" body—is used to justify women's underrepresentation in better-paying jobs. Let us turn to this question of "difference," this time in terms of woman's supposed gender difference of moral character, personality, and individual choice.

Gender "Difference" and Sex Discrimination

Descriptions of gender "difference" often portray women as more nurturing, more sensitive, more connected to their feelings than men are. The explanation—whether explicit or implicit—is that woman's particular relation to her (pregnant) body and her family make this so. It assumes that woman's body, among other things, affects her personality and place in society; woman's body as ultimately the mother's body assigns her her "difference." This view is held by feminists and antifeminists alike. Feminists usually argue that these differences of personality are more cultural than biological—but not always. When they do not argue this way, feminists use descriptions of gender "difference" to view women as homogeneous and to replace awareness of the diversity of women, some of whom are nurturing and some not, with the notion of mothers.

Feminists such as Carol Gilligan and Sara Ruddick recognize the significant role that culture plays in equating the female body with the mother's body.[67] Woman is more nurturing than man because of this mix of influences. Because society plays an important part in defining motherhood, women will interpret motherhood differently. Although woman's body is constitutive of her personality, individual choices cannot be reduced to the effects of the body. This viewing of gender "differences" begins to recognize the complex interconnection between sex and gender and between the pregnant body and the mother's body. A recognition of gender "difference" need not deny women their individuality and be used to oppose their claim for equality, as it is in antifeminist rhetoric. The problem, however, is that it can be, has been, and is being used this way. Whether this is done in the name of biology or culture— or feminism or antifeminism—matters little in the end.

It is because I have argued that sex equality must recognize difference(s) that I think it is so important to acknowledge the dangers of such an approach to gender "difference." Rather than try to reconstruct a notion of equality that recognizes woman's particularity, as feminists of the special treatment or gender difference(s) approach would do, New Rightists and neoconservatives use "difference" as a reason to reject the concept of equality.

The neoconservative argument runs something like this: If women are different from men, why treat them the same way? Their "difference" and not sex discrimination is used to explain their position in the family and the labor force. As I will examine more fully in Chapter 4, the crisis of liberalism, which in large part

67. See Carol Gilligan, *In a Different Voice: Psychological Theory and Women's Development* (Cambridge, Mass.: Harvard Univ. Press, 1982); and Sara Ruddick, "Maternal Thinking," *Feminist Studies* 6 (Summer 1980): 342–67. Also see Janet Sayers, *Biological Politics: Feminist and Anti-Feminist Perspectives* (New York: Tavistock Publications, 1982).

concerns sex equality, requires a rearticulation of sex "difference" and with it of the phallocratic dualisms that undergird legal discourse.

We can see the use of "difference" to justify sex discrimination in the case of *Equal Employment Opportunity Commission* (EEOC) v. *Sears, Roebuck and Co.*, which was filed in U.S. district court for the Northern District of Illinois, Eastern Division in 1979 and covered the years 1972–1980. The case charged Sears with discrimination against women in promotions of commission sales staff.[68] The EEOC accused Sears of a pattern of "sex discrimination in recruitment, selection, assignment, transfer, training, and promotion of women."[69] Sears, the world's largest retailer and the nation's largest private-sector employer of women, maintained that the underrepresentation of women in commission jobs and its work force in general was a result not of discrimination but of women's own job preferences.[70] The legal question at issue was whether discrimination was a plausible explanation for the statistical disparities between men's and women's positions in the company.[71] The EEOC held that the statistical disparities reflected the limited job options for women at Sears. Sears contended that women's goals and values, as wives and mothers, led to their preference for lower level, noncompetitive jobs. The obverse question was whether women's "difference," defined by their so-called job preference, could explain their unequal position in the Sears work force.

Rosalind Rosenberg, a feminist historian and one of the "expert" witnesses for Sears, argued that women's traditional values explained their positions in the Sears work force. The primary reason that women did not receive commission sales jobs was that women try to balance family responsibilities with work, and the commission jobs made it more difficult to do this. "The assumption that women and men have identical interests and aspirations regarding work is incorrect."[72] According to Rosenberg's testimony, women

68. 628 F. Supp. 1264, 39 FEP 1672 (N. D. Illinois, 1986).

69. From Rosalind Rosenberg's statement "The Sears Case: An Historical Overview," 25 November 1985.

70. See Ruth Milkman, "Women's History and the Sears Case," *Feminist Studies* 12 (Summer 1986): 375–400.

71. See Alice Kessler Harris, "Women's History and Public Advocacy" (Paper delivered at the Organization of American Historians Meetings, 13 April 1986).

72. Offer of Proof Concerning the "Testimony of Dr. Rosalind Rosenberg," *EEOC* v. *Sears*, U.S. District Court for the Northern District of Illinois, Eastern

who work outside the home see this work as their secondary responsibility. Women retain their historic commitment to the home, even when large numbers of married women enter the labor force. "Because housework and child care continue to affect women's labor force participation even today, many women choose jobs that complement their family obligations over jobs that might increase and enhance their earning potential" ("TRR," pp. 8–9). Whereas men derive their self-esteem from their jobs, women derive their self-image from their roles as wives and mothers.

Although Rosenberg argued that women shy away from the competition and financial risk of commission jobs, Sears could not name one female applicant who had actually turned down a job.[73] And although Sears claimed that women are not interested in non-traditional jobs, during the years at issue AT&T hired ten times as many women to climb up poles and go down manholes as Sears hired to sell home improvements.[74] Nevertheless, Rosenberg argued that differences in female and male self-perception prevent women from entering traditionally masculine occupations. "It is naive to believe that the natural effect of these differences is evidence of discrimination by Sears" ("TRR," p. 18; and see p. 14). She considered Sears innocent of discrimination on the ground that women chose their job situations on the basis of their own preferences.

My testimony has emphasized the complexity of the world in which women make decisions—choices—about their work, and I reject the temptation to blame employers for everything I do not like about the condition of women. Too many factors have shaped women's work force participation for such a monocausal view to be convincing. Among these factors are the restraints on women imposed by cultural norms and values and the socialization process that re-creates generations of women many of whom continue to share traditional notions about the meaning, requisites, and responsibilities of womanhood, gender, and femininity.

("TRR," pp. 18–19)

Division, 79–C–4373, p. 1; all further references to this work, abbreviated as "TRR," will be included in the text.

73. See Alice Kessler Harris, "Equal Opportunity Employment Commission v. Sears, Roebuck and Company: A Personal Account," *Radical History Review* 35 (April 1986): 61.

74. Jonathan Weiner, "Women Fall One Step Back in Sears Case," *In These Times*, 9–22 July 1986, p. 6.

Rosenberg's analysis does not seem to me to recognize the complexity of women's choices. If it did, she would have had to acknowledge how discrimination plays a part (at least) in constituting her notion of difference in the first place. The patterns she described, which are not entirely accurate, do not exist in isolation from the structural patterns of discrimination in the labor force. She—not the EEOC—constructed a monocausal view of women and the choices they make. She wrote, "Disparities in the sexual composition of an employer's work force, as well as disparities in pay between men and women in many circumstances are consistent with an absence of discrimination on the part of the employer."[75] We must ask why anyone would posit such a finding, unless he or she is looking for a solo causal factor rather than a series of interrelationships with which to define "difference."

It is important to note that in her book *Beyond Separate Spheres* Rosenberg acknowledges the complexity of the issue of sex "difference" more than she did in the courtroom. She describes the way women students often reject the ideals of womanhood. "The values of individualism, egalitarianism, scientific objectivity and careerism that characterized the scholarly outlook in the emerging American university turned many women students away from the ideals of womanhood that had shaped their upbringing—ideals like selflessness, feminine purity, and social reform" (*BSS*, p. 110). In this instance, she recognizes how environment helps to construct sex "difference"; yet in her testimony she did not view Sears as a part of women's environment delimiting their choices. Rosenberg also recognizes the debilitating role that the notion of sexual spheres has played in women's lives and even criticizes early feminists for insisting that "women are innately nurturant, supportive, community minded beings" (*BSS*, p. 246). Yet she asserts a static vision of sex "difference" that is, at least in part, implicit in her testimony.

Alice Kessler Harris, like Rosenberg a feminist historian, testified in behalf of the EEOC. She argued that women's underrepresentation at Sears was best explained by the employer's discrimination. She submitted that women's choices must be seen in the context of available opportunities. "What appear to be women's

75. Written Rebuttal Testimony of Dr. Rosalind Rosenberg, *EEOC* v. *Sears*, p. 1.

choices and what are characterized as women's 'interests' are, in fact, heavily influenced by the opportunities for work made available to them. . . . Opportunities offered to women have been conditioned by society's perceptions of women and assumptions about them."[76] Choice is structured, limited, and in some sense predefined; this is exactly what discrimination is about in the first place, the limiting of a person's options. Kessler Harris stated that the problem is not that women do not take advantage of opportunity but that opportunities are not made available to them. "Where opportunity has existed women have never failed to take the jobs offered. When opportunities have been closed to them, women have rationalized their inability to participate fully in the world of work with notions of domesticity."[77]

The fact that women are not found in nontraditional jobs in significant numbers reflects not their chosen "difference" but employers' preference for a sexually differentiated work force. Heidi Hartmann and Barbara Reskin's study of women's participation in the labor force bears out Kessler Harris's position. They found that "women's occupational choices and preferences play a limited role in explaining occupational segregation by sex." Employers have the real impact on structuring their workplaces: they most often "establish and reinforce job segregation, but [they] also respond to changes in women's and men's attitudes as well as to government initiatives[;] . . . as opportunities have expanded in the past, women have rapidly responded."[78]

Kessler Harris did not deny that domestic roles and domestic ideology play a part in defining women's position in the labor market. However, she stated her belief that Rosenberg had failed to understand the relationship between institutional barriers and women's aspirations and choices. Nor did she think Rosenberg understood the complicated relationship between domestic ideology and wage-earning women. Rosenberg assumed, according to Kessler Harris, that "if women are revealed to adhere to some form of domestic ideology, then they cannot as a matter of course also be

76. Written Testimony of Alice Kessler Harris, *EEOC* v. *Sears*, p. 3.
77. Ibid., p. 9.
78. Heidi Hartmann and Barbara Reskin, *Women's Work, Men's Work: Sex Segregation on the Job* (Washington, D.C.: National Academy Press, 1986), pp. 80, 81.

competitive, [be] willing to take risks and be income oriented."[79] Kessler Harris did not deny differences, but she did deny that women always affirm traditional family values, or that differences definitively determine women's participation in the labor force. She clarified her position further in an article she wrote after the *Sears* trial. Instead of relegating women to their "difference," or denying that differences exist, she wants women to move toward equality without either negating or reifying their identification with their family. "Ignoring difference tends to perpetuate existing inequality."[80]

Judge John Nordberg, a Reagan appointee, decided the case in favor of Sears. In his opinion the EEOC statistics were flawed by two assumptions: that male and female applicants were equally interested in commission sales jobs, and that male and female applicants were equally qualified for such jobs.[81] Nordberg felt that disparity in the number of men and women in a job category can exist without discrimination, particularly if it is true that women avoid jobs that are unfamiliar and competitive. In his opinion, the EEOC failed to identify specific discriminatory practices. "Instead, E.E.O.C. contends that there is 'something in the process' at Sears which causes the disparities shown in the statistical evidence" ("JNO," p. 1682). In contrast, "Sears has proven, with many forms of evidence, that men and women tend to have different interests and aspirations regarding work and that these differences explain in large part the lower percentage of women in commission sales jobs in general at Sears" ("JNO," p. 1702).

Nordberg questioned the validity of Kessler Harris's testimony that women are influenced "only" by the opportunities presented to them ("JNO," p. 1708). He viewed her examples of women choosing nontraditional jobs as the exceptions. He found Rosenberg much more convincing. "She offered the more reasonable

79. Alice Kessler Harris's Response to the Written Rebuttal Testimony of Rosalind Rosenberg, *EEOC* v. *Sears,* 27 November 1985, p. 1.

80. Alice Kessler Harris, "Recognizing Difference: The Debate over Equality for Women in the Workplace," in *Women and Work: An Annual Review,* vol. 1, ed. Laurie Larwood, Ann H. Stromberg, and Barbara A. Gluck (Beverly Hills, Calif.: Sage Publications, 1986), p. 144.

81. See Judge John Nordberg's Opinion, *EEOC* v. *Sears,* 39 FEP Cases 1679; all further references to this work, abbreviated as "JNO," will be included in the text.

conclusion that differences in the number of men and women in a job could exist without discrimination by an employer" ("JNO," p. 1709). Whereas Nordberg was unwilling to reduce women's participation in the labor force to the criterion of sex discrimination, he was willing to reduce their activity in the labor force to one criterion—their preference. The court never explored the reasons for women's so-called preference for traditional jobs. Family—through the circuitous route to the mother's body—was assumed to explain women's choices.

The decision in favor of Sears reduces women to their engendered "difference." It treats them as a homogeneous class differentiated from the class of men by their gender. The decision conceptualizes their gender in static, unitary, and causal terms. It refuses to view familial orientation as characteristic of "some" but not all women or as, in part, a reflection of sex discrimination itself—that is, as a response to closed alternatives. Instead the decision posits familial orientation as universally true of women and prescribed by nature. By this reasoning, women's inclination toward family life explains their subordinate place in the labor market. The complex or subtle relationships between sex and gender, family and market, childbearing and child rearing are ignored.

The dualistic perspective of the court—the *either* discrimination *or* woman's "difference" approach—distorts the issue at hand from the start. It allows room for no more than one answer. The question of employers' discrimination is constructed in the "scientific" discourse of causality. The court wanted to know whether discrimination was *the* explanation for statistical disparities; it was not enough to prove that discrimination was a part of the explanation. Nor was it possible to try to show that some women are more involved in familial obligation than others and consequently, that women and their work patterns vary. The choice was seen as strictly between women's sameness and their "difference"; women were not acknowledged to be both categorically similar and particular or to have their behavior and situations explained in relation to both sets of characteristics. The court's standpoint distorted testimony on both sides of the issue.

The *Sears* case is an example of what proponents of the ACLU position most fear. Arguments about women's "difference" are open to the interpretation of the courts. "Difference" in the *Sears* case was used to disguise and protect discriminatory practices. Duality, as the epistemological stance of law, made it possible for Judge Nordberg to overlook the subtle and intricate relations of sex and gender, similarity and difference(s), society and women's choices. The dualistic framework negated the notion of difference(s) representing diversity. Instead it protected "difference" as an inequality. Such a view denies discrimination—meaning the unacceptable and real difference of treatment—and with it a claim for equality that recognizes differences as individual and multiple rather than unitary and determined by sex class.

As we have seen, discourses concerning sex "difference" shift, as do their articulations in law. Their changeability and subjectivity affect how the courts interpret evidence. And this is why we cannot allow the notion of equality to be limited to the existing dualistic discourse. The neoconservative interpretation of sex "difference" had a significant impact on the *Sears* decision, the dualistic framework of sameness/difference helped make it possible to distort the complex relations involved in sex discrimination.

I have argued that equality based on sameness of the sexes is problematic because the female body has a particular identity resulting from its reproductive capacity and its gendered meaning. Its needs cannot be met by present law. Unlike the neoconservatives, however, I do not opt for "different" treatment. Instead, I seek to initiate a radical transformation of the present interpretations of sex equality. But before we explore the policy implications for a reconstructed theory of sex equality any further, we need to examine the present assault on sex equality. Let us therefore turn to a discussion of the Reagan administration's attempt to shift the political discourse of sex equality toward engendered "difference" in order to reverse the progress made during the 1970s toward a sex equality rooted in "sameness." We must understand the administration's attempt to limit the radical egalitarianism inherent in a notion of diversity that pluralizes the meaning of equality.

Chapter Four

Reconstituting the Phallus I: Reaganism and the Politics of Inequality

Sex equality, however we define it, has become a radical demand in the 1980s. As a consequence, liberal feminism—the view that women should be treated as the same as men—has become more subversive than it was in the 1970s. Through that decade affirmative action was institutionalized and abortion legalized. Black and white women and black men made strides toward equality of opportunity.[1] But by the late 1970s and early 1980s these gains were opposed by neoconservatives and New Rightists, who had gained a firmer hold inside the state.

This political background contributes to the context of a discussion about sex equality in the 1980s. I therefore turn my attention to other sites where the state's discourses on sex equality are articulated. I will specifically examine the privileged neoconservative and New Right stances in the Reagan administration that have shaped current thinking about difference, equality, and ultimately the pregnant body. I extend my focus especially to the imagery and rhetoric used in discussions concerning family life, because here we uncover the prevalent view of woman as one and the same as mother. More generally I argue that these discourses construct as well as reflect shifts in contemporary power relations.

1. My discussion of racial minorities is limited to black men and women because most of the data available through polling and survey research does not consistently apply to other Third World groups.

As we shall see, the politics of sex equality in the 1980s has been defined by multiplicity and contradiction concerning the meanings of "difference" and its relation to equality between the sexes. But politics is not of one coherent voice, and this incoherence is what this chapter and the next discuss. Hence my examination in this chapter of the tensions within and between state discourses. I will show how these discourses both intersect with, and differ significantly from, public consciousness. My discussion of the gender gap focuses particularly on the conflict between political discourses that exist simultaneously. The gender gap reflects the power of liberal and feminist discourses, embodies gender difference at the same time that it critiques it, and also stands in stark contrast to neoconservative rhetoric about "difference." I will further argue that gender consciousness among women is plural and yet was markedly distinct (from that of men) in its criticism of Reagan administration policies. In Chapter 5, I will argue that the politics of antipornography is contradictory at best and that the 1986–87 Supreme Court decisions on abortion and affirmative action did not simply endorse the Reagan state's position. But neither is it true that the Court's progressive position on affirmative action extends to the sexual practices of homosexuals.

Rather than a single dismissal of sex equality within the state, there has been a series of discussions that attempt to restrengthen phallocratic privilege. This multiplicity of rhetoric is seen in the "pro-family" stance of both Democratic and Republican parties; the antipornography findings of the Meese Commission; the antiabortion position taken by President Reagan and continually articulated by the New Right; and the assault, primarily instigated and endorsed by neoconservatives, on affirmative action programs.

We need to recognize this discontinuity, without either forgetting the privileged status of neoconservatism or overstating its homogeneity. This awareness involves not only recognizing the variety of political discourses that coexist within the state but distinguishing between these discourses and the political consciousness of the American public. Although the public is obviously not of one mind, the range of its political positions appears to be much less antiegalitarian than that of the state. Yet public consciousness is marked by conflicting viewpoints. People believe in the importance of liberal democratic values but criticize the social welfare state; people believe that a pregnant woman has the right to choose whether she will have an abortion but are bothered by what they see as a promiscuous society and seem to believe that the availability of abortions encourages sexual activity. In the 1984 presidential election, people believed that the Democrats were more committed to fairness as a policy guide, but they voted for Reagan anyway.

Over the past twenty-five years, the liberal democratic politics of the state—its commitment to increased equality for white and black women and black men through an active social welfare state—has been both established and in large part dismantled. The language of the state has shifted with these changes from a liberal democratic rhetoric of equality to a neoconservative (and neoliberal) rhetoric of opportunity. The appeal of the liberal feminism that grew during this period remains visible alongside these shifting discourses despite the neoconservatives' and New Right's rejection of the feminist commitment to sex equality. The American public expresses and has internalized these conflictual positions. This is the context—of contradictory images and embattled consciousness—in which we need to explore the crisis of liberalism as a crisis about the meaning of equality. To the degree that consciousness, as a part of political discourse, occupies a spot on the continuum between the "real" and the "ideal," it remains an important inhibitor of rightward moves by the state.

Liberal feminism was more a part of the political discourse of the state in the early 1970s than in the late 1980s, when it had been displaced in large part by what can be termed a neoconservative feminism or a New Right antifeminism. In both instances the vision of equality was revised to mean "opportunity"; woman's sameness to man has been replaced by her "difference" from him. In this view women need freedom to choose how they will be women, which is quite different from needing equality with men.[2] Although this viewpoint was the dominant one in the Reagan administration, its dismissal of liberal feminism was not as simple as it might first appear. The political discourse concerning equality— the notion that women and men are equal and have the same rights—remains very much a part of the consciousness of the

2. See Midge Decter, *The New Chastity and Other Arguments against Women's Liberation* (New York: Capricorn Books, 1972); and Phyllis Schlafly, *The Power of the Positive Woman* (New York: Jove/HBJ Books, 1977).

American public. The discourse about equality constrained the Reagan administration's policies on family life, pornography, affirmative action, and abortion. It established what people expected and thought was fair treatment. Discourse, as ideas that establish consciousness as part of the real, cannot be easily discarded because it helps constitute the relations of power that we must address.

To the degree that liberal law authorizes the idea of sex equality, the Reagan administration was constrained by law. This is why affirmative action and abortion law became the administration's chosen targets. Liberal feminism and its expression in law stunted the neoconservative and New Right politics of the 1980s. Liberal feminism and its commitment to an equality between the sexes based on sameness of treatment remain significant obstacles to the recentering of the phallus and the politics of engendered sex "difference."

Sex Equality
and the Crisis of Liberal Discourse

Discussions of sex equality are completely intertwined with liberal doctrine. Liberalism—by which I mean the commitment to individual freedom of choice, privacy, and equality of opportunity—was the dominant discourse of the American state in the 1960s. Hostility toward the discourse of liberalism and its commitment to the welfare state gained increasing credibility under the Nixon and Carter administrations and continued under Reagan. The New Right's rejection of liberalism calls for the dismantling of the social welfare state. For the neoconservative, the revision of liberalism requires a redefinition of equality: equality of opportunity is to be distinguished from equality of conditions. Equality of conditions supposedly involves a false egalitarianism that destroys the needed hierarchy of "difference." According to the neoconservative, liberals have confounded the meaning of equality: equality of opportunity has come to mean equality of outcome.

The demand for sexual equality and sexual freedom is central to both the crisis of liberalism and the consolidation of neoconservatism and the New Right that occurred in the Reagan state. The critique of liberalism—the rejection of the notion of equality and

its political form, the welfare state—seeks to establish the "opportunity" state, which does not guarantee equality through affir-
ative action, quotas, and so forth but rather requires that individuals make their own "opportunities."

The New Right, as radically antiliberal, argues that women are
different from men: women are intended, by God and nature, to
bear and rear children. Men, in contradistinction, are supposed to
provide for and protect their wives and families.[3] Neoconservatives, as revisionist liberals, do not assign woman her "difference"
as a mother and homemaker, as the New Right does, but argue
that women's "difference" from men requires a notion of equality
that does not presume sameness. The language of neoconservatives stresses "personal freedom and independence for women; not
equality, but an equality of opportunity, which recognizes sexual
difference. Neoconservatives do not argue that women are not
equal to men; they say rather that women are different from men.
Therefore equality of opportunity for women is fine; equality of
conditions, which assumes sameness, is not."[4] The sameness between men and women is replaced by "difference." Women may
very well work in the labor force, but they should not expect governmental programs to intervene and treat them as *like* (equal
to) men.

Neoconservatives argue that there is already too much equality.
Daniel Patrick Moynihan, a leading neoconservative, approvingly
quotes his colleague Nathan Glazer to make this point. "The demand for economic equality is now not the demand for equality of
opportunity for the equally qualified: it is now the demand for
equality . . . of results, of outcomes."[5] Moynihan argues that in the
end this demand creates a culture of dependency, that we will have

3. For a fuller treatment of the New Right, see Zillah Eisenstein, *Feminism
and Sexual Equality: Crisis in Liberal America* (New York: Monthly Review
Press, 1984), esp. ch. 2. See also Pamela Johnston Conover and Virginia Gray,
Feminism and the New Right: Conflict over the American Family (Westport,
Conn.: Praeger, 1983); Barbara Ehrenreich, Elizabeth Hess, and Gloria Jacobs,
Re-Making Love: The Feminization of Sex (Garden City, N.Y.: Doubleday, Anchor
Books, 1986), esp. ch. 5; and Connaught Marshner, "How Jerry Falwell Is Driv-
ing the Left to an Early Grave," *Conservative Digest* 11 (June 1986): 93–104.

4. Eisenstein, *Feminism and Sexual Equality*, p. 82.

5. Nathan Glazer, qtd. in Daniel Patrick Moynihan, *Family and Nation* (New
York: Harcourt Brace Jovanovich, 1986), p. 27; all further references to this work,
abbreviated as *FN*, will be included in the text.

"a disproportionate number of persons not equal to their opportunities. In consequence there would not be equal results" (*FN*, p. 27). According to him, the problem with the welfare state is its egalitarian model. He quotes disapprovingly from President Johnson's speech at Howard University in 1964, which Moynihan himself helped write:

You do not take a person who for years has been hobbled by chains and liberate him, bring him up to the starting line of a race and then say, "You are free to compete with all the others," and still justly believe that you have been completely fair. Thus it is not enough just to open the gates of opportunity. All our citizens must have the ability to walk through the gates.

(*FN*, p. 31)

Equality in this view was to mean equality of results. Although this doctrine has never been fully practiced in the United States, it is significant that it was articulated as a part of state discourse in the 1960s, and such statements were absent from state rhetoric in the 1980s. In the 1980s policies committed to promoting sexual and racial equality have been considered highly suspect. The white male is explicitly privileged in New Right and neoconservative rhetoric. The American public is asked to reassess public welfare programs because they ostensibly create a culture of dependency for the black family. It is interesting that Governor Mario Cuomo of New York noted in 1987 that when he raised the issue of a culture of dependence ten years ago, he was called a conservative; today he's called a liberal.[6] This change reflects the new positioning of these ideas in relation to the state's degree of support for them. At the beginning of the 1960s, poverty was seen as a structural problem: the individual was not held solely responsible—hence, the affirmative action policies of the mid- and late 1960s. In the late 1980s the policies have been blamed as the source of the problem, and individuals have been asked once again to take responsibility for their place in the economic class structure. The welfare state is said to have failed: neoconservatives say that in the war on poverty, poverty won (see *FN*, p. 69).

The crisis of liberalism, which involves rejecting equality be-

6. See quotation of Cuomo in Lena Williams, "Democrats Urged to Reassess Impact of Public Welfare Programs," *New York Times*, 24 June 1986, p. A23.

cause equality was, according to neoconservatives, wrongly extended into the realms of family life, sexuality, and the meaning of "difference," has led to a rejection of equality (meaning egalitarianism), particularly although not exclusively between the sexes. This critique extends to the notion of freedom itself when it is specifically applied to sexual freedom, especially in relation to abortion, homosexuality, and premarital, extramarital, or nonmarital sex. For George Gilder of the New Right, "there are no human beings; there are just men and women, and when they deny their divergent sexuality, they reject the deepest sources of identity and love."[7] The sexual constitution of society is as important as the legal constitution, for "sex is the life force—and cohesive impulse of a people, and their very character will be deeply affected by how sexuality is managed, sublimated, expressed, denied, and propagated" (*SS*, p. 1; and see p. 131). Gilder attacks feminism because he feels that it is hostile to sexual difference and family life and that "as a movement it is devoted to establishing the career woman as the American ideal, supported by federal subsidies and celebrations" (*SS*, p. 67).

Neoconservatives opt for the homogeneous view of engendered sex "difference" as well; women are "different" as a class from men. Michael Levin, in the noted neoconservative journal *Commentary*, criticizes the feminist movement for assuming that there are no important biologically based differences between men and women and for inferring that if men and women were raised identically, they would develop identically. He argues that "we come into the world not as bits of prime matter, but as males or females," and he assumes that culture plays no part in this process of definition.[8] In another leading neoconservative journal, *The Public Interest*, woman's "difference" from man is used to challenge the validity of affirmative action policy. "We should strive for equal treatment [i.e., opportunity] of individuals rather than equal results [i.e., conditions] for men and for women."[9] The problem of women's lack

---

7. George Gilder, *Sexual Suicide* (New York: Quadrangle/New York Times Book Co., 1973), p. 43; all further references to this work, hereafter abbreviated as *SS*, will be included in the text.

8. Michael Levin, "The Feminist Mystique," *Commentary* 70 (December 1980): 25, 28.

9. Carl Hoffman and John Shelton Reed, "Sex Discrimination?—The XYZ Af-

of advancement is understood not as a lack of opportunity but rather as a reflection of the natural "difference" of women from men. Hence, neoconservatives contend that we need a reward system that recognizes initiative, leadership, knowledge of the job, and competitive spirit rather than one that tries to equalize the sexes (see "SD," p. 38). "The law should open opportunities and expand the range of choices for individuals—not interfere with rational business practice, individual decisions, or the fundamental institutions of society" ("SD," p. 23). Neoconservatives assume that the "race of life" will not be the same for women as it is for men. Unlike members of the New Right, neoconservatives do not stipulate that the home is the only proper place for women. Women can enter the market, as long as they do not expect to operate as men do in it.

Neoconservatives wish to reinstate the "difference" of woman from man and the "difference" of homosexual from heterosexual because they view these "differences" as crucial to the smooth functioning of the social order. Order is established through hierarchical differentiations and is destroyed by a commitment to "too much" equality—that is, too much similarity. Sameness between the sexes leads to homosexuality on the one hand and a social welfare state out of control on the other. Given this kind of analysis, the significant restructuring of the social welfare state as well as the systematic assault on homosexual rights that took place under Reagan are not surprising.

The restructuring of the social welfare state was premised on the rejection of sexual and racial as well as economic equality. It has affected poor, working-class, and middle-class black and white women in very particular, yet similar, ways. Poor and working-class women have lost welfare benefits, food stamps, and such, while middle-class women have lost their jobs *in* the social welfare state. Through the 1970s the government employed 49.9 percent of all female professionals. With the Reagan administration cutbacks, "minority employees of the federal agencies have been laid off at a rate of 50% greater than nonminority employees, women administrators have been laid off at a rate of 150% higher than male admin-

---

fair," *Public Interest* 62 (Winter 1981): 23; all further references to this work, abbreviated as "SD," will be included in the text.

istrators."[10] By 1984 the number of federal employees had fallen by 22 percent. Minority women accounted for only 12.3 percent of the federal work force but suffered nearly half (49 percent) of the reductions.[11]

Similarly, as a result of work incentive programs, the labor-force participation rate of welfare mothers rose 28 percent from 1967 to 1973 because the market and the state encouraged the mixture of wage earning and welfare during this period.[12] Since that time, however, such gains have been lost. The reorganization of the welfare state has attacked women across economic class and racial lines. This attack sought to *re*establish the privilege of white men against women as a sex class while attempting to increase the economic and racial inequities among women. As a result, black women fared the worst of any group as allocations shifted from public to private agencies.

The first term (1981–1985) of the Reagan administration initiated the rearticulation of the patriarchal state through the restructuring of the social welfare state and the realignment of the state's relationship to the family. Two tendencies mark the policies of the state in this attempt. First, control was established over parents/women as mothers, for example, in issues of child custody and compulsory fetal or neonatal surgery. Second, the authority of parents/men as fathers was reinforced, for instance, in parental notification or consent requirements regarding abortion, birth control for minors, textbook censorship, sex education censorship, and so forth.[13] Moynihan argues for the second tendency, for the establishment of a welfare state that is conservative in form, in order to make clear what is legitimate and what is not. "There must be an acknowledged providing male" (*FN*, p. 181). Reconstituting the social wel-

10. Augustus F. Hawkins, "Minorities and Unemployment," in *What Reagan Is Doing to Us*, ed. Alan Gartner, Colin Greer, and Frank Riessman (New York: Harper & Row, 1982), p. 134.

11. Federal Government Service Task Force, comp., *Report on Fiscal 1984 Reduction-in-Force Activity and Summary Report for Fiscal Years 1982–1984*, p. 1.

12. See Steven Erie, Martin Rein, and Barbara Wiget, "Women and the Reagan Revolution: Thermidor for the Social Welfare Economy," in *Families, Politics, and Public Policy: A Feminist Dialogue on Women and the State*, ed. Irene Diamond (New York: Longman, 1983), p. 98.

13. I am indebted to Rosalind Petchesky for helping me clarify this point.

fare state was recentering the phallus and the politics of inequality. In the assumptions behind this effort, the male head of household needs to be at the center of the family and the market and the state. Men and women are "different": men are providers, women are provided for and engendered by their "difference."

Recentering the Phallus
in "the" Family

Although sometimes the Reagan white-male-identified administration presented itself for what it was—for instance, when it adopted New Right rhetoric, which was most often explicitly antiegalitarian—it more often presented itself in terms of a "pro-family" stance that cloaked this politics. The New Right initiated the "pro-family" position in the 1980 election, but "pro-family" arguments have since become part of mainstream politics and been embraced by Democrats and Republicans alike. They have affected feminist politics, and other radical politics as well.[14] The problem is that the mainstreaming of family-life issues asserts the importance of familial values without recognizing or resolving their conflict with the individualist priorities of liberalism, neoconservatism, neoliberalism, or the New Right. In the end, "pro-family" politics assumes that women will resolve the conflict: when familial needs, which presume collectivity or community, conflict with the needs of the individuals in families, women (as mothers and wives) are to resolve the conflict in favor of the family. All family needs—such as love, caring for children, maintaining a household, earning a living—are not always in conflict with individuals' equivalent needs but they often are.

The tension between individual needs and family needs does not arise for New Right "pro-family" politicians, because they assume that the individuals with needs are men and that women are "different"—women's needs are one and the same as the needs of the

14. See Greg Calvert, "Why Are Leftists Leaping to the Family's Defense?" *In These Times*, 10–16 March 1982, pp. 12–15; Barbara Ehrenreich, "Family Feud on the Left," *Nation* 234 (13 March 1982): 303–6; Barbara Epstein, "Family Politics and the New Left," *Socialist Review* 12 (May–August 1982): 141–61; and Lynne Segal, ed., *What Is to Be Done about the Family? Crisis in the Eighties* (Harmondsworth: Penguin Books, 1983).

family. Hence, there is no conflict between individualism and familism. Individuals are men. The family, though headed by a man (who is *also* a father and husband) is constituted by a wife and mother. Engendered sex "difference" and the separate spheres it supposedly creates resolve any conflict. The neoconservative "profamily" politics is somewhat different from that of the New Right because it recognizes women not only as mothers but as "working" mothers. The woman, as mother, however, is still the one who must resolve the conflicts between her work and her family's needs through day-care arrangements, after-school programs, and so on. This is why such concerns are often identified as women's issues rather than family issues.

Strong families are the heart of the "opportunity" society. Or, as President Reagan said in his 1986 State of the Union address:

We must also look to the condition of America's families. Struggling parents today worry how they will provide their children the advantages that their parents gave them. In the welfare culture, the breakdown of the family, the most basic support system, has reached crisis proportions: in female and child poverty, child abandonment, horrible crimes, and deteriorating schools. After hundreds of billions of dollars in poverty programs, the plight of the poor grows more painful. But the waste in dollars and cents pales before the most tragic loss—the sinful waste of human spirit and potential.[15]

Reagan, supposedly speaking about family life, launched an attack on the social welfare state, which he held responsible for creating poverty and destroying "the" family. He argued in this same address that we must "create a ladder of opportunity" that is not burdened "by horse and buggy programs that waste tax dollars and squander human potential." Family and community must be reconstituted as the core of society; "private values must be at the heart of public policies." With no clarification of what a "pro-family" policy might be, Reagan argued: "True reform means a tax system that at long last is pro-family, pro-jobs, pro-future, and pro-America." His imagery is positive but empty.

Reagan chose to develop this theme further later that month in one of his weekly radio addresses. He argued that current govern-

15. Ronald Reagan, "The State of the Union Address," *New York Times*, 5 February 1986, p. A20.

ment programs were creating "a permanent scar on the nation by perpetuating poverty and contributing to the breakdown of the family." He blamed the crisis of family breakdown on a welfare system that paid higher benefits to homes where fathers were not present, saying, "government programs have ruptured the bonds that held families together."[16] A "pro-family" policy obviously requires fathers to be present and government systems to support the father as head of household. As Reagan collapsed the issues of family, welfare, and poverty, he underlined the racist aspect of his argument. "Welfare" and "poverty" function as code words for the black family in "pro-family" rhetoric.

Moynihan argues in his *Family and Nation*, "American arrangements pertained to the individual and only in the rarest circumstances did they define the family as the relevant unit" (*FN*, p. 5). This is true of liberalism in general: the focus is on individual rights and not familial needs. That is why the individual so often meant the man; the woman saw to familial needs. Alexis de Tocqueville believed that the family would moderate individualism, but instead individualism and feminism, to the extent that they derive from individualist claims for women, have challenged the traditional meaning of family life.[17] Moynihan, instead of recognizing the important challenge of feminism to the patriarchal arrangements of traditional family structure, wants to reinstate this structure. "A community that allows a large number of young men to grow up in broken families, dominated by women, never acquiring any set of rational expectations about the future—that community asks for and gets chaos" (*FN*, p. 9).

Moynihan thinks the government must establish programs that enhance traditional (patriarchal) family life. The problem with Reagan's destruction of many of the social-welfare policies pertaining to family life is that they did have a positive effect on the problem of poverty, even if they also "contributed to family breakups, welfare dependency, and a large increase in births out of wedlock" (*FN*, p. 69). Because Moynihan believes that "poverty is inextricably associated with family structure," he asserts that programs that

16. Ronald Reagan, qtd. in Ellen Warren, "Reagan: Welfare Helps Split Families," *Philadelphia Inquirer*, 16 February 1986, p. A20.

17. For an interesting discussion of this point, see Robert Bellah et al., *Habits of the Heart* (New York: Harper & Row, 1985).

help sustain families must be kept in place (*FN*, p. 46). These programs do, however, need to be changed so as not to undermine the authority of the father in relation to the state. Today these concerns are accepted as commonplace, especially when speaking of the black family. When Moynihan first articulated some of these concerns in his report "The Negro Family: The Case for National Action,"[18] this was not the case. The rejection of liberalism has entailed the *re*articulation of racist and phallocratic privilege. And black culture, rather than structural joblessness, is blamed for black poverty.[19]

The Democratic party has also aligned itself with a neoconservative stance on family life. "Indeed, virtually every successful Democratic candidate of the Senate [in 1986] made it clear from the start that he opposed wasteful spending on social programs, opposed using tax reform as a way to raise taxes and supported government policies to encourage economic growth and traditional American family values."[20] *New Choices in a Changing America,* the report of the Democratic Policy Commission to the Democratic National Committee, identifies strong, independent families as the centerpiece of the party's domestic policy. The report argues that self-sufficient families are necessary if children are to be nurtured appropriately. "Democrats favor pro-family policies that will raise family incomes, help keep families together, and provide some assistance to parents in their day-to-day lives."[21] Specific proposals of this report include pro-family tax reform that raises exemptions for children, removal of the working poor from tax rolls, increased

18. See Daniel Patrick Moynihan, "The Negro Family: The Case for National Action," in *The Moynihan Report and the Politics of Controversy,* ed. Lee Rainwater and William Yancey (Cambridge, Mass.: MIT Press, 1967).

19. For further discussion of this issue, see Nicholas Lemann, "The Origins of the Underclass," *Atlantic Monthly* 257 (June 1986): 31–55; Charles Murray, *Losing Ground: American Social Policy, 1950–1980* (New York: Basic Books, 1984), and "White Families, White Trash," *National Review* 38 (28 March 1986): 30–34; David Osborne, "Winning Battles, Losing the War," *Mother Jones* 11 (June 1986): 13–21; Alphonso Pinkney, *The Myth of Black Progress* (New York: Cambridge Univ. Press, 1984); Jan Rosenberg, "An Interview with William Julius Wilson," *Democratic Left* 14 (September–October 1986): 27–30; and William Julius Wilson, *The Declining Significance of Race* (Chicago: Univ. of Chicago Press, 1978).

20. Mark Penn and Douglas Schoen, "Reagan's Revolution Hasn't Ended," *New York Times,* 9 November 1986, p. E23.

21. The Democratic National Committee, *New Choices in a Changing America* (Washington, D.C., 1986), p. 17.

child-care credits, creation of "pro-family" workplaces, and assurance of greater income security (through a strengthened economy). The report mentions the importance of job security for pregnant women and parental leave. It also calls for the expansion of child care, particularly employer-assisted, on-site care. The Democratic call for better day-care facilities recognizes the families in which both parents work.

The "pro-family" discourse has moved from a vision of the traditional patriarchal family to a more pluralist view of multiple family forms. Day care is supposedly part of this package, although the government appears to be expected to have little role in financing such endeavors. Neoconservatives in both parties have endorsed this view. In contrast, the New Right has no need for day-care policies given its commitment to the traditional (patriarchal) form of family life.

The language of "pro-family" policy has shifted and is in flux today. Families with single parents and with both parents working outside the home are recognized as widespread. The problem is that the traditional family form, which makes up only a minority of families today, was nonetheless privileged as the preferred model by the radical right factions of the state and was the model that prevailed in state discourse. Thus the model of woman as exclusively wife and mother was preferred to the model of woman as family member and wage earner. Thus day care is something needed by wage-earning mothers, not wage-earning fathers. Care of the children and the responsibilities of the home remain in large part women's concerns. The pregnant body is still a problem because the female is seen as one and the same as the mother, engendered by her sex "difference." The man is preferred as the head of household, and the woman is unequal, as in "different." She is not a provider, she is the mother, and the mother is therefore the unprivileged parent. This analysis is not to deny that state discourse sometimes embraces the idea of parent rather than simply mother and by so doing reflects a changing political context. In this instance, however, the shift in discourse was an insufficient rearrangement of power.

We have to look not only at the rhetoric used in politics but at the actual policies if we are to assess what such shifts in discourse really mean. A discourse remains viable only as long as it is useful and can make sense of things. When it seems unreal, when what it states is in obvious conflict with what we experience, discourse loses its effectiveness. Although Reagan spoke of "pro-family" policies, his administration supported only the traditional form of the family. His reorganization of the social-welfare state has led to more poverty and family disintegration in all family forms. The number of poor children increased during his administration, while aid for them decreased. "After a high of 83.6% of poor children receiving AFDC [Aid to Families with Dependent Children] in 1973, by 1983 only 53.3% were recipients."[22] Ruth Sidel points out that budget cuts alone increased the number of poor people in 1982 by at least 557,000 and increased the number of poor children by 331,000. As of 1984, the reduction or elimination of AFDC support caused the percentage of wage-earning mothers living below the poverty line to more than double. It would seem that the contradictions in Reagan's "pro-family" discourse will instigate yet another shift in state discourse. This may be true for anti–welfare state rhetoric as well.

Reagan said that the war on poverty was lost by the welfare state, but government statistics show that whereas the number of Americans living below the poverty level dropped virtually every year between 1964 and 1979, from 1979 to 1986 it increased by 41 percent. Moynihan reiterates this point: during the Johnson–Nixon years, from 1965 to 1974, poverty as officially measured fell from 17.3 percent to 11.6 percent (see *FN*, p. 72). By 1983, the poverty rate had reached its highest level in eighteen years. This fact did not, however, prevent the Reagan administration from arguing that the welfare state institutionalized poverty, and this depiction allowed them to dismantle poverty programs. The administration spoke about the preciousness of human life and of young children while it took away their food programs and day care. Federal funds for day care were cut significantly in fiscal year 1982: Title XX, the largest program providing federal support for child care, was cut by 20 percent. The Public Service Employment Program of the Comprehensive Employment and Training Act (CETA), which helped provide staff for child-care centers, was abolished. The

22. Ruth Sidel, *Women and Children Last: The Plight of Poor Women in Affluent America* (New York: Viking Press, 1986), p. 87.

child-care cuts during the first three years of the Reagan administration eliminated care for at least 150,000 children.[23]

The Phallus and 1984

What does it mean to argue that Reagan administration politics
strove to recenter the phallus? It means that current politics seeks
to reestablish the white male as the privileged standard and, using
this standard, to undermine claims for equality for black men and
women and white women. The phallus had not been successfully
decentered before the Reagan administration, but the challenges
to its dualistic structuring of men's and women's lives were clearly
under way and making progress. Reagan's politics was about reaf-
firming sex "difference" and sharpening the distinction between
genders. There was no one vision within the state on how best to
attain these ends, hence the conflicts between and varied concerns
of the neoconservatives, New Rightists, neoconservative feminists,
antifeminists, and others on questions such as abortion, "the" family, pornography, AIDS, the ERA, aid to the Contras, arms ship-
ments to Iran. These questions are not all of the same order, but
they all have significance for establishing the phallocratic aspects
of state rule.

International politics, although not obviously related to issues of
sex equality, is often the arena in which the phallocratic state establishes its credibility. President Reagan's macho image was seriously
damaged by the Iran-Contra scandal—the selling of weapons to
Iran in exchange for American hostages and the diversion of funds
from the sale to the Contras in Nicaragua. Strong men do not get
caught lying and covering up secret dealings with supposed ene-
mies. The Iranian hostage situation made President Carter look
impotent and contributed to his loss of the 1980 presidential election. President Johnson decided not to seek reelection when it became clear that he could not win the Vietnam War. The American

23. Sidel, *Women and Children Last,* p. 127. And see Gartner, Greer, and
Riessman, eds., *What Reagan Is Doing to Us,* and *Beyond Reagan: Alternatives
for the '80's* (New York: Harper & Row, 1984); John L. Palmer and Isabel V.
Sawhill, eds., *The Reagan Record* (Cambridge, Mass.: Ballinger Publishing,
1984); and Lester Salamon and Michael Lund, eds., *The Reagan Presidency and
the Governing of America* (Washington, D.C.: Urban Institute Press, 1984).

state, given its phallocratic underpinnings, must appear strong and determined and hegemonic: as in man, husband, father. Instead, the United States has been decentered as a major international power by its post-Vietnam ineffectuality in foreign affairs, economic crisis, and the politics of terrorism. The American state, and with it liberalism, has been made to seem "wimpy."

The phallocratic aspects of the liberal state—the privileging of the white male through the dualistic structuring of public/private and state/family established in the opposition of man/woman—were more bluntly stated as a part of state discourse during the Reagan administration than at any other time in recent U.S. history. This development has created significant problems for a liberal democratic state that is supposed to applaud the basic universalist claims of liberal individualism for both men and women. It is not surprising that disaffection and hostility developed among women toward both the administration's attack on their newly won gains in equality and its protection of the white male.

I want to examine this disaffection to elucidate further how liberal discourse, and more particularly liberal feminist discourse, not only reflects but affects society. The ideas of liberal feminism are more than empty rhetoric; they guide expectations and influence the way we live. Once again, the rigid distinction between the real (concrete) and the ideal (nonconcrete) does not hold, because the idea of women's right to equality is both less than "true" equality and more than a complete misrepresentation of reality. The idea of equality occupies a space on the continuum of the real/ideal that allows it to affect the relations of power. These relations would be different—even if not wholly different—if liberal feminist claims for equality did not exist.

The Reagan state in its first term was openly hostile to liberal feminist concerns such as abortion and the ERA. By the 1984 election this was so much the case that members of the Republican party feared that Reagan would be defeated by what the media termed the "gender gap," the fact that women were more disaffected than were men with Reagan's policies. More interesting than the media's description of this gap is the understanding of the contradictory nature of women's supposedly gendered "difference" implied by it. Whereas women's disaffection with Reagan was based in part on his relegation of women to their "difference" as mothers, the gender gap was largely depicted as a reflection of women's gendered "difference" as mothers, as more peaceable and nurturing. The media treatment of the gender gap assumes some aspects of the neoconservative discourse about women's engendered sex "difference"; both view women's "difference" as homogeneous. The gender gap, however, stands as a critique of this viewing, as we shall see.

A White House memorandum confirms the Reagan administration's concern about the gender gap. The memo, dated 5 November 1982, states that "the continued growth of the 'gender gap' in its current form could cause serious trouble for Republicans in 1984."[24]

In 1981, partly as a response to the acknowledged gender gap in the 1980 election, Reagan had appointed Sandra Day O'Connor justice of the Supreme Court and Jeane Kirkpatrick ambassador to the United Nations. He continued this tactic of appointing women to visible positions before the 1984 election: Elizabeth Dole was made secretary of Transportation and Margaret Heckler, secretary of Health and Human Services. Policy initiatives concerning abortion, affirmative action, day care, and similar issues changed little if at all.

By the time the 1984 presidential campaign began, women's disaffection with the Reagan administration had increased. In an attempt to reverse this trend, the Republicans mobilized a media campaign to change women's ideas about Reagan's positions on nuclear war and on the economy. In contrast to their 1980 presidential campaign, Republicans in 1984 focused little on issues such as abortion and the ERA; instead they emphasized international peace by stressing American strength and patriotism. In this way they hoped to court enough of the women's vote to win. The Republican strategists developed a media campaign that replaced specific policy proposals with masculinist imagery of a virile economy and a strong international stance. It was an election of images, and the imagery was phallic. This tactic—projecting the image of

24. Memorandum for White House Coordinating Council on Women and Working Group Members from Emily Rock, subject: Gender Gap, Ronald Hinckley Report, 9 November 1982, p. 3. The memo was first revealed by Adam Clymer, in "Warning on 'Gender Gap' from the White House," *New York Times*, 3 December 1982, p. A18.

Reagan as an embodiment of the patriarchal state—seems to have appealed to the residual male identification of the men and women who voted for him. The strategy appears to have been effective with some white women: support for Reagan among women as a whole increased from 38 percent in 1982 to 57 percent in 1984. The gender gap on the national level dipped from 8 percent in 1980 to 4 percent in 1984.[25] This was not true for black women, however, who overwhelmingly voted for Walter Mondale.

Blacks voted against Reagan: 85 percent of black men as well as 93 percent of black women voted for Mondale, making the gender gap between black men and women 8 points. Only 36 percent of white women voted for Mondale. More married men and women voted for Reagan than for Mondale (63 to 51 percent); more married men than married women voted for Reagan (65 to 60 percent). Sixty-three percent of homemakers voted for Reagan; 53 percent of blue-collar workers did so as well, as did 59 percent of white-collar workers. Seventy-one percent of southern whites voted for Reagan. Mondale, by contrast, won 52 percent of the women's vote in the East, 73 percent of the Jewish women's vote, 65 percent of the Hispanic women's vote, and the majority of the women's vote among the poor and jobless.[26] There are obviously different dimensions to the gender gap and its relation to gender consciousness. The gap itself bespeaks a "difference" of gender in the electoral arena, but it does not specify the meanings of this multiple difference for politics.

In relation to other issues, 69 percent of women who opposed

25. Gender gap statistics in and of themselves do not specify race, class, age, and so on. There is variation in these percentages when categories are specified further; the most dramatic variation is for black women. And even the general gender gap statistics vary, depending on what data base is used. The 1984 *New York Times*/CBS poll revised the gender gap upward from 4 to 6 percent. Other polls showed an even higher gap in comparison with that of 1980: ABC/*Washington Post* and the National Election Studies noted an 8 percent gap, and NBC noted a 9 percent gap. See also Ethel Klein, "The Diffusion of Consciousness in the United States and Western Europe," in *The Women's Movements of the United States and Western Europe,* ed. Mary Fainsod Katzenstein and Carol McClurg Muller (Philadelphia: Temple Univ. Press, 1987).

26. See Warren Miller [principal investigator], *American National Election Data, 1984: Pre- and Post-Election Survey File* (Ann Arbor: Center for Political Studies, University of Michigan, 1985). Available from Inter-University Consortium for Political and Social Research, P.O. Box 1248, Ann Arbor, Mich. 48106.

the legalization of abortion voted for Reagan, 29 percent for Mondale. Of women who believed that abortion should be legal only under extreme circumstances, 64 percent voted for Reagan, 36 percent for Mondale. Conversely, women who thought abortion should be legal and not limited to extreme circumstances voted for Mondale in greater proportions than for Reagan: 54 versus 45 percent. Beliefs about the legalization of abortion obviously did not determine people's votes, yet these beliefs are strongly held. Of women who identified war in Central America and arms control as the issues that mattered most to them, 47 percent voted for Mondale, 19 percent for Reagan. Clearly gender and feminist consciousness cannot be correlated with the 1984 vote.

Geraldine Ferraro's nomination as the first woman vice-presidential candidate of a major political party could have been used to mobilize the women's vote for the Democratic ticket, but the Democrats would have had to develop a politics sensitive to gender issues. Instead of articulating a platform consistent with this purpose, they assumed that the women's vote was theirs because of Ferraro's candidacy. This strategy was not sufficient, especially in the view of women who identified themselves as feminists—they had moved beyond thinking that isolated women in electoral and appointed offices constitute genuine equality between the sexes. This is not to belittle the importance of feminist politicians in the state apparatus. A woman vice-presidential candidate legitimates women in the public/political sphere. Unfortunately, though, a woman vice-presidential candidate does more to remind us that all the other candidates are men than she does to help us imagine that all the others could be women.

Feminist concerns such as day care, pay equity, parental leave, abortion, and so forth were largely silenced in the 1984 election. The Democrats apparently chose Ferraro as the symbol of these concerns, and they banked on this choice being a sufficient policy initiative.[27] She was to represent the party's commitment to "opportunity" for women, and this representation replaced specific proposals. She was expected to bring in the women's vote but quietly, indirectly, without further developing a consciousness

27. See Geraldine Ferraro, *Ferraro: My Story* (New York: Bantam Books, 1985); and Gloria Steinem, "The Ferraro Factor: What Difference Can One Woman Make?" *Ms.* 13 (October 1984): 43–49, 146–48.

among women of their sex-class status. For women who recognized their needs as women but not necessarily as feminists, Ferraro's candidacy was not a meaningful symbol in and of itself. They did not see Ferraro as representing a party commitment to women's equality. These women, who—in terms of their interest as wage earners, single parents, financially disadvantaged people—might have voted for Mondale, did not vote at all, or voted for Reagan, and did not see a link between themselves, their needs, their vote, and the Mondale-Ferraro ticket. Dottie Lynch, a top adviser to Democratic presidential candidate Gary Hart and a pollster for Mondale, has said of the Democrats: "They've missed opportunities. . . . They were afraid of [Ferraro's] power—to do harm or do good. . . . They made the decision that they had the women's vote and were terrified of a male backlash."[28]

The Democratic party was frightened that a great deal of the excitement over the Mondale-Ferraro ticket after the 1984 national convention would backfire on Mondale, damaging his image particularly among white males. They feared that Ferraro would make Mondale appear ineffectual; if she seemed too smart and too strong, Mondale could seem dumb and weak. The contrasts were predefined by the engendered sexual differentiation of woman from man. The Ferraro nomination demonstrates how politics limits the possibilities of mobilizing women electorally; at the same time, it highlights the possibility of developing gender consciousness for feminists. Ferraro represented both these realities: her candidacy was far from meaningless, yet it was not meaningful enough. She was different because she is a woman, but she was not different enough for feminists (she had no agenda particularizing the needs of women), and she was too "different" for white males (she was not a man).

The Ferraro nomination posed a problem for the Republicans as well. They paraded their few women officials before the American public and even said they would entertain the possibility of a woman vice-presidential nominee in 1988. (We should not, however, fail to note that there was no discussion of a woman as a presidential candidate.) The Reagan administration was proof that

28. Dottie Lynch, qtd. in Joan Walsh, "How Reagan Bridged the Gender Gap," *In These Times* 9 (21 November–4 December 1984): 6.

women can be appointed to positions of electoral power within a discourse of antifeminism or neoconservative feminism: sexual opportunity and "difference" replace sexual equality (meaning sameness).

At this point the discourse of neoconservatism, which applauds the "opportunity" society, and the discourse of mainstream feminism, which is committed to sex equality, interface in both contradictory and mutually exclusive ways. Liberal feminism, which initially saw sex equality in "opportunity" terms, was never limited to this view, because feminism criticizes the exclusion of women as a sex class from equality with men.[29] Inasmuch as women are excluded from equality of opportunity in running the "race of life," or at least are disadvantaged in the race, liberal feminists cannot embrace the view of individual opportunity that neoliberals and neoconservatives espouse. This disadvantage, however, has not impeded the development of neoconservative feminism, which rejects policies based on sex class, such as affirmative action and comparable worth, and instead promotes the merits of individual (i.e., unaided) achievement. Neoconservatives have rejected liberalism—as the promise of equality of opportunity (economic, sexual, racial)—for the promise of "opportunity." The concern with equality per se has been dropped. And the neoconservatives hope to reroute feminism away from equality as well. This redefinition of liberalism and liberal feminism rejects equality (meaning sameness of treatment) and favors the opportunity to be "different." The "opportunity" society assumes individual freedom within the hierarchical relations of sexual, racial, and economic differentiation. A woman can achieve on her own. "Difference" in these instances, however, means inequality, not a recognition of diversity or radical pluralism. Thus this redefinition sees "difference" as being in opposition to equality.

This language of the "opportunity" society presents real problems for a feminist discourse committed to equality. According to this language, opportunity exists in order for women to explore their "difference" from men, not their sameness. Because the discourse of liberalism has shifted and the concept of equality is being

29. See Zillah Eisenstein, *The Radical Future of Liberal Feminism* (Boston: Northeastern Univ. Press, 1981), for a fuller explication of this point.

revised, both the Democrats and the Republicans, who have come to adopt similar versions of this neoconservative, neoliberal stance, have a freer hand to limit the meaning of "sex equality." The Republicans have articulated their individual "opportunity" platform as anti-ERA, antiabortion, and anti–affirmative action. The Democrats remain symbolically supportive of the ERA, abortion, affirmative action, day care, and comparable worth, but what this support will actually mean as they move closer to a neoconservative stance on the economy is unclear.

At best, we can characterize current political discussion of sex equality as conflictual and shifting. Neither party has blatantly rejected the liberal feminist discourse of equality, but both have redefined equality to mean not sameness but different opportunities. A woman's "difference," her "separate but equal" status, and her "need for protection" are all aspects of a language that attempts to deny woman her similarity with man. These multiple political meanings exist alongside another language and a public consciousness that can be characterized as liberal feminist. In their view "equal treatment" means treatment that is the same for women and men.

There are multiple radical feminisms that remain largely outside the electoral arena. Liberal feminism is poised uneasily on the outskirts of the arena. There are different versions of a sexual "opportunity" discourse of neoliberalism and neoconservatism privileged in the state. And the antifeminism of the New Right has defined much of the radical rhetoric in the Reagan administration. The effect of feminism remains, despite its exclusion from the revisions of liberalism; its influence was evident in both parties' anxiety over their "manliness," the neoconservative Democrats' fear of feminist influence within the party, and so forth.

The Reagan administration's neoconservative and New Right stances were often expressed in a sloppy phallocratic imagery that began to reveal the administration's "opportunity" language and views for what they really were. One example was Vice-President Bush's usage of overtly phallocratic language during the 1984 campaign. Bush described his part in the televised vice-presidential candidates' debate as having "kicked a little ass." During the debate Bush insisted on calling his opponent Mrs. Ferraro, which is not even correct; her husband's name is Zaccaro. Former White

House Chief of Staff Donald Regan dismissed women as not being interested in the U.S.-Soviet armament talks. President Reagan himself repeatedly spoke out against abortion. In his 1986 State of the Union address, he remarked, "We are a nation of idealists, yet today there is a wound in our national conscience; America will never be whole as long as the right to life granted by our creator is denied to the unborn. For the rest of my time, I shall do what I can to see that this wound is one day healed."[30]

This phallocratic viewing of women and issues pertaining to their lives characterized the Reagan administration even more in its second term. Margaret Heckler was removed from her cabinet position to become ambassador to Ireland. United Nations Ambassador Jeane Kirkpatrick resigned in protest over being stalemated by the administration. What could the opposition to her really have been, given that she was one of those rare individuals in the administration who had the support of both the New Right and the neoconservatives? Kirkpatrick herself was critical of the sexism in the White House. "Sexism is alive in the U.N., in the U.S. government, in American politics—where it is bipartisan—but it is not unconquerable."[31]

Muriel Siepert, a leading Republican woman, criticized the administration for its insensitivity toward women at a 1986 Gotham luncheon, a meeting of New York moderate Republicans, that convenes four or five times a year to discuss party issues.

If the party would simply reaffirm its traditional commitment to equal economic, social and political rights for men and women; if the party would show the same kind of enthusiasm for education and nutrition that it shows for missiles and bombs; if the idea of dignity and respect for women, rather than condescension and neglect, played a more prominent part in the deliberation of the party—then I think the Republican party . . . could expect a lot more women to march in its ranks.[32]

Journalist Ellen Goodman describes the Reagan administration as a white male bastion. After Elizabeth Dole resigned from her po-

30. Reagan, "The State of the Union Address."

31. Jeane Kirkpatrick, qtd. in *National N.O.W. Times* 18 (January–February 1985): 5.

32. Muriel Siepert, qtd. in Sydney Schanberg, "The G.O.P. vs. Women," *New York Times*, 5 April 1986, p. A27.

sition as secretary of transportation to join her husband's presidential campaign, there were no women left in the administration's top ranks. And there were never any black men. Nancy Reagan was said to have been in the inner circle of decision makers, but her role and priorities were always those of the adoring wife. Apart from the First Lady, as of 1985, "not a single woman attends senior staff meetings at the White House. Not one regularly sits at National Security meetings any more. Nor, since Faith Whittlesey's departure from the job of public liaison to be ambassador to Switzerland, is there any woman who reports directly to the president."[33] Goodman quotes a statement by Whittlesey, once ranking woman in the White House and an anti-ERA conservative, to the *Wall Street Journal:* "'All I saw was a sea of men coming and going in those cars. I began to think, maybe they're right. Women aren't welcome in the White House.'"[34]

Eleanor Smeal, president of the National Organization for Women (NOW), makes it clear, however, that antifeminist politics and white male privilege are not limited to the Republicans. "There is too little vigor from the Democrats and too many Democrats who are willing to tell us that we have to go to the right, that they have to get the Southern white male, that it was the blacks and the women and the progressives that caused their defeat in 1984."[35]

Women's absence from the Reagan administration represented and reflected the administration's rejection and dismissal of the idea of equality for women. Their absence also reflected and established the shifts in state discourse that denied the claims of liberal feminism. It should be no surprise that an administration that articulated the needs of the white male was dominated by white men. Those who are not white men were excluded by the state's language, its images and symbols, and the state's practice. When the discourse makes women absent by denying a language and a practice of equality, it is harder to claim "equality." We lose the capacity to critique the duality of engendered "difference" when

33. Ellen Goodman, "Showcasing Women Is Out of Style," *Boston Globe,* 8 October 1985, p. 19.

34. Ibid.

35. Eleanor Smeal, qtd. in Robin Toner, "N.O.W. Marks 20th Year amidst a Strategy Debate," *New York Times,* 13 June 1986, p. A19.

we lose the idea of equality—this is why the discourse of sex equality is so important. Even though it has never been fully exercised,
it remains real as a critique of state practices; it affects and expresses the relations of power, "difference," and inequality.

Phallic Contradiction and
Feminist Consciousness

The images of family and their residual meanings for people have
granted the Reagan administration more credibility than we might
expect, but the American public has not been as accepting of Reagan's New Right politics or neoconservatism as we might think.
Americans as a whole still support most of the programs of the New
Deal and the Great Society. Public skepticism of the Reagan administration was increasing even before the 1986 Iran-Contra scandal broke. In 1984 only 6 percent of those polled said that they
voted for, or cared about, Reagan's conservatism. In the same year,
a Louis Harris poll found that 67 percent of the respondents supported federal laws requiring affirmative action for women and minorities, provided that rigid quotas were not used.[36] In a series of
ABC News/*Washington Post* polls taken between 1981 and 1983
that support for increased domestic spending was found to have
grown from 49 to 67 percent for programs directed to the poor,
from 43 to 75 percent for education programs, and from 49 to 66
percent for health programs—all contrary to the effects of Reagan's
policies. According to Thomas Ferguson and Joel Rogers, this increase coincided with declining public support for military spending. Two-thirds of Americans believed the United States should let
the Soviets have their system of government, while 53 percent
thought the United States would be safer if it stopped trying to halt
the spread of communism. "In general, religion, feminism, civil
liberties, abortion and race relations are the policy areas in which
the public has shown the sharpest increase in liberalism since the
Second World War."[37]

36. See Thomas Ferguson and Joel Rogers, "The Myth of America's Turn to
the Right," *Atlantic Monthly* 257 (May 1986): 46. See also their *The Hidden Election: Politics and Economics in the 1980 Presidential Campaign* (New York: Pantheon Books, 1982).

37. Ferguson and Rogers, "The Myth of America's Turn to the Right," p. 45;
and see p. 48.

All these findings confirm my point that although the American state has been shifting to the right, the American public has not. Liberalism—both as evidenced in the social-welfare state and as a discourse about individual rights to equality and privacy—is still very much a part of the public's consciousness. Samuel Bowles and Herbert Gintis have spoken of the "impressive hegemony of liberal discourse,"[38] a discourse that applauds personal rights to privacy, freedom of choice, and equality (of opportunity and of conditions). Further, although it is said that the feminist movement is dead and that we have moved into a postfeminist era, a majority of American women identify themselves as feminist and think that the women's movement has improved their lives. In a 1986 *Newsweek* poll, 64 percent of nonwhite women, 59 percent of white women, and 48 percent of non-wage-earning women identified with feminism.[39] In a Media General/Associated Press poll, also conducted in 1986, women's participation in the labor force was seen as a positive trend by nearly half of those questioned, but only one-third thought that women had equal chances with men of being promoted. Fifty-eight percent of those polled thought that women should have an equal chance to do any job a man can do. More than nine out of ten respondents stated that spouses should share household cleaning equally when both spouses work full-time outside the home, even though in most families in which both partners were wage earners the housework was not shared.

In the 1984 election, "three fifths of Reagan voters agreed with him on issues that mattered to them, from arms control to abortion, but at the same time, a fifth had important disagreements and another fifth had no strong feelings on issues one way or the other."[40] These findings limit the degree to which any clear legis-

38. Samuel Bowles and Herbert Gintis, *Democracy and Capitalism: Property, Community, and the Contradictions of Modern Social Thought* (New York: Basic Books, 1986), p. 62. For a discussion of the crisis of the hegemony of liberalism, see G. William Domhoff, *Who Rules America Now? A View for the 1980s* (Englewood Cliffs, N.J.: Prentice-Hall, 1983); Douglas MacLean and Claudia Mills, eds., *Liberalism Reconsidered* (Totowa, N.J.: Rowman & Allanheld, 1983); and Linda Medcalf and Kenneth Dolbeare, *NeoPolitics: American Political Ideas in the 1980s* (New York: Random House, 1985).

39. See Barbara Kantrowitz et al., "A Mother's Choice: How Women View Work, Motherhood, and Feminism," *Newsweek* 107 (31 March 1986): 51.

40. Adam Clymer, "Long Range Hope for Republicans Is Found in Poll, No Sure Policy Mandate," *New York Times*, 11 November 1984, p. A30.

lative mandate toward conservatism can be discerned. Two-fifths of those who voted for Reagan did not support his policies enthusiastically, and this is not an insignificant number, especially when we add to it the large number of people who didn't vote at all.

A partial explanation for Reagan's reelection, even though a majority of Americans did not identify with his conservative policies, is that individuals have a conflictual and contradictory consciousness concerning the validity of liberalism as a guide for public policy. Although Americans remain very committed to the individual values espoused by liberalism—freedom of choice, equality before the law, and equality of opportunity—they appear to be less clear about how these values can be assured by government. Everett Carl Ladd, director of the Roper Center for Public Opinion Research at the University of Connecticut, has stated,

Contemporary political conflict is not so much between social groups where politicians must bring together enough groups to establish a majority, as it is within individuals, where they must appeal to contrasting predispositions in the very same people. . . . Most people have been led by their practical experience to view government as a persisting mix of the helpful and the harmful.[41]

People are both committed to an expansive government and deeply troubled by it; they believe in the freedom of individual choice, particularly in relation to abortion, but they also believe that there are problems with this position.

This contradictory consciousness is clearly evident in the survey data compiled from the 1984 presidential election.[42] The proportion of respondents who identified themselves as moderate or conservative was three times that of those who saw themselves as liberal. This kind of political labeling, however, has less clear meaning than we might think. When asked whether "this country

41. Everett Carl Ladd, qtd. in Richard Reeves, "America's Choice: What It Means," *New York Times Magazine*, 4 November 1984, pp. 31–32. See also John Patrick Diggins, *The Lost Soul of American Politics: Virtue, Self-Interest, and the Foundations of Liberalism* (New York: Basic Books, 1984); and Thomas Byrne Edsall, *The New Politics of Inequality* (New York: Norton, 1984), and "Reagan's Triumph, Election '84," *Time* 124 (19 November 1984): 38–98.

42. The following discussion is based on data from the American National Election Data, 1984: Pre- and Post-Election Survey File. There were 2,257 respondents: 989 male, 1,268 female; 1,946 white, 250 black. I wish to thank David Lansky for his computer assistance in helping me sort through the data.

would be better off if we worried less about how equal people are," slightly more of the respondents agreed than disagreed. When approached with the statement that "if people were treated more equally in this country we would have many fewer problems," however, considerably more respondents agreed than disagreed.[43] An overwhelming number of individuals believed that "our society should do whatever is necessary to make sure that everyone has an equality of opportunity to succeed."[44] Yet a majority of the respondents agreed that "most people who don't get ahead should not blame the system; they have only themselves to blame." Yet again, slightly more agreed than disagreed that "hard work offers little guarantee of success." The respondents were split down the middle on the statement "We have gone too far in pushing equal rights in this country." Yet slightly more agreed than disagreed that "one of the big problems in this country is that we don't give everyone an equal chance." Most respondents thought that "even if people try hard, they often cannot reach their goals."

These responses evidence a complicated perspective on the issue of equality and individual opportunity. It is interesting that this confused political consciousness led the respondents to identify themselves as moderates or conservatives rather than liberals, a result that suggests a troublesome shift in the political discourse of the 1980s. The mainstream label—the one an individual identifies with most easily, even through contradictory feelings—is conservatism, *not* liberalism. The term "liberal," as a representation of a coherent discourse, has lost much of its legitimacy, even though many of the ideas of liberalism are still very much a part of American consciousness. This loss of credibility and authority limits the effectiveness of liberalism as a political force. But liberalism also remains a presence to be reckoned with.

Liberals used to support issues because they believed they were right, according to columnist Richard Reeves, but now stances have to be justified economically and be "cost effective."[45] People

43. The actual breakdown of the respondents to this question was 652 agreed strongly, 769 agreed somewhat, 272 neither agreed nor disagreed, 378 disagreed somewhat, and 136 disagreed strongly.

44. Of the respondents, 1,475 agreed strongly with this statement, and 541 agreed somewhat; only 35 disagreed strongly, and 105 disagreed somewhat.

45. See Richard Reeves, "America's Choice: What It Means," p. 36.

who judged President Reagan as unfair voted for him anyway if they thought he could improve the economy. A series of more specific policy positions reflect this kind of conflicted politics as well. In the 1984 election, the voters thought Republicans could secure a stronger economy than could Democrats (54 percent for the Republicans, as compared with 27 percent for the Democrats). However, 43 percent of the voters thought the Democrats would run a government that was fair to all, while only 34 percent thought the Republicans would. A majority of voters thought the Democrats would not reduce the deficit, were less likely to maintain a strong defense, and were more likely to preserve Social Security and Medicare. In the end, a majority of voters believed that the Democrats were more concerned with the needs of the people; however, 51 percent entrusted the future to the Republicans whereas only 37 percent chose the Democrats. This kind of evidence supports the conclusion that the Reagan administration's politics of imagery worked in the 1984 election. The American public, which remains torn but still committed to the liberal democratic values of individualism and equality of opportunity, voted for a president who fundamentally challenged American liberalism. It did so while expressing a complicated consciousness about liberalism as an effective discourse.

Consciousness is hardly ever of one piece, and women's consciousness, though critical of Reagan, evidences multiple meanings as well. A *Woman's Day* magazine survey of 115,000 women in April 1984 found that while they desired peace, 75 percent of the women thought that America's position as a world power was slipping and that its decline was worrisome; a majority thought that the U.S. posture toward the Soviets was correct; a majority supported a nuclear freeze only if other nuclear powers agreed to a verifiable pact; 79 percent supported abortion; 68 percent supported the ERA; 61 percent supported federally subsidized day care. In a CBS News poll of 1,367 people, also taken in April 1984, only 25 percent of the women polled approved of U.S. policy in Latin America, whereas 34 percent of the men did; 22 percent of the women favored the overthrow of the pro-Soviet government in Nicaragua, whereas 31 percent of the men did; and only 8 percent of the women supported the harbor mining in Nicaragua, whereas 19 percent of the men did. Sweeping generalizations about the gender gap—about women's "difference" from men as pro-peace or pro-militarization—need to be narrowed. Although there clearly were differences in consciousness between men and women in the 1984 election, the "difference" was not homogeneous.

The treatment of women as a homogeneous unity, as the media's use of the term "gap" implies, denies important heterogeneities among women while it points to an important similarity among them. Differences of race, economic class, marital status, age, and so on exist among women, and these differences had some effect on the way women voted in the 1984 election. These differences also affect women's gender consciousness—the way they think about themselves as women and about their right to equality—which may, or more likely may not, materialize into a vote. It is this question of consciousness (more than the vote) that allows us to examine the complex relation between being female (as in biological body), being a woman (as in culture), and being a feminist.

The focus on gender (and gender gap) consciousness, contrasted with the narrower focus of the vote, also allows us to see how being female intersects with women's more specific identities. For the most part, the media's coverage of the gender gap was reduced to the issue of the women's vote rather than the more interesting question of women's mixed consciousness. The voting gap between men and women was described as not feminist: women were said to have voted on the issue of sex equality not as *women* but as *mothers, "different" from men.* In this sense the depiction of the 1984 gender gap is internally contradictory. It operates in part as integral to the neoconservative state discourse on engendered sex "difference": *woman as mother,* a homogeneous category, is more peaceable than man. In part, however, it documents many women's disaffection with the Reagan administration's position on women: women reject the phallocratic positioning of *woman as mother.*

The absence of a unified women's vote in the 1984 election does not mean that unity cannot exist among women despite differences; rather there was little place for a women's vote or a feminist vote to develop. In an election based on imagery, in which most of the images were masculinist, it is not clear where a women's vote or a feminist vote could have been directed. A vote for Mondale was more a vote against Reagan than a vote for women. The more important question, then, is not What happened to the gender gap in terms of the women's vote in 1984? but What are the meanings of gender consciousness among women that initially defined a "gap"? Does consciousness derive from being female in a biological sense? From being a woman in a cultural sense? From being a feminist in a political sense? I would argue that it is a complicated response to all three.

In this neoconservative era, which attempts to assign women to their engendered "difference," it should be no surprise that the gender gap was popularly characterized as a homogeneous unity, by a circuitous logic that led back to the pregnant mother's body. Feminist activists such as Eleanor Smeal and Bella Abzug reject this view and argue that the gender gap reflects women's particular economic interests and their commitment to the feminist issues of the ERA and abortion rights. Smeal thinks that women's rights issues were given short shrift as a principal cause of the gender gap. For her, sex discrimination runs through all the issues of the gap. She and Abzug both argue that what is often described as woman's compassion and commitment to peace can be better understood in economic terms. Smeal believes that women are antimilitaristic because military spending cuts social spending, thereby affecting the services women need, and the military offers few job options for women.[46]

On the other side, Jean Elshtain, a self-described feminist, argues that women's traditional values—their commitment to peace and social compassion—and not feminist concerns are what best explain the gap. She posits that women's opinions about the ERA and abortion are really no different from men's. The "difference" rather appears on war-related and foreign policy issues.[47] Frances Fox Piven, an analyst of working-class politics, also argues that "the emphasis on peace, economic equality and social needs associated

46. See Eleanor Smeal, *Why and How Women Will Elect the Next President* (New York: Harper & Row, 1984), pp. 14–15; and Bella Abzug, with Mim Kelber, *Gender Gap: Bella Abzug's Guide to Political Power for American Women* (Boston: Houghton Mifflin, 1984), p. 45. See also Ethel Klein, *Gender Politics* (Cambridge, Mass.: Harvard Univ. Press, 1984).

47. See Jean Bethke Elshtain, "The Politics of Gender," *Progressive* 48 (February 1984): 22–26, and "Reclaiming the Socialist-Feminist Citizen," *Socialist Review* 14 (March–April 1984): 21–27.

with the gender gap suggests the imprint of what are usually taken as traditional female values." In addition, she states (and Elshtain concurs), "There is not much correlation between the largely middle class constituency of the movement and the cross class constituency of the gap, or between the issues emphasized by the movement and the issues highlighted by the gap."[48]

Why do we need to adopt the either/or standard for explaining gender consciousness? Women are never simply their bodies (female sex), or simply a product of culture (gendered women), or simply a reflection of their politics. They are a mix of these aspects. To the extent that women live in society, they reflect its engendered aspects—the particular history, traditions, activities, and differences of being women in society. No woman can ever be completely outside the engendered context of her sex. Consequently no woman can ever just be female. Women always, though, have the potential to challenge aspects of their engendered being: to live not only in society but against it as well. The resulting challenge for equality is both engendered and *un*engendered, as is feminism itself. Gender and feminist consciousness reflect the facts that we live both in and against society at the same time, that we are part of an engendered system even as we challenge it, that gender consciousness is heterogeneous, contradictory, and complicated, even when it takes feminist shape.

The differences in gender consciousness between men and women reflect the multiple aspects of women's lives as experienced through their sex-class status, which is always further mediated by such factors as race, economic class, and age. Women's consciousness reflects the way their female and gendered aspects affect each other. Part of the process of developing consciousness occurs alongside and through a liberal feminist discourse that has legitimated the idea of sex equality. This discourse is as real as the body, which is always part interpretation. Liberal feminist discourse is real, if real means "having impact," if real means "mattering," and the gender gap is proof that a gendered consciousness exists through and in the discourse(s) of engendered "difference" and

48. Frances Fox Piven, "Women and the State: Ideology, Power, and the Welfare State," *Socialist Review* 14 (March–April 1984): 13.

feminism. The differences and similarities among women simultaneously indicate gender and challenge engendered "difference."

The aspect of gender consciousness that challenges existing phallocratic arrangements has been stunted by the neoconservatism of the Reagan administration, but the phallocratic stance of Reaganism has *also* been challenged. In 1986 Reagan's foreign policy initiatives came under close scrutiny when it was learned that the White House had carried out a disinformation campaign against Libya's Muammar al-Qaddafi to gain support for the earlier U.S. bombing of Libya. The failed summit meeting between the United States and the USSR in Reykjavík, Iceland; the swap of an accused Soviet spy for an American journalist; an American plane filled with weapons shot down over Nicaragua, of which Reagan denied any knowledge; and finally the Iran-Contra scandal all furthered a crisis for the macho Reagan state. Even before the Iran-Contra scandal broke in April 1986, a CBS/*New York Times* poll found 62 percent of the American public was critical of aid to the Contras. Nearly half of those who opposed aid said that the money could be better spent on domestic programs.

The New Rightist and neoconservative aspects of the Reagan administration, to the extent they were evidenced in international politics through the symbolization of the phallus (represented as the strong, aggressive, interventionist state) were in crisis well before the administration ended. The phallic imagery on which Reagan's credibility rested had been significantly damaged. The weaker the phallus, the weaker the state; the weaker the state, the weaker the phallus—because the state defines the relation between itself and the family, between public and private life, and between man and woman through the phallus that engenders each of these realms. To undermine the phallocratic basis of the state is to undermine the politics of duality, which interprets "difference" as inequality and characterizes women by their "difference" from men.

The American public never fully endorsed the policies of Reagan. The problem is that aspects of New Right and neoconservative politics became institutionalized during the Reagan administration—whether or not they had the support of the public—and they will continue to affect American society long after 1988. This New Right and neoconservative legacy, which rejects equality in favor of hierarchical "difference," affects the way we think and speak about a multitude of issues related to sexual equality and sexual freedom. It is important to remember, though, that although this discourse elicits significant power and privilege, it is not thoroughly hegemonic. It has cracks and contradictions that allow challenge.

Chapter Five

Reconstituting the Phallus II: Reaganism and the Courts, Pornography, Affirmative Action, and Abortion

The Reagan administration focused on the courts and the judicial system to institutionalize further its New Rightist and neoconservative policies. In Reagan's first term, the administration significantly altered affirmative action law through legislative initiatives and Justice Department policy statements. Reagan also appointed conservative Sandra Day O'Connor to the Supreme Court; her antiabortion stance presumably played a large part in his choice.

In his second term, Reagan successfully appointed two more conservatives to the Supreme Court: Antonin Scalia and Anthony Kennedy as associate justices. He also appointed William Rehnquist chief justice. Although Reagan was unable to gain confirmation for his nominee Robert Bork, who represented the New Right's political agenda, the New Right stance remained a powerful political force in the administration, represented by Attorney General Edwin Meese and the numerous federal judges appointed by Reagan who passed the New Right or neoconservative litmus test. The administration's objective was to reestablish the "traditional" meaning of the phallus in law as a discourse that rejects sex equality, applauds sex differentiation and its protective stance toward women, and denies abortion as a woman's right. It is to these concerns that we now turn.

The neoconservative anti–affirmative action stance fully dominated the Equal Employment Opportunity Commission (EEOC) in 1987: the commission abandoned the use of numerical hiring goals in settling discrimination cases against private employers. This bias is clearly evident in the case against Sears, Roebuck and Company that I discussed in Chapter 3. The Reagan administration continued, however, to seek a more sweeping indictment of affirmative action by the Supreme Court. New Right antifeminist, antiabortion politics also preoccupied the Reagan administration in its second term. New Right rhetoric continued bluntly to assert a commitment to the traditional patriarchal family—man as wage earner and provider, woman as homemaker and one provided for. Affirmative action is less relevant to this model, because in this model women are not a part of the public labor force. In fact, to the extent that affirmative action allows women to overcome their "difference" in the labor force, it poses a problem for New Right family policy. Abortion is the major concern for the New Right, because it directly relates to the New Right's views of womanhood, motherhood, and woman's "difference." Legalized abortion helps make the pregnant body less definitive; it helps women be less "different." Women can engage in heterosexual intercourse "like" men can because women too can *not* bear a child—if they choose—but still be sexually active.

These different views concerning sex equality—the neoconservative assault on affirmative action and the New Right attack on abortion—defined much of the agenda of the Reagan administration. In the second Reagan term, these two issues further intersected with the administration's concerns about pornography, drugs, and Acquired Immune Deficiency Syndrome (AIDS) in a complicated fashion that mixed people's concerns about a moral and healthy society with their feelings about sex equality and sexual freedom. Just as it is difficult to distinguish between sex and gender while trying to analyze women's particularities and biological potentials, it is difficult to distinguish between the problem of pornography and the importance of the erotic, between the problem of drugs and the state's use of that problem to justify foreign interventions, and between the importance of sexual freedom and its dangers. The New Right's evangelical mode of thinking in terms of absolute good and evil does not help; the lines are not easy to draw, and the multiple sites where sexual equality and sexual freedom are discussed in elusive, partial, moralistic, and contradictory ways do not make the distinctions any easier to sort out.

Sex, Promiscuity, and Equality

It might be argued that whether or not women became more equal through the 1960s and 1970s, they became more free, and their freedom has been largely a sexual freedom, albeit within a heterosexual context. Sexual freedom, as much as (if not more than) sexual equality, is the concern of the New Right and neoconservatives. Freedom to exercise sexual variety, freedom to express homosexuality, and freedom of sexual practice undermine the clear distinctness of woman and man: "difference" in heterosexuality is always already in place as an opposition. Heterosexuality, as expressed through the phallus, makes clear woman's "difference" from man, and that "difference" is needed to establish the hierarchy of differentiation along gender lines.[1]

Barbara Ehrenreich, Elizabeth Hess, and Gloria Jacobs argue in *Re-Making Love: The Feminization of Sex* that "the fear of women's sexual independence has become a major theme of the 80's, one that indicates not only the growing strength of the Christian right, but the powerful, lingering influence of sexism in American culture."[2] They present the interesting argument that the sexual revolution of the 1960s and early 1970s really affected the sexual practices of women more than men and that the casual sex and nonmonogamous relationships of that revolution were new for women, not for men—who had long engaged in casual sex. Therefore, when the right wing attacks the promiscuity that came out of this period, they are really arguing against the increase in sexual freedom for women. And the sexual freedom of women is inti-

1. See Stephen Heath, *The Sexual Fix* (New York: Schocken Books, 1984); Jane Root, *Pictures of Women: Sexuality* (London: Pandora Press, 1984); Ann Snitow, Christine Stansell, and Sharon Thompson, *Powers of Desire: The Politics of Sexuality* (New York: Monthly Review Press, 1983); Jeffrey Weeks, *Sexuality and Its Discontents: Meanings, Myths, and Modern Sexualities* (London: Routledge & Kegan Paul, 1985); and Monique Wittig, "The Straight Mind," *Feminist Issues* 1 (Summer 1980): 103–11.

2. Barbara Ehrenreich, Elizabeth Hess, and Gloria Jacobs, *Re-Making Love: The Feminization of Sex* (Garden City, N.Y.: Doubleday, 1986), p. 160.

mately linked with women's equality: freedom without equality means only that one is free to be unequal. Equality without freedom means one is equally not free. Gains in the realm of (hetero)sexual freedom underscore the need for sex equality as well.

President Reagan continually portrayed the 1970s as a time of sexual promiscuity, rampant pornography, and drug abuse. In addressing the National Association of Evangelicals in Columbus, Ohio, he stated: "Americans are turning back to God. . . . We must denounce liberal attitudes ranging from governmental disarray to sexual license."[3] He argued that "liberal attitudes view promiscuity as acceptable, even stylish. Indeed, the word itself was replaced by the term 'sexually active.' And in the media, what we once thought of as a sacred expression of love was often portrayed as something casual and cheap."[4]

Phyllis Schlafly, leading spokeswoman for New Right antifeminist politics, continually criticizes the "sexual license" of American society.[5] In a pamphlet entitled "The ERA-Gay-AIDS Connection," published and distributed by the Eagle Forum (a New Right anti-ERA lobbying group that Schlafly founded), she argues that the Equal Rights Amendment, if passed, would leave Americans defenseless against homosexuality and, as a result, against the threat of AIDS. "Since E.R.A. prohibits all discrimination 'on account of sex,' if E.R.A. were put in the U.S. Constitution, how could society protect itself against a class of people who have a high rate of various contagious diseases (some fatal), but whose only identifiable difference is sex?"[6] In the pamphlet, Schlafly writes that the ERA will put "gay rights" into the Constitution. In her circuitous, homophobic way, Schlafly rejects sex equality, promiscuity, homosexuality, and AIDS as all the same thing.

3. Ronald Reagan, qtd. in Francis X. Clines, "Reagan Sees U.S. Regaining 'Moral Bearings,'" *New York Times*, 7 March 1984, p. 1.

4. Ronald Reagan, qtd. in "Excerpts from President's Address to the 42nd Annual Convention of the National Association of Evangelicals," *New York Times*, 7 March 1984, p. A20.

5. For a fuller discussion of Schlafly's politics, see Zillah Eisenstein, *Feminism and Sexual Equality: Crisis in Liberal America* (New York: Monthly Review Press, 1984), esp. ch. 7; Carol Felsenthal, *The Sweetheart of the Silent Majority: The Biography of Phyllis Schlafly* (Garden City, N.Y.: Doubleday, 1981); and Phyllis Schlafly, *The Power of the Positive Woman* (New York: Jove/HBJ Books, 1977).

6. "The ERA-Gay-AIDS Connection" (Alton, Ill.: Eagle Forum, n.d.).

Schlafly's campaign against sex education in the schools is similarly fearful and illogical. She criticizes the liberal pluralist approach to sex: it does not tell students what is right and what is wrong. Rather, they "are instructed 'to identify and evaluate the choices involved in sexual expression.' The choices then listed for the student are 'abstinence, sexual fantasy, masturbation, hugging, kissing, petting, exploration, intercourse, nocturnal emission or wet dreams, sexual preference, homosexual preference, homosexual experience, gay, lesbian, bisexual, transvestite, transsexual.'"[7] Schlafly thinks such pluralistic discussions are an invasion of private family life and undermine its authority—such pluralism, in her opinion, only creates confusion. Her worries about sexual permissiveness are not entirely about sex or gender "difference"; she is also concerned with parental power, including maternal power—that is, parents' control over children and parent-child authority relations. Ultimately, what concerns her most is the authority of the heterosexuality of her male god and his rights to privacy.

On the question of sexual freedom—especially in terms of homosexuality and promiscuity—the neoconservatives' views are very similar to those of the New Right. They fear sexual license, which they think undermines heterosexuality and the natural order that they believe stems from it. Homosexuality is unnatural; AIDS is "their" punishment. Norman Podhoretz, discussing the AIDS crisis in his *New York Post* column, wrote,

Curious is it not, that in an age of ubiquitous pornography and blunt speech, it should be hard to say in plain English that AIDS is almost entirely a disease caught by men who bugger and are buggered by dozens or even hundreds of other men every year? . . . Not only do these men refuse to assume responsibility for their own sexual habits, they demand that society undertake a crash program to develop a vaccine (or what one activist called a "one-tablet cure") that would allow them to resume buggering each other by the hundreds with complete medical impunity.[8]

7. Phyllis Schlafly, "Classes in Sex, Nuclear War, Harm Students" [excerpted from testimony by Phyllis Schlafly at the Department of Education Hearing on the Protection of Pupil Rights Act, 17 March 1984], *Conservative Digest* 10 (May 1984): 38.

8. Norman Podhoretz, qtd. in Christopher Hitchens, "A Modern Medieval Family," *Mother Jones* 11 (July–August 1986): 56.

This mixing of homophobia, antiegalitarian attitudes toward sexuality, sex equality and freedom, sickness, drugs, and pornography has characterized the dominant state discourse on sex in the 1980s. This language set the images and imagery for thinking about sex equality in the Reagan administration. By now it should be clear that I do not think any one discourse, even when dominant, is ever hegemonic to the point of silencing competing and conflicting standpoints. Nevertheless, the multiple standpoints do not have equal weight. The privileged discourse today defines sex equality as a problem loosely connected to homosexuality, abortion, promiscuity, and pornography.[9]

Our sexuality and sexual practices, much like the rest of our personalities, are defined in and through the social frames we live in. As Jeffrey Weeks writes, "Sexuality is as much about words, images, ritual and fantasy as it is about the body; the way we think about sex fashions the way we live it." Sexuality—homosexuality or heterosexuality—is in part a social construction. "The mediating elements are words and attitudes, ideas and social relations."[10] Although the New Right and neoconservatives speak as if sexuality were predefined through nature, written in and on our bodies, they fight to maintain the privileged position of phallic heterosexuality, because sexual practices can and do shift. Foucault understood that "our epoch has initiated sexual heterogeneities" and that these heterogeneities challenge the homogeneity of the dominant heterosexual discourse.[11] A radical sexual pluralism that is not

9. The Reverend Jerry Falwell, evangelical leader of the Liberty Foundation (once the Moral Majority), recognizes that the New Right's attempt to dismiss abortion as a problem of sexual promiscuity has serious problems. As a result, he has compromised on his position supporting a constitutional amendment against abortion. He now argues that the amendment should allow for exceptions in the cases of rape and incest and if the life of the mother is threatened. Otherwise, he says, the amendment will have little chance of adoption. See Connaught Marshner, "How Jerry Falwell Is Driving the Left to an Early Grave," *Conservative Digest* 11 (June 1986): 93–104. I doubt the amendment has much of a chance anyhow, but it is significant that even the evangelical Right seems to understand that its antisex, antiabortion stance lacks the support it needs and must be tempered.

10. Weeks, *Sexuality and Its Discontents*, pp. 3, 4.

11. Michel Foucault, *The History of Sexuality. Volume 1: An Introduction*, trans. Robert Hurley (New York: Pantheon Books, 1978), p. 37.

dominated by any one sexual viewpoint does not yet exist. Conservative forces want to make sure that it never does.

Sexual variety and pluralism attack the dichotomous hierarchy of woman and man, homosexual and heterosexual, wife and husband, as the authors of *Re-Making Love* make clear.

Where, for example, is the great drama of domination and submission when a woman buys masturbation aids from a mail order catalog? What happens to the meaning of that drama when two women—butch and femme lesbians—can play all the parts? More profoundly, perhaps, S/M—by making domination and submission into a consciously chosen and deliberately scripted ritual—deprives these venerable themes of their "natural" role in heterosexuality . . . because it is now widely *known* as a potential option or variation.[12]

Thoughts about sex and sexuality as well as sexual practices, expressed as discourses, change, but they do so within the context of power relations, which is partially constructed through sexuality itself. Although sex is supposedly related to the body and privacy, Foucault notes that "what is peculiar to modern societies, in fact, is not that they consigned sex to a shadow existence, but that they dedicated themselves to speaking of it ad infinitum, while exploiting it as *the* secret."[13]

The way we think about sex and sexual freedom is part of what sexuality is, and it affects the way we think about the question of sex equality. If we accept a notion of "sexual heterogeneities"—in the realm of sexual practices or physical potentialities—our vision of sex equality will not be limited to a notion of woman's sameness. Difference and sameness will no longer necessarily be seen as opposites. This is exactly what conservative forces fear: the loss of a hierarchical, oppositional sexual order.

Laws, as legal discourse, help to establish the way we think about legitimate and illegitimate sex. Law attempts to differentiate between rape, consensual sex, legitimate sex, and so forth, through distinctions such as marriage, prostitution, and pornography. Law also constructs images of sex equality through legislation pertaining to affirmative action, sexual harassment, and equal rights. The Reagan administration located much of its attention

12. Ehrenreich, Hess, and Jacobs, *Re-Making Love*, p. 204.
13. Foucault, *History of Sexuality*, p. 35.

here—right where law had endorsed a notion of sex equality for women. It sought to direct the courts away from the commitment to equality they made in the 1970s and establish a vision of society premised in the "difference" of woman from man. This concern with "difference" is ultimately what has been at issue in the discussions about pornography, affirmative action, and abortion in the 1980s, and these issues affected extralegal discourses. To understand these influences, we must examine a series of Supreme Court decisions related to these concerns.

Edwin Meese and the Courts

Edwin Meese, who espouses the politics of the New Right, was appointed by President Reagan in 1985 to replace William French Smith as attorney general. His appointment was part of the administration's attempt to reverse the direction of the courts. "Pornography or drug smuggling, abortion or school prayer, the Attorney General's legal agenda is the President's political agenda."[14] Charles Fried was appointed solicitor general, replacing Rex E. Lee, and shortly afterward Fried filed a brief with the Supreme Court urging it to overturn the 1973 decision in *Roe* v. *Wade*, which legalized abortion. The administration's position was that the Supreme Court should not "invent" rights—such as the right to abortion on demand—but should hold to a "jurisprudence of original intention." Meese maintains that "the" meaning of the Constitution is to be found in "the" *original* text: his argument presumes that there is one text, that it has one meaning, and that this meaning should not be applied by the Supreme Court to the states. According to Meese, the Constitution permits New York to ban newspapers, California to establish a state religion, and Kansas to deny its citizens the right to assemble for the purpose of protesting government misconduct.[15] Meese said that he would promote "truth" in the courtroom, and that, for him, there is one truth. Law, in Meese's mind, is unambiguous, objective, and neutral.

14. John A. Jenkins, "Mr. Power: Attorney General Edwin Meese Is Reagan's Man to Lead the Conservative Charge," *New York Times Magazine*, 12 October 1986, p. 19.

15. See Floyd Abrams, "Mr. Meese Caricatures the Constitution," *New York Times*, 25 July 1986, p. A31.

Meese supported congressional efforts to limit substantially the Freedom of Information Act, thereby to restrict the amount of government information available to the public; he handpicked the members of a government commission on pornography, which called for sweeping restrictions on constitutionally protected freedom of speech; he proposed lifetime censorship agreements for government workers; he used "judicial litmus tests" to determine acceptable (to him) candidates for federal judgeships; he attacked *Roe* v. *Wade* as a wrong decision that should be overturned and asserted that states should have the right to make abortion a crime; he opposed the Voting Rights Act Amendment of 1982, which outlawed intentional discrimination; and he continually urged the president to revoke a twenty-year-old executive order that promotes minority employment in the federal government.[16]

By the time Reagan's second term ended, he had appointed more than half of the 743 federal judges then seated, more appointments than any recent predecessor has made to the federal bench. These judges were chosen only after "close ideological inspection."[17] Reagan, like Meese, wanted the courts to override precedents he disliked but was unable to change through Congress. The administration looked to the judges to overrule "judge-made law." As one White House official stated to a *Newsweek* reporter, "It became obvious to us that the courts were the only recourse we have for the issues we care about" ("RJ," p. 15). Nominations and appointments to the Supreme Court, for instance, the nomination of Robert Bork, reflect this kind of thinking. William Rehnquist was chosen to be chief justice because he has been more predictable than any other conservative in his stances against affirmative action and sex equality. In contrast, Sandra Day O'Connor has occasionally disagreed with the administration on religious and affirmative action cases.

Reagan's appointments have political import for the Court. Harvard law professor David Shapiro says that Chief Justice Rehnquist is guided by three basic propositions: "Conflicts between the indi-

16. See the American Civil Liberties Document "The American People v. Edwin Meese" (New York: n.d.).

17. See Aric Press, with Ann McDaniel and Margaret Garrard Warner, "Reagan Justice," *Newsweek* 107 (30 June 1986): 14–19; all further references to this work, abbreviated as "RJ," will be included in the text.

vidual and the government should be resolved against the individual; conflicts between state and federal authority should be resolved in favor of the states; and questions of the exercise of the jurisdiction of the federal courts should be resolved against such exercise" ("RJ," p. 18). The appointment of Antonin Scalia to the Court reflects a similar judicial politics. Although it was clear that Rehnquist's and Scalia's appointments were based on ideological grounds, the Senate Judiciary Committee approved them by a vote of 13–5. Not all Reagan's judicial appointments, however, have met with similar approval. Whereas the legal credentials of Rehnquist, Scalia, and even Bork were never questioned, other judicial candidates have been closely scrutinized and have had either their appointments to the bench denied or only narrowly confirmed on the basis of their questionable judicial competence.

Daniel Manion is a case in point. A lawyer from Indiana, Manion was nominated by Reagan for a seat on the U.S. Court of Appeals in Chicago. He was chosen on ideological grounds, had questionable legal credentials, and barely acquired Senate approval. His father was a founding member of the John Birch Society, and the younger Manion identified with the society's views, even though when testifying before the Senate Judiciary Committee he said, "I could not tell you what the policies of the John Birch Society are." According to *New York Times* writer Anthony Lewis, Manion has never argued a case in the Seventh Circuit—to which he was nominated—or any other federal court of appeals. The briefs he submitted to the Senate Judiciary Committee for examination were "lacking in legal craftsmanship, spelling, and grammar."[18] When asked to list ten of his most significant cases, he included his defense of a client sued for poorly repairing a Volkswagen Rabbit and a case involving damages resulting from the building of a fence. It is remarkable that the Senate confirmed Manion's appointment, even by the slim margin 48–46.

Other Reagan appointees have not made it through the confirmation process. Pertinent to their rejection, no doubt, is the fact that at least half of Reagan's twenty-eight nominees to the appeals court since January 1985 were given the American Bar Associa-

18. Anthony Lewis, "They Don't Like Ike," *New York Times*, 30 June 1986, p. A19.

tion's lowest possible passing rating. In 1985–86 alone, the Senate rejected the nomination of William Bradford Reynolds as associate attorney general, Jeffrey Zuckerman as general counsel to the Equal Employment Opportunity Commission, and Jefferson Sessions III as federal district judge in Alabama. In Sessions's case, incompetence, along with his racist record, ended his candidacy.

Despite these actions by the Senate, New Right politics has gained a stronger presence in the court system than it had before 1980, and it profits from all the support that Meese as attorney general provided it. There also appears to be a growing conservative presence on the Supreme Court.

Before looking more specifically at the Supreme Court decisions of 1986–87—which do not endorse the New Right view—let us examine the Meese Commission Report on Pornography. This examination will allow us to view a significant discussion about sex and to become aware of the discourse on "difference" that in part set the tone for the discussion of sex equality in the 1980s. We will discover an epistemological framework that favors duality over diversity, homogeneity over multiplicity, and simplicity over complexity.

The Politics of Porn

The first meetings of the Attorney General's Commission on Pornography were held in June 1985. Meese appointed all commission members; Alan Sears was executive director. The purpose of the commission was to study the effect of pornography on society. My concern here is with how the commission report's treatment of pornography reflects New Right and neoconservative politics related to sex equality—in other words, with how antipornography politics helps to establish the New Right and neoconservative political discourse on sex equality.[19] The preoccupation with pornography as a

19. For a broader discussion of the relation between feminism and pornography, see Varda Burstyn, ed., *Women against Censorship* (Toronto: Douglas and McIntyre, 1985); Andrea Dworkin, *Pornography: Men Possessing Women* (New York: Putnam, Perigee Books, 1979); Susan Griffin, *Pornography and Silence: Culture's Revenge against Nature* (New York: Harper & Row, 1981); Laura Lederer, ed., *Take Back the Night* (New York: Morrow, 1980); Alan Soble, *Pornography: Marxism, Feminism, and the Future of Sexuality* (New Haven, Conn.: Yale Univ. Press, 1986); Carol Vance, ed., *Pleasure and Danger: Exploring Female*

social problem is indicative of New Right politics. The belief that pornography is "the cause" of sexual violence and promiscuity leads to a protectionist stance toward women, which allows the New Right to argue for women's protection rather than their equality. This New Right stance treats women as "different" from men: men like pornography, women do not. The New Right imagery of sex and violence and promiscuity rolled into one presents pornography as "the" problem for a moral society.

Why didn't the Reagan administration set up a commission to study day care or job sharing or comparable worth? Why was pornography advanced as the most pressing issue? How does the concern with pornography bear on the concern with establishing controls on sexuality in general? On sex "difference" in particular? On the pregnant body as the mother's body? I am not saying that pornography is not *a* problem. Nor do I mean that all forms of pornography are acceptable. Nor do I mean that in the best of all possible worlds, violent pornography would still exist. Rather, my point is this: the Reagan administration used pornography as a political issue to establish a context in which arguments for sexual freedom, sexual equality, and sexual pluralism would be curtailed. Through the equations of pornography and sex, and sex and violence, the administration attempted to reorient the public discussion of sexual expression away from sex equality and toward sex "difference" in the context of phallocratic heterosexual sex.

Pornography is an easy issue for conservatives to manipulate because it so readily conjures up anxiety and confusion about our own bodies and our sex and gender identities. Pornography is very much tied to the meaning of engendered sex: in it females are displayed as subjugated, objectified women. Pornography's scope, however, is broader than this; it includes fantasy and rebellion as well. Multiple meanings coexist within pornography, and they crisscross the realms of real and ideal. Females are subjugated by masochistic fantasies, yet some females may feel pleasure in imagining both being subjugated and subjugating others. Because sexual pleasure can be experienced as a liberating feeling (liberation from inhibition), fantasies of subjugation can be emancipatory.

Sexuality (Boston: Routledge & Kegan Paul, 1984); and Marianna Valverde, *Sex, Power, and Pleasure* (Toronto: Women's Press, 1985).

Thus, pornography is not a homogenized discourse expressing only women's oppression.

This, however, is not the New Right's reading of pornography. Their concern is not with women's sexual pleasure or subordination, or with pornography's multiple meanings, but rather with the problem of "sexual license" that pornography represents to them. They use the antipornography campaign for their own purposes: to reestablish traditional forms of heterosexuality and gender delineation. The antipornography campaign aims ultimately to reassign woman to her female body as the mother's body. The engendered mother's body exists within marriage; pregnancy replaces sexuality. Not only is the right-wing antipornography stance antisex but it is antiegalitarian: the female is supposed to be the woman as wife and mother.

The Reverend Greg Dixon, a leader of the right-wing antipornography movement in Indianapolis, reportedly believes that "abortion is murder, ERA would destroy the family and the free enterprise system, homosexuality ought to be a felony." According to Lisa Duggan, he is convinced that "there is a conspiracy of 'elitists' to control the world's population through advocacy of a 'six pronged program of contraception, abortion, homosexuality, euthanasia, suicide, and even war and terrorism.'"[20] Jerry Falwell, evangelist president of the Liberty Federation, praises the Meese Commission report on pornography as "a result of grass roots repudiation of the garbage called pornography which has too long exploited the women and children of America." Rabbi Hirsch Ginsberg also applauds the report, stating that it represents the "defense of decency for women *and* children."[21] Pornography is thus seen as an assault on women and children, who are grouped together. The woman is the mother with child. She and her children must be protected—which is to say, protected by men.

Neoconservative Irving Kristol, when writing about pornography, says that he does not want to get involved in distinguishing essential from cultural differences between men and women. Yet he states, "But I do know—and I take it as a sign that has mean-

20. Lisa Duggan, "Censorship in the Name of Feminism," *Village Voice* 29 (16 October 1984): 16.
21. Jerry Falwell and Hirsch Ginsberg, qtd. in Barbara Gamarekian, "Report Draws Strong Praise and Criticism," *New York Times*, 10 July 1986, p. B7.

ing—that pornography is, and always has been, a man's work; that women rarely write pornography; and that women tend to be indifferent consumers of pornography."[22] He uses pornography, somewhat inaccurately, to establish the "difference" of woman from man; men are pornographic, women are not. Hence, he argues that "pornography is a form of sexism" (*RN*, p. 48), although, of course, the method he has employed to establish pornography as such is itself sexist. Pornography, in his view, differentiates woman from man while making women a homogeneous class, "different" from men. Kristol assumes that *the* "difference" lies in the fact that women are more emotional about sex than men are. "My own guess, by way of explanation, is that a woman's sexual experience is ordinarily more suffused with human emotion than is man's, that men are more easily satisfied with autoerotic activities, and that men can therefore more easily take a more 'technocratic' view of sex and its pleasures" (*RN*, p. 47).

The antipornography campaign not only creates the vision of woman as "different" from man but provides a major site where the discussion of engendered "difference" gains legitimacy. Whereas the claim of woman's "difference" from man is usually used to deny women's right to equality, in this instance the discourse about "difference" is employed to enhance the supposed rights of women.

The problem is that the rights being enhanced are rights to protection against violence and aggression rather than rights to equal treatment. If pornography treats women as victims, arguing against it seems to mean challenging women's status as victims. This is not necessarily the case, though, and it is absolutely not the case in the right wing's perspective. The right wants to establish controls on sexual expression: their real fear is that pornography represents women as sexual beings rather than as mothers. Whereas the misogynist stance has often tolerated the dichotomy between whore and mother, in fact, has created it, the New Right uses this distinction to criticize pornography. The fact is that pornography represents engendered sexual beings more than sexual ones, but the engendered meaning of sex is not as close to the "mother" in a heterosexual marriage as the New Right would like.

22. Irving Kristol, *Reflections of a Neoconservative: Looking Back, Looking Ahead* (New York: Basic Books, 1983), p. 47; all further references to this work, abbreviated as *RN*, will be included in the text.

The methods used to examine pornography express a politics as much as the findings themselves do. The Meese Commission adopted the so-called scientific, objective method to study the relationship between pornography and violence. Its report adopted a cause-effect model and tried to present social science data, which is open-ended at best, as conclusive evidence that pornography causes violence. Barry Lynn, legislative counsel for the American Civil Liberties Union, states that the Meese Commission report "tries to deceive Americans into believing that there is a sound scientific and legal basis for suppressing sexually oriented materials. It is little more than prudishness and moralizing masquerading behind social science jargon."[23] The course, at least up to the time of the report, had not taken this social science data—whatever it is—seriously.[24]

Even the pornography commission members themselves recognized that the standard of proof—that pornography causes harm—is difficult to assess. They asked, How much evidence is needed before we can conclude that sexually explicit material *causes* harm? They answered, "Whenever a causal question is even worth asking, there will never be *conclusive* proof that such a causal connection exists, if 'conclusive' means that no other possibility exists."[25] They therefore "reject[ed] the suggestion that a causal link must be proved 'conclusively' before [they could] identify a harm" (*PR*, p. 307). All they needed to do was show that pornography is one of many harmful factors. The problem is that the commission did not examine what the other factors might be or how they intersect with pornography. Instead they isolated the issue of pornography as causing violence while noting that "the world is complex, and most consequences are 'caused' by numerous factors" (*PR*, p. 309). What then does the report mean by "causal relationship"? It means that "if there were none of the material being tested, then the incidence of the consequences would be less" (*PR*, p. 310).

The commission members undermine their own cause-effect methodology and then continue to seek authority for their findings

23. Barry Lynn, qtd. in Gamarekian, "Report Draws Strong Praise and Criticism," p. 7.
24. See Neil Malamuth and Edward Donnerstein, eds., *Pornography and Sexual Aggression* (New York: Academic Press, 1984).
25. *Attorney General's Commission on Pornography: Final Report* (Washington, D.C.: U.S. Dept. of Justice, 1986), p. 306; all further references to this work, abbreviated as *PR*, will be included in the text.

from it. Pornography is harmful; the objective scientific method says so. The report uses dualistic/scientific methodology to indict the violence of pornography even though it acknowledges the limitations of this analysis. "We have concluded, for example, that some forms of sexually explicit material bear a causal relationship both to sexual violence and to sex discrimination. But we are hardly so naive as to suppose that were these forms of pornography to disappear the problems of sex discrimination and sexual violence would come to an end" (*PR*, p. 309).

The report states that, because we live in a world of "multiple causation," changing any one cause will only lessen, not solve, the problem. And it admits that identified causes may often be of less significance than those that remain unidentified. "When faced with the phenomenon of multiple causation, cause is likely to be attributed to those factors that are within our power to change. Often we ignore large causes precisely because of their size" (*PR*, p. 311). Nevertheless, the authors of the report all but admit that pornography may not really be *the* significant cause of violence. "We take confidence in the fact that lessening those causes will help alleviate the problem, even if lessening other causes might very well alleviate the problem to a greater extent" (*PR*, p. 312).

In the end, the Meese commission report admits that a positive correlation between pornography and sex offenses does not itself establish a causal connection between them. Still, "the fact that correlational evidence cannot definitively establish causality does not mean that it may not be *some* evidence of causality, and we have treated it as such" (*PR*, p. 317; emphasis mine). Even though the report provides a multicausal description of pornography and its relation to violence, the commission concludes that "substantial exposure to sexually violent materials as described here bears a causal relationship to anti-social acts of sexual violence and, for some subgroups, possibly to unlawful acts of sexual violence." They validate this assessment in the name of their "scientific, empirical evidence," and their evidence "says *simply* that the images that people are exposed to bears a causal relationship to their behavior" (*PR*, p. 326, my emphasis).[26]

The commission's definition of pornography includes all materi-

26. See Philip Shenon, "Pornography in U.S. Linked to Violence, Meese Panel Asserts," *New York Times*, 14 May 1986, p. 1.

als that are sexually explicit and intended primarily for the purpose
of sexual arousal. The report groups pornography in four categories: (1) sexually violent; (2) nonviolent, depicting degradation,
domination, subordination, or humiliation; (3) nonviolent and non-
degrading; and (4) nudity. The commission focused on violent
forms of pornography and argues that exposure to sexually violent
materials increases the likelihood of aggression. They then shift
their findings to pornography as a whole and argue that it causes
violence.

Edward Donnerstein, the psychologist whose research on aggression is often cited to support this antipornography position and
whose work is discussed in the Meese Commission report, is much
more cautious than his supporters on the commission in evaluating
the relationship between pornography and violence. "We would
be[,] perhaps, on safe ground therefore to say that aggressive pornography does have a negative effect. But, what about the other
type of pornography? The problem here is what we mean by pornography. Are we discussing just sexually explicit material?" Donnerstein questions the very use of the term "pornography" and suggests that we avoid it. "In other words, the issue of whether or not
pornography is related to aggression against women might best be
served by doing away with the term pornography. There is no
question that the term encompasses portrayals from mere sexual
explicitness to scenes of rape, torture, and mutilation."[27] It is interesting, to say the least, that the author of the studies most often
cited to indict pornography states that categorizing all sexually explicit materials as pornographic is not useful. Pornography is not a
homogeneous category with a homogeneous message.

The Meese Commission, composed of eleven individuals, had
its disagreements as well. Judith Becker, a behavioral scientist, and
Ellen Levine, a journalist and editor, wrote a dissenting opinion
on the commission's findings. They argue that the "commission's
methods themselves have hindered the adequate pursuit of information" (*PR*, p. 196).[28] They also claim that the commission over-

27. Edward Donnerstein, "Pornography: Its Effect on Violence against
Women," in Malamuth and Donnerstein, *Pornography and Sexual Aggression*,
p. 79.
28. See Philip Shenon, "Two on U.S. Commission Dissent on a Pornography
Link to Violence," *New York Times*, 19 May 1986, p. A17.

emphasized violent pornography, which dominated the materials presented at hearings and "distorted the commission's judgment about the proportion of such . . . material in relation to the total pornographic material in distribution" (*PR*, p. 199). Critics of the report also note its misuse of so-called scientific causal methodology noted earlier. In Becker and Levine's words, "Social science research has not been designed to evaluate the relationship between exposure to pornography and the commission of sexual crimes; therefore efforts to tease the current data into proof of a causal link between these acts simply cannot be accepted" (*PR*, p. 204).

Becker and Levine's objection to the commission's findings goes even further. They criticize its right-wing paternalistic protectionist stance, which makes women appear to be powerless victims. "We abhor the exploitation of vulnerable people and condemn those who profit from it. We respect, however, the rights of all citizens to participate in legal activities if their participation is truly voluntary. We reject any judgmental and condescending efforts to speak on women's behalf as though they were helpless, mindless children" (*PR*, p. 194).[29] And although the National Organization for Women (NOW) supported the findings of the commission— that pornography harms "women and children"—it specifically disassociated itself from the right-wing agenda attached to the Meese report. "N.O.W. does not support the commission's emphasis on obscenity law enforcement. Feminists are wary that the religious right, in particular, will use the revulsion that many Americans feel against the violence and subjugation of pornography as an excuse to spread bigotry and hatred against lesbians and gay men."[30]

The Meese Commission report both reflects and encourages New Right and neoconservative attitudes toward sex, sexuality, and sexual practices. Their preoccupation with the opposition between good and evil is masked by an antipornography position, which applauds motherhood, family, and the moral life. While not

29. Commission member Deanne Tilton-Durfee joined in this statement.

30. Gamarekian, "Report Draws Strong Praise and Criticism," p. B7. For other reaction to the report, see Lindsy Van Gelder, "Pornography Goes to Washington," *Ms.* 14 (June 1986): 52–83; Philip Shenon, "A Second Opinion on Pornography's Impact," *New York Times*, 18 May 1986, p. E8; and Carol Vance, "The Meese Commission on the Road," *Nation* 243 (2–9 August 1986): 1–82.

conflating the issue of pornography with the New Right agenda, we must realize that this agenda is precisely what gives the commission's findings their particular meaning for the 1980s. The Johnson-appointed Commission on Obscenity and Pornography, which reported to President Nixon in 1970, found no causal relationship between pornography and aggressive behavior. It suggested that the American public is "permissive about permissiveness" and therefore recommended against restrictive legislation for adults; however, it did recommend that restrictions on public display and unsolicited mail be enacted and that age-appropriate sex education materials be developed.[31] The Meese Commission, in contrast, recommended vigorous enforcement of obscenity laws and confinement of the distribution of pornography. The political climate evidently affects the interpretation of findings—and the interpretation of "evidence" affects the political climate.

Before leaving this discussion, I want to stress that an antipornography position is not necessarily New Rightist or neoconservative in spirit or purpose. There has been a long history of feminist antipornography political activity, and Andrea Dworkin and Catharine MacKinnon are currently leading a vigorous radical feminist antipornography campaign. Although radical feminist and New Right concerns about pornography dovetail in certain respects, their focuses differ significantly. Dworkin and MacKinnon have attempted in an Indianapolis antipornography ordinance to make pornography illegal by viewing it as a matter not of the pornographers' freedom of speech but of women's civil rights. According to them, pornography, defined as "the sexually explicit subordination of women, graphically depicted, whether in pictures or words," is "central in creating and maintaining the civil inequalities of the sexes."[32] Pornography in this instance is seen as a form of discrimination based in and on sex. It affects women's equality of rights in employment, education, and property, to mention only the most obvious realms. When pornography is defined as a problem of sex

31. *The Report of the Commission on Obscenity and Pornography* (New York: Bantam Books, 1970), p. xi; and see p. 444.

32. Lisa Duggan, Nan Hunter, and Carole S. Vance, "False Promises: Feminist Legislation in the U.S.," in Burstyn, *Women against Censorship*, p. 134. And see the Indianapolis City-County General Ordinance No. 35, 1984, Proposal No. 298, 1984.

discrimination, one which denies women equality, it becomes clear that radical feminists' motive for eliminating pornography is not to protect women ("difference") but to empower them ("sameness"). This is a far cry from the purpose of the New Right's indictment of pornography.

But the distinction between the radical feminist and New Right critiques of pornography is not always so clear. Both the radical feminists and the right wing assume that pornography is something men enjoy and women do not, that it is something men do to women, that woman is the victim and man is the aggressor. And both feminists and the right wing assume that pornography is the same as violence, an assumption that makes it difficult to avoid thinking about sex in other than protective terms. MacKinnon states that "pornography sexualizes women's inequality. It makes the inequality of women sexy. It sexualizes most broadly speaking, dominance and submission."[33] If we assume this stance, it is difficult not to negate sex by assuming that it is the same thing as pornography. Thinkers adhering to this perspective can only support equality by recognizing that there is more than one message in pornography. As Lisa Duggan, Nan Hunter, and Carol Vance, feminists critical of the antipornography stance, have written, "Pornography carries many messages other than woman-hating: it advocates sexual adventure, sex outside of marriage, sex for no reason other than pleasure, casual sex, anonymous sex, group sex, voyeuristic sex, illegal sex, public sex."[34] If pornography is not universally victimizing, then a sweeping indictment of it can create a new problem—denial of the freedom to engage in multiple sexual practices.

Andrea Dworkin denies the multiplicity of views within pornography. For her, pornography is identical to the sexual subordination of women. In reacting to feminists who criticize her view on this point, she says, "If part of what women are pissed about is that we're suggesting that there are things that are right and things that are wrong, and one of the things that is wrong is the sexual subordination of women, that's accurate. Politics is about making those

33. Catharine MacKinnon, in Edward Donnerstein, Cheryl Champion, Cass Sunstein, and Catharine MacKinnon, "Pornography: Social Science, Legal, and Clinical Perspectives," *Law and Inequality* 4 (May, July, October 1986): 41.

34. Duggan, Hunter, and Vance, "False Promises," p. 145.

kinds of distinctions."[35] MacKinnon agrees with Dworkin. "A critique of pornography is to feminism what its defense is to male supremacy."[36] But this view holds only if pornography treats women exclusively as victims. According to this perspective, the equations are clear. "Pornography . . . is a form of forced sex, a practice of sexual politics, an institution of gender inequality" ("NMI," p. 325). MacKinnon reduces sex to its engendered form. "Gender is sexual. Pornography constitutes the meaning of that sexuality" ("NMI," p. 326). To equate sex and gender in this fashion, however, is to let the phallus win. It is like saying that the female body is one with the mother's body. We lose track of a lot with this reductionist thinking, for instance, the difference between the engendered sex of pornography and a truly free radically pluralist sex.

MacKinnon's reductionist and oppositional mode of thinking excludes the possibility of seeing pornography in terms of its multiplicity. Her stance becomes quite similar to that of the right wing, albeit through a very different politics. She fails to see the interconnections between the ideal and the real and sex and gender. For MacKinnon as well as Dworkin, "pornography is not imagery in some relation to a reality elsewhere constructed. It is not a distortion, reflection, projection, expression, fantasy, representation or symbol either. It is sexual reality" ("NMI," pp. 326–27). The problem is that pornography is *both* image and reality, and it is at this intersection that its multiplicity is evident in pornography's heterogeneous interpretations. MacKinnon accepts the oppositional method and is constrained by it.

Pornography is not an idea. . . . Pornography is more act-like than thought-like. The fact that pornography, in a feminist view, furthers the idea of the sexual inferiority of women, a political idea, does not make the pornography itself a political idea. That one can express the idea a prac-

35. Andrea Dworkin, qtd. in Mara Math, "Andrea Dworkin Talks about Feminism and Pornography," *Gay Community News*, 28 December 1985–4 January 1986, p. 8. And see Andrea Dworkin, *Pornography,* and *Intercourse* (New York: Free Press, 1987).

36. Catharine MacKinnon, "Not a Moral Issue," *Yale Law and Policy Review* 2 (Spring 1984): 321; all further references to this work, abbreviated as "NMI," will be included in the text. And see her *Feminism Unmodified: Discourses in Life and Laws* (Cambridge, Mass.: Harvard Univ. Press, 1987), which reproduces much of this argument.

tice embodies does not make that practice into an idea. Pornography is not an idea any more than segregation is an idea, although both institutionalize the idea of the inferiority of one group to another.

("NMI," p. 335)

I would agree that pornography should not be reduced to the realm of ideas, but pornography does operate as a series of ideas and thus as a discourse on sex inequality: as ideas with a practice. But as a discourse—as both real (the actual picture) and ideal (interpretation), occupying a space on the continuum between—it has a multiplicity of meanings. The antipornography position does not recognize this and therefore with uncomplicated simplicity can reduce sex to its engendered form: pornography is reduced to violence; sexual equality is reduced to a protectionist stance.

MacKinnon believes that "women live in the world pornography creates. We live its lie as reality" ("NMI," p. 335). I would add that women live in a world that they have helped create. Thus women are not only victims who need protection from sex but human beings who need the freedom and equality to explore sex as well. And pornography may be a part of what women want to explore. It may be that in the discourse of pornography we can find that sexual freedom exists alongside sexual inequality, in which case we may want to eliminate the inequality without sacrificing the sex or the freedom.

The problem with treating pornography as a unity—which creates violence and further establishes sexual discrimination against women—is that pornography as a discourse affects society in a variety of ways. The issue is whether that impact is *all* bad—or bad in the ways that the Meese Commission report or MacKinnon and Dworkin depict it. Some forms of pornography have a positive effect in depicting sex as not necessarily tied to pregnancy, marriage, or heterosexuality. Pornography can help to create a multiplicity of sexual imagery that enhances women's equality by differentiating the female body from the mother's body.

The New Right and neoconservative fear of plural sexualities and practices has defined one of the dominant political discourses of the 1980s, through which the Supreme Court ruled on affirmative action and abortion. This standpoint has affected the way the public and the courts think about equality and discrimination.

However, the Court's recent decisions have been mixed and somewhat unclear. Women's sexual "difference," as well as their equality, emerges as a theme but in no coherent fashion. Other legal decisions—related to AIDS patients, the physically handicapped, victims of sexual harassment, and homosexuals—reflect a way of thinking about "difference" (in general) and its relation to discrimination, while seeming to be about something else.

The general concept of "difference" (as inequality) affects the way we think about the concept of sex "difference." And the converse is true as well. Although each policy issue, and each court's decision, or the Justice Department's stance on it, constitutes much more than the single concern with sex "difference," the decisions articulate the context in which the treatment of "difference" and therefore of sex "difference" is established. We will see that the lower courts and the Supreme Court have used the general notion of "difference" both to justify discrimination of all sorts and to undermine it, whereas the Justice Department chooses only to justify discrimination. Although the question of the relationship between "different" treatment and discrimination has come before the courts in a plurality of forms, decisions which have found that "different" treatment on a variety of issues does not constitute discrimination have begun indirectly to justify the New Right's position on homogeneous sex "difference." "Different" treatment (according to sex) is then judged not to be discriminatory.

Discrimination, "Difference," and the White Man

The Reagan administration was more concerned with what it termed "reverse discrimination" against white men than it was committed to remedying past inequities of treatment of black and white women and black men. The administration took the neoconservative stance that these groups have gained too much equality to the detriment of white men, that white men have been unfairly asked to redress "past" discrimination. "The enforcement of civil rights and equality of opportunity has gone too far in recent years, resulting in remedies that discriminate against the majority population."[37] Affirmative action law and policy were seen as having cre-

37. D. Lee Bawden and John Palmer, "Social Policy: Challenging the Welfare

ated the problem. The EEOC and Title VII of the Civil Rights Act of 1964 came under intense criticism for their bias in favor of women.[38]

Affirmative action, once defined as "giving preferential treatment to a sub group of the population whose current circumstances *as a group* have been adversely affected by past discrimination," was reassessed as "simply another form of discrimination" ("SP," p. 207). The administration stance argued that many of those who benefit from affirmative action did not personally suffer from past discrimination and that, therefore, "no justice is really being served by affirmative action" ("SP," p. 207). According to its perspective, only specific, individual acts of discrimination should be redressed. This led to a redefinition of federal responsibility in enforcing civil rights and equality of opportunity. The new policy was to "assure that individuals qua individuals, are protected against present, *intentional* discrimination only when individual victims can be identified" ("SP," p. 208). The intent to discriminate became the crucial criterion rather than the effect of discriminatory practice. This formulation of policy exempted many more government contractors from filing affirmative action plans and significantly relaxed the standards for hiring white women and minority men and women. By reducing federal involvement in enforcing and regulating equality of opportunity and encouraging "voluntary" compliance, by requiring proof of intent to discriminate before the government would take remedial action, and by rejecting the use of quotas, numerical goals, and timetables as means of redressing the consequences of past discrimination (see "SP," p. 204), the Reagan administration gutted affirmative action as government policy.

The Presidential Executive Order on Affirmative Action, which was a part of the civil rights program initiated by President Kennedy, encouraged by President Johnson, and retained by Presidents Nixon, Ford, and Carter (however unenthusiastically), required federal contractors to set numerical goals—as guidelines

---

State," in *The Reagan Record*, ed. John L. Palmer and Isabel V. Sawhill (Cambridge, Mass.: Ballinger Publishing, 1984), p. 208; all further references to this work, abbreviated as "SP," will be included in the text.

38. For a discussion of the history of the EEOC, see Patricia Zelman, *Women, Work, and National Policy: The Kennedy–Johnson Years* (Ann Arbor: Univ. of Michigan Press, 1980).

rather than quotas—for their hiring. Attorney General Edwin Meese instituted an attack on the executive order. He argued that goals are quotas and that they discriminate against white men. Secretary of Labor William Brock opposed Meese on this issue, stating that goals are not rigid and inflexible quotas but needed targets. Several organizations, including the National Black Republican Council, backed Brock on this issue, as did Secretary of Transportation Elizabeth Dole and Secretary of Health and Human Services Margaret Heckler. Nevertheless, the EEOC, as stated earlier, abandoned the use of numerical hiring goals in settling discrimination cases, the Justice Department opposed these guidelines, the Civil Rights Commission remained divided in its support for them, and, as we shall see, the Supreme Court hesitantly endorsed them. Obviously, there was little agreement about what constitutes discrimination against white women and minority women and men, as well as how affirmative action affects white men.

President Reagan said he opposed quotas, but he did not say whether he thinks quotas are the same as guidelines. When asked at a news conference to state his views on goals and timetables, he replied, "I think we must have a color blind society. Things must be done for people neither because of nor in spite of any differences between us in race, ethnic origin or religion. . . . So I want to tell you that I don't want to do anything that is going to restore discrimination of any kind."[39] Reagan's statement rejects affirmative action while ostensibly taking an antidiscrimination position. Affirmative action makes discrimination, past or present, on the basis of an individual's "difference" in terms of sex, race, ethnic origin, religion, age, or handicap illegal. It also urges "different" treatment (which some have termed "reverse discrimination") on the basis of these characteristics in order to redress past and present discrimination. Affirmative action policy forbids "different" treatment that denies equality of opportunity; it allows such treatment to create equality of opportunity. When Reagan said that he was against discrimination "of any kind," he rejected the very idea of affirmative action.

39. Ronald Reagan, qtd. in "Reagan Tells of Weighing Plans to Revise Minority Hiring Rules," *New York Times*, 12 February 1986, p. A13.

In contrast to the administration's position, the Supreme Court, in a series of 1986 decisions, upheld the constitutionality of affirmative action. It found that remedies could be applied for those who had not personally suffered racial discrimination. *Wygant v. The Jackson [Michigan] Board of Education,* concerned an affirmative action program that dismissed white, tenured teachers while retaining black, probationary teachers during a series of layoffs.[40] The Supreme Court reaffirmed its support for the limited use of racial preference to redress specific job discrimination. In a 5–4 decision, the Court deemed it unconstitutional to lay off white teachers before minorities with less seniority, but—contrary to the administration—it said that public employers could make limited use of numerical hiring goals favoring minorities when such goals are intended to remedy past discrimination. Justice Powell stated for the Court, "We have recognized, however, that in order to remedy the effects of previous discrimination, it may be necessary to take race into account. As part of this Nation's dedication to eradicating racial discrimination, innocent persons may be called upon to bear some of the burden of the remedy."[41] In the decision, the Court specifically distinguished between guidelines and quotas: whereas guidelines must be used sparingly, quotas are unconstitutional.

Similarly, *Local 28 of the Sheetmetal Workers v. E.E.O.C.* reaffirmed the Supreme Court's authority to order relief to members of racial minority groups who themselves had never been discriminated against. Basing its decision on Title VII, the Court stated, "Courts may utilize certain kinds of racial references to remedy past discriminations."[42] In these two cases the Supreme Court, however cautiously, interpreted the use of racial guidelines as constitutional in redressing past discrimination and did not endorse the administration's view of so-called reverse discrimination. We may find out more about the caution of the Court in interpreting racial discrimination when it restudies and reviews (as it de-

40. 106 S. Ct. 1842 (1986).

41. Ibid., p. 1850.

42. 106 S. Ct. 3019 (1986), p. 3044; and see p. 3023. Six members of the Court agreed "that a district court may, in appropriate circumstances, order preferential relief benefiting individuals who are not the actual victims of discrimination as a remedy for violations of Title VII" (p. 3054).

cided to do in spring 1988 in a 5–4 decision) *Runyon* v. *McCrary* (1976), which established the rights of minorities to sue private parties for racial discrimination.[43]

In *Johnson* v. *Santa Clara Transportation Agency* (1987), the Court found in favor of affirmative action policy applying specifically to women.[44] The 6–3 decision upheld a California city's affirmative action plan for employees that had effected the promotion of Diane Joyce to road dispatcher over Paul Johnson. The majority opinion, written by Justice Brennan, states,

Given the obvious imbalance in the Skilled Craft category, and given the Agency's commitment to eliminating such imbalances, it was plainly not unreasonable for the Agency to determine that it was appropriate to consider as one factor the sex of Ms. Joyce in making the decision. . . . The plan sets aside no positions for women. . . . Rather, the plan merely authorizes that consideration be given to affirmative action concerns when evaluating qualified applicants.[45]

Affirmative action is a positive step in limiting white men's privilege as a politics of differentiation and discrimination based on individual "difference." It is no longer acceptable to treat white and black women, or black men, differently from white men, if this treatment relegates women and black men to their "difference" from white men and thereby limits their equality of opportunity. But different treatment, when it enhances equality, is legal. It is this kind of thinking about the notion of reverse discrimination that also led to the Court's progressive decision in the *Cal Fed* case, discussed in Chapter 3. In a 6–3 vote, the Court decided that pregnancy leave for women did not constitute discrimination against men, that special treatment need not conflict with equality of opportunity between women and/or (white) men. The specific issue in this case, which in part reflects the impact of neoconservatism, was the concern with reverse discrimination: What consti-

43. Similar decisions were also reached in *Local 93 of the International Association of Firefighters* v. *Cleveland* (106 S. Ct. 3063 [1986]), in which the Court ruled that lower federal courts have discretionary room in settling discrimination suits based on preferential hiring or promotion of minority group members; and in *United States* v. *Paradise* (106 S. Ct. 3331 [1987]), in which the Court ruled that quotas, when used to cure "egregious" past discrimination against blacks, are constitutional. *Runyon* v. *McCrary*, 427 U.S. 160 (1976).

44. 107 S. Ct. 1442 (1987).

45. Ibid., p. 1455.

tutes discrimination against (white) men? Pregnancy leave was found to be nondiscriminatory toward men, as well as toward non-pregnant women. Any differential impact on men was deemed not discriminatory, because it does not relegate men to a "different" status; such impact is rather an unintended effect of redressing past discrimination against women. As for women, pregnancy reflects a "real difference." Treating it specially is not discriminatory. "Any state laws based on 'stereotypical notions' that pregnant workers suffered from an inherent handicap, or denying opportunities to them, would violate Federal Law."[46]

Another aspect of the issue of sex discrimination is sexual harassment. In *Meritor Savings Bank, FSB* v. *Vinson et al.* (1986), the Court held that sexual harassment on the job violates Title VII, which prohibits discrimination in employment.[47] The Court ruled that the language of Title VII is not limited to economic loss but is meant to apply to the entire spectrum of disparate treatment between men and women. Differentiating women in terms of their sex by unwelcome sexual activity in the workplace was declared discriminatory.

Not all recent legal decisions, however—in the lower courts, the Justice Department, or the Supreme Court—have been as progressive as those just cited. The interpretation of "discrimination" has been mixed. When neoconservative discourse prevails, discrimination is masked by a politics of "difference" that supposedly justifies unequal treatment. Given this stance—that "difference" allows disparate (unequal) treatment—the existence of discrimination as such is denied. This stance was evident in the Supreme Court's ruling on sodomy, which assumed that rights of privacy belong exclusively to heterosexuals engaged in procreative sex. In *Bowers, Attorney General of Georgia* v. *Hardwick et al.* (1986), the Court, in a 5–4 decision, found the Georgia statute criminalizing even consensual sodomy constitutional.[48] The Court argued that "the issue presented is whether the Federal constitution confers a fundamental right upon homosexuals to engage in sodomy

---

46. Stuart Taylor, Jr., "Rights Backed in Pregnancy Case," *New York Times*, 14 January 1987, pp. A1, B10.

47. 106 S. Ct. 2399 (1986).

48. 106 S. Ct. 2841 (1986); all further references to this work, abbreviated as 106, will be included in the text.

and hence invalidates the laws of the many states that still make such conduct illegal and have done so for a very long time" (106, p. 2843). They found that it does not. Justice Harry Blackmun dissented.

This case is no more about "a fundamental right to engage in homosexual sodomy" as the Court purports to declare, than Stanley v. Georgia, 394 US 557 (1969), was about a fundamental right to watch obscene movies. . . . Rather, this case is about the most comprehensive of rights and the right most valued by civilized men; namely the right to be let alone.

(106, p. 2848)

Blackmun argued that the Georgia statute at issue denies "individuals the right to decide for themselves whether to engage in particular forms of private, consensual sexual activity." If the right to privacy means anything, it means that "before Georgia can prosecute its citizens for making choices about the most intimate aspects of their lives, it must do more than assert that the choice they have made is an 'abominable crime not fit to be named among Christians'" (106, p. 2848). Blackmun urged the Court to reconsider its decision and concluded that "depriving individuals of the right to choose for themselves how to conduct their intimate relationships poses a far greater threat to the values most deeply rooted in our Nation's history than tolerance of nonconformity could ever do" (106, p. 2856).

The Court's decision in effect differentiates between the rights of homosexuals and heterosexuals in the practice of sex. Although the decision differentiates between the rights of homosexuals and those of heterosexuals, the distinction is not between "no sexual rights for homosexuals" and "sexual freedom for heterosexuals," because the Court did not uphold sexual rights for any group. Rather, the distinction is between sexual rights for anyone and procreative rights for heterosexuals only.[49] Thus, heterosexual procreative sex falls within the zone of privacy; homosexual nonprocreative sex does not. Whereas the Court has used privacy doctrine and the individual right to choose progressively in its abortion rulings, it has not done so in the case of sodomy. "Difference" of treatment according to sexual practices is not deemed discriminatory. It should come as no surprise that the right wing hailed this decision

49. I am indebted to Rosalind Petchesky for this point.

and interprets it as it wishes. Jerry Falwell thinks it is about time that the Court "recognize[s] the right of a state to determine its own moral guidelines."[50] In his view a moral society requires the differentiation of woman from man; the "difference" of homosexuality from heterosexuality underlies the engendered "difference" of the sexes.

A similar legitimation of discrimination on the basis of "difference" is evident in *U.S. Department of Transportation* v. *Paralyzed Veterans of America* (1986).[51] Here the Court found that federal law barring discrimination against the handicapped does not apply to commercial airlines, even though they may indirectly benefit from federal funding to airports. A federal appeals court panel had earlier ruled that the law covered all commercial air travel because commercial airlines benefited so pervasively from federal assistance to airports. But the Supreme Court argued that this was an erroneous reading of the law, which would give almost limitless coverage, drawing in "whole classes of persons and businesses with only an indirect relation. . . . The airlines do not actually receive the aid, they only benefit from airports' use of the aid."[52] This ruling (which exempts these airlines from Section 504 of the Rehabilitation Act of 1973, which bars discrimination against handicapped people in any program receiving federal financial assistance) is somewhat similar to the ruling in the 1984 *Grove City College* case.

In *Grove City College* v. *Bell*, the Court accepted the administration's narrow reading of sex discrimination. It ruled that the law bars sex discrimination only in those departments of the college that receive federal aid, not in the college as a whole. Because the student financial aid office was the only part of Grove City College receiving federal funding, it alone was subject to the anti–sex discrimination provisions of Title IX of the Education Amendment of 1972.[53]

50. Jerry Falwell, qtd. in Larry Rohter, "Friend and Foe See Homosexual Defeat," *New York Times*, 1 July 1986, p. A18.

51. 106 S. Ct. 2705 (1986).

52. Ibid., p. 2712. And see Stuart Taylor, Jr., "Most Airlines Held Exempt on Handicapped Rights Rule," *New York Times*, 28 June 1986, p. A8.

53. The *Grove City* decision, 465 U.S. 555 (1984), instigated the Civil Rights Restoration Bill of 1985, H.R. 700, which was finally passed in January 1988. This positive step was, however, tempered by an amendment proposed by Senator

In both instances, discriminatory practices were endorsed through a narrow reading of the law, which in effect limits equality of opportunity for those who are said to be "different." Although the Court's argument in both cases is not about the meaning of discrimination per se, the justices in effect adopted the neoconservative approach to the definition. We could argue that neoconservative discourse significantly affected how the Court thinks about the meaning and interpretation of discrimination.

The Justice Department adopted a similar position but through a different method. Its ruling on the civil rights of AIDS patients is a case in point. Limiting the opportunities of AIDS patients is justified on the basis of their "difference." The department has stated that federal civil rights law does not protect those suffering from AIDS from dismissal by employers who fear the spread of the disease. Assistant Attorney General Charles Cooper held in 1986 that employees with AIDS are not protected by civil rights law "if discrimination against them [is] based on fear of the individual, real or perceived, ability to spread the disease."[54] This ruling applies to all federal agencies and federally financed programs, even though federal health officials have issued a statement stressing that the AIDS virus cannot be spread through casual contact in the workplace.

As a result, the justification of discrimination—that is, treating individuals differently on the basis of their departure from a male, heterosexual, able-bodied standard and limiting their opportunities for equality—gained a significant foothold in the Reagan administration. This discourse on "difference" has affected the interpretation of discrimination and has been used to deny the similarity between rights of homosexuals, AIDS patients, and the physically handicapped and those of the privileged standard. These decisions in turn affect the discourse itself in a very specific way: the treatment of illness and handicap in a dualistic framework of "difference" allows for the reification of difference as "less than," "unequal," or "other." Such treatment is used to deny the notion of

---

John Danforth (Missouri), under which refusal to provide abortion services would not be considered discrimination against women.

54. Charles Cooper, qtd. in Erik Eckholm, "Ruling on AIDS Provoking Dismay," *New York Times*, 27 June 1986, p. A17.

differences in the sense of the richness of diversity and plurality. And it is used to confine the discourse not only of difference but of freedom as well.

Obviously, AIDS is not a difference anyone wishes to experience, but this does not mean that discrimination against AIDS patients is justifiable or that the present association between AIDS and sexual conservatism is completely warranted. According to an internal White House memorandum, President Reagan decided to support a federal campaign to educate "the public about the dangers of AIDS, but only if the campaign stresses 'responsible sexual behavior' within marriage and teaches children to avoid sex."[55] Reagan criticized Surgeon General C. Everett Koop's plan to educate children in the schools about using condoms to reduce the risk of contracting or transmitting AIDS, and he opposed advertising of condoms on television; instead, Reagan proposed sexual abstinence as the solution. Thus AIDS is used to encourage a sexually conservative discourse that associates homosexuality and sexual diversity with drugs and disease.[56]

Finally we need to examine abortion in terms of the issue of "difference" and sexual freedom and its particular impact on women's lives. In this realm progressive gains have been upheld. Although the language of the Court does not address abortion as a question related to discrimination or "difference" or sexual freedom, the Court's 1986 decision to uphold *Roe* v. *Wade* and affirm the legality of abortion significantly affects women's right to sex equality and heterosexual (if not homosexual) freedom. It has allowed individual women the opportunity to exert a certain amount of control over their pregnant bodies, making them less "different" from men in sexual freedom, rights as wage earners, and other

55. Philip M. Boffey, "Reagan to Back AIDS Plan Urging Youths to Avoid Sex," *New York Times*, 26 February 1986, p. A14.

56. For an interesting discussion of the incomplete and distorted reporting on AIDS, see Peter Davis, "Exploring the Kingdom of AIDS," *New York Times Magazine*, 31 May 1987, pp. 32–40; Richard Goldstein, "The Hidden Epidemic: AIDS and Race," *Village Voice* 32 (10 March 1987): 23–30; Jonathan Lieberson, "The Reality of AIDS," *New York Review of Books* 32 (16 January 1986): 43–48; Gary Null, with Trudy Golobic, "The Secret Battle against AIDS," *Penthouse*, June 1987, pp. 61–68; and "Facing AIDS: A Special Issue," *Radical America* 20 (November–December 1986).

aspects of their lives. Women's right to abortion involves their right to sex equality, whether or not the Court has explicitly argued as much.

Abortion and Sex Equality

The debates surrounding the abortion issue today are very much a part of the discussion about women's right to equality and its relation to woman's "difference," her pregnant body. According to Kristin Luker, it was not until the late 1960s that the demand for abortion came to include the issue of sex equality, that the right to abortion was seen as essential to women's right to equality as "individuals."[57] The demand for abortion as a right was tied up with women's demand for equality at work. "The mobilization of significant numbers of women around the issue of abortion laws can therefore be seen as an attack on a symbolic linchpin that held together a complicated set of assumptions about who women were, what their roles in life should be, what kinds of jobs they should take in the paid labor force, and how those jobs should be rewarded" (*APM*, p. 118). Abortion became a prerequisite for other choices in women's lives. The demand to legalize abortion was "an attack on both the segregated labor market and the cultural expectations about women's roles. It allowed women to argue (and symbolically demonstrate) that although childbearing was important, it was not the single most important thing in a woman's life" (*APM*, p. 120).

It is impossible to understand abortion as an issue related to equality without recognizing that it is also tied up with the issues of sexual freedom and sex "difference." Abortion developed as a demand not only in relation to women's entrance into the labor market but also as a part of women's new relation to sexuality and sexual practices, which developed during the 1960s and 1970s. Abortion was a part of the sexual revolution; it catalyzed the revolution at certain stages and reflected it at others. Abortion allows women to engage in heterosexual sex more the way men do, because they can be freer of the risk of having an unwanted baby.

57. See Kristin Luker, *Abortion and the Politics of Motherhood* (Berkeley and Los Angeles: Univ. of California Press, 1984), p. 92; all further references to this work, abbreviated as *APM*, will be included in the text.

Abortion simultaneously creates greater freedom for sex, lessens the sex "difference" of a woman from a man, and focuses attention on woman's "difference." It highlights the pregnant body, which is invariably a woman's body. Difference and sameness are both at issue in abortion.

We have seen that the liberal discourse of equality shifted, albeit unevenly, throughout the Reagan administration toward a focus on "difference." Women's right to abortion was attacked in the course of this process, although the New Right does not explicitly attach abortion to the equality issue. Rather, as Rosalind Petchesky argues, they link abortion with a religious and moral standpoint that they term "pro-life."[58] They see abortion as denying the rights of the unborn, being a "referendum on the place and meaning of motherhood" (*APM*, p. 193). The "pro-life" activists Luker interviewed did not want equality with men if equality meant having exactly the same rights and responsibilities as men. Their "pro-life" language cloaks their antiegalitarian stance.

Much of the "pro-life" message is presented through an imagery that obscures its antiequality politics. According to Petchesky, the religious Right uses television and video imagery to capture political discourse—and power.

Along with a new series of "Ron and Nancy" commercials, the Reverend Pat Robertson's "700 Club" (a kind of right-wing talk show) and a resurgence of "good vs. evil" kiddie cartoons, American television and video viewers [have been] bombarded with the newest "pro-life" propaganda piece, "The Silent Scream." "The Silent Scream" marked a dramatic shift in the contest over abortion imagery. With formidable cunning, it translated the still and by now stale images of fetus as "baby" into real-time video thus (1) giving those images an immediate interface with the electronic media; (2) transforming anti-abortion rhetoric from a mainly religious-mystical to a medical/technological mode; and (3) bringing the fetal image to life.[59]

Petchesky argues that the politics of style makes surface impressions the whole message. "The Silent Scream," which is really a cultural representation of the issues involved, treats the issue of

58. See Rosalind Pollack Petchesky, *Abortion and Woman's Choice: The State, Sexuality, and Reproductive Freedom* (Boston: Northeastern Univ. Press, 1984).

59. Rosalind Pollack Petchesky, "Fetal Images: The Power of Visual Culture in the Politics of Reproduction," *Feminist Studies* 13 (Summer 1987): 264.

personhood as a scientific question. "Its appearance as a medical document both obscures and reinforces a coded set of messages that work as political signs and moral injunctions." The viewer's impression is of an autonomous fetus (as person) and an absent and peripheral woman: "It is this abstract individualism, effacing the pregnant woman and the fetus' dependence on her," that leaves the viewer with blurred images of fetus and baby, "as if it were outside a woman's body, because it can be viewed."[60] When it becomes part of discourse, this kind of "politics as imagery," for which the Reagan administration was noted, further blurs the lines between the real and ideal and as a result has significant impact on our ability to think clearly about this complicated issue.

President Reagan identifies himself with the New Right stance on abortion. He has likened abortion to murder of the unborn, supported a constitutional amendment against abortion, and had the Justice Department ask the Supreme Court to reverse its *Roe* v. *Wade* decision. In the Justice Department brief on this issue, Charles Fried urged the Court to overturn *Roe* and leave state legislatures free to regulate—read prohibit—abortion. He argued that it was time for the Court to declare that giving women a constitutional right to abortion has proved inherently unworkable. Senator Jesse Helms stated that the *Roe* decision was "an erroneous interpretation of the Constitution, and that the law should provide protection for unborn human beings." Representative Jack Kemp (New York) sponsored the Unborn Children's Civil Rights Bill, introduced by Representative Robert Dornan (California), which would prohibit any federal involvement in funding for, or encouragement of, abortion.[61] However, this position has not been upheld by the Supreme Court.

As I mentioned earlier, the Supreme Court reaffirmed its 1973 abortion decision in June 1986. In *Thornburgh* v. *American College of Obstetricians and Gynecologists*, by a 5–4 ruling, the Court struck down a Pennsylvania law that it determined was designed to deter women from having abortions.[62] The law required doctors to provide women seeking abortions detailed information about the

60. Ibid., pp. 267, 270, 272.
61. Jesse Helms, letter to author, 11 September 1985; see Jack Kemp, "Why Abortion Is a Human Rights Issue," *Conservative Digest* 12 (August 1986): 39–44.
62. 106 S. Ct. 2169 (1986).

risks of and alternatives to abortion. Justice Blackmun's majority opinion rejected the state's role in regulating abortion; it held that the decision to have an abortion is beyond the scope of government. "Few decisions are more personal and intimate, more properly private, or more basic to individual dignity and autonomy, than a woman's decision—with the guidance of her physician and within the limits specified in Roe—whether to end her pregnancy. A woman's right to make that choice freely is fundamental."[63] Thus the Court upheld, albeit narrowly, women's right to privacy—their freedom to decide their bodies' destiny.

Privacy doctrine laid the basis for the legal right to abortion, and although this has been a successful strategy, it also has severe limitations.[64] Privacy doctrine does not argue for abortion on the basis of a woman's right to reproductive control, or her right to equality, or her right to freedom of sexual expression. Nor does it challenge the patriarchal/phallocratic dimension of privacy. Instead, it works within the confines of the opposition of public and private, which obfuscates the political nature of the private realm.

Feminists have long argued that the private realm—the realm of sex and sexual decision making—is at least as political as the public realm.[65] The right to abortion, based solely on the right to privacy, therefore remains tenuous. Instead of discussing abortion as an issue of reproductive freedom, privacy doctrine makes it, as Kristin Glen states, "a debate about the constitutional protection of a 'medically assisted right to choose abortion freed from unwarranted governmental interference.'"[66] Concerns with reproductive freedom and sex equality are displaced by this line of reasoning. However, this is not the whole story. Privacy doctrine and its role in the contemporary debate about abortion are more complicated.

63. Ibid., p. 2185.

64. See Petchesky, *Abortion and Woman's Choice*, for a full discussion of this point. See also Catharine MacKinnon, "The Male Ideology of Privacy: A Feminist Perspective on the Right to Abortion," *Radical America* 17 (July–August 1983): 22–35; and Petchesky's response, "Abortion as 'Violence against Women': A Feminist Critique," *Radical America* 18 (March–June 1984): 64–70.

65. See Catharine MacKinnon, "*Roe* v. *Wade*: A Study in Male Ideology," in *Abortion: Moral and Legal Perspectives*, ed. Jay Garfield and Patricia Hennessey (Amherst: Univ. of Massachusetts Press, 1984), pp. 45–54.

66. Kristin Booth Glen, "Understanding the Abortion Debate," *Socialist Review* 16 (September–October 1986): 67.

Although the courts have limited the abortion issue to the realm of privacy, the dialogue on abortion has extended to equality. Today the right to abortion, which is accepted by a majority of the public as an individual's right to freedom of choice, is seen as a part of women's right to equality of opportunity.[67] Petchesky warns feminists not to depend on the courts, because "except in rare instances, [feminists'] language does not become the courts' language, nor their reasons the courts' reasons."[68] Yet she understands that the widespread approval in society for liberal feminist ideas about equality and self-determination has led to a broader interpretation of the meaning of *Roe* v. *Wade* than the Supreme Court intended. Abortion is viewed as a fundamental right of women, and it is linked, however loosely, with a vision of women's equality.

Given the politics of the 1980s, perhaps we should be glad that the legality of abortion has been grounded in privacy doctrine rather than in a commitment to equality. Many of the feminist litigators who have dealt with the issue would agree with this assessment. They have argued for abortion as a right of privacy, because that strategy works; it is effective in the confines of a liberal discourse that privileges individual privacy as a universal right. Feminist litigators have thus helped to shape the legal discourse surrounding abortion: they have stretched the discourse of privacy to legitimize abortion. I wonder whether they could stretch the issue of abortion to include the legal discourse of equality and equal protection, or whether the dominance of neoconservatism—and its rejection of equality—makes this impossible.

Nevertheless, without a commitment to equality, abortion rights remain partial. A case in point is the 1977 Hyde Amendment, which stopped the federal funding of abortions for Medicaid recipients; privacy doctrine has not extended itself to ensure *their* right to abortion. And in 1985 federal funding to international family-planning organizations that offer or support abortion was cut off. Attempts to extend this exclusion to domestic agencies continue.

67. For an important analysis of the history of abortion, see Linda Gordon, *Woman's Body, Woman's Right: A Social History of Birth Control in America* (New York: Grossman Publishers, 1976); Frederick Jaffe, Barbara Lindheim, and Philip Lee, *Abortion Politics: Private Morality and Public Policy* (New York: McGraw-Hill, 1981); and James C. Mohr, *Abortion in America: The Origins and Evolution of National Policy, 1800–1900* (New York: Oxford Univ. Press, 1978).

68. Petchesky, *Abortion and Woman's Choice*, p. 319.

Still, Representatives Vic Fazio (California) and William Green (New York) have initiated the Reproductive Health Equity Act (RHEA), which would amend basic Medicaid law "to insure that services related to abortion are made available in the same manner as are all other pregnancy-related services under federally funded programs."[69]

The discourses about abortion are complex and pluralist.[70] The Reagan administration's New Right view was held in tenuous check by the Supreme Court on the basis of privacy doctrine. The American public supports a woman's right to abortion on demand as a part of her right to equality of opportunity. The administration rejected the notion of equality in favor of recognizing "difference." The Court, however, does not recognize abortion as part of the equality debate. As Stephanie Wildman points out, "The failure to see this issue of access to reproductive freedom as involving the potential denial of equality of rights under law reveals a serious problem about contemporary [legal] equality theory. The court has not conceptualized the reproductive freedom issue as an equality issue, undoubtedly because of the poverty of the comparison mode. Since men cannot biologically bear children," equality doctrine supposedly cannot hold in this instance.[71]

Sex equality, or its opposite, discrimination, can hold only when a comparison of likeness can be made. If discrimination were at issue in the abortion debate, then treating women as "different" from men in a way that limits women's opportunity would not be acceptable. Abortion would then be grounded in a woman's right *not* to be sexually discriminated against as a reproducer, as a pregnant body, or in terms of her "difference." This is why sex equality remains for women a radical, even if incomplete, demand.

As I've pointed out in various contexts throughout this book, the dominant state discourse of the 1980s shifted from a language of equality to a language of "difference." The Reagan administration

---

69. Planned Parenthood Washington Memo, 1984, H.R. 5745, p. 1.

70. See Adam Clymer, "Abortion and Ambivalence: One Issue That Seems to Defy a Yes or No," *New York Times*, 23 February 1986, p. E22.

71. Stephanie Wildman, "The Legitimation of Sex Discrimination: A Critical Response to Supreme Court Jurisprudence," *Oregon Law Review* 63 (1984): 265–307.

focused on the courts and their interpretation of affirmative action and abortion law to institutionalize this standpoint more thoroughly. Although the result was mixed, I think it is safe to say that the administration was largely unsuccessful in gaining greater dominance for its position. It was countered by the power of liberal discourse and liberal feminist discourse.

The rejection of Robert Bork's nomination to the Supreme Court, as well as his confirmation hearings themselves, is an example of this power. During the hearings Bork attempted to disassociate himself from his previously stated right-wing constructionist views of the Constitution. Had he been confirmed, it would have been as someone of the center conservative position and not the radical right, as became true of the eventual confirmation of Anthony Kennedy. In this sense, existing political discourses that have legitimated civil rights legislation and rights to privacy (including abortion) forced Bork to distance himself from his former antiliberal writings in order to be acceptable. And it forced Reagan to choose Kennedy, as a centrist, as his next nominee.

It may be simply the incoherence of politics that explains why Antonin Scalia was confirmed as an associate justice while Bork was not. Scalia is said to be as right wing as Bork—he rejects affirmative action, believes sexual harassment is not actionable, and so on. Or it may be that the public was not made aware of Scalia's right-wing orientation. No questions concerning Scalia's illiberal judicial opinions were raised. Hence there was no organized fight against his confirmation. But through either its absence or its presence, the impact of liberal discourse and its potential for political effect is a "reality" to be reckoned with.

Chapter Six

Beyond the Phallus
and the Mother's Body

I argue here that a politics of sex equality that recognizes the female body as the potentially pregnant body has to recognize the importance of abortion and reproductive choice; maternity and paternity leave; infant-care, child-care, and day-care needs; parental sick-day leave policy; and related issues. Because the pregnant body is also the gendered mother's body, policies committed to sex equality need to apply to both childbearing and child rearing.[1] But whereas policy related to childbearing affects only females, policy related to child rearing applies to both men and women. We shall see that much of the equality legislation and policy-making in the United States does not focus on the needs of the childbearer or child rearer. Instead, most of the legislation and policy-making focuses on the market, where men and women appear to be the same.

1. For interesting discussions of the concept of motherhood, see Nancy Chodorow, *The Reproduction of Mothering: Psychoanalysis and the Sociology of Gender* (Berkeley and Los Angeles: Univ. of California Press, 1978); Dorothy Dinnerstein, *The Mermaid and the Minotaur: Sexual Arrangements and Human Malaise* (New York: Harper & Row, 1976); Ann Ferguson, "Motherhood and Sexuality: Some Feminist Questions," *Hypatia* 1 (Fall 1986): 3–22; Ann Oakley, *Women Confined: Towards a Sociology of Childbirth* (New York: Schocken Books, 1980); Mary O'Brien, *The Politics of Reproduction* (Boston: Routledge & Kegan Paul, 1981); Adrienne Rich, *Of Woman Born: Motherhood as Experience and Institution* (New York: Norton, 1976); and Joyce Trebilcot, ed., *Mothering: Essays in Feminist Theory* (Totowa, N.J.: Rowman & Allanheld, 1983). For a critical and feminist revisionist viewing of these sources, see Germaine Greer, *Sex and Destiny: The Politics of Human Fertility* (New York: Harper & Row, 1984).

Issues of economic and legal equity substitute for sex equality. Economic and legal equality of opportunity are likened to sex equality, but we should not assume from this equation that equality in these realms is available to women. Women are far from equal to men and do not even share similar opportunity with them in the market. But more to the point is the fact that as long as the concept of sex equality is subsumed under the non-sex-specific category of economic or legal equality, the phallus will remain the referent. Only in the shift away from the phallus can a radical pluralism develop. In this perspective pregnant bodies would no longer be engendered; parenting would no longer be equated exclusively with the mother's body through a connection engendered in "difference."

The importance of differentiating the female body from the mother's body is a key point of this book. Not until this happens can women and men both be considered equal in the task of parenting, equally able to nurture. This view would recognize that men and women have similar, though not always identical, responsibilities as parents. Women bear children; men do not. Although this biological fact sets up an apparently dualistic relationship, it can be construed with much more flexibility. But the continuum I have in mind is not that of the surrogate motherhood relationship represented in the infamous "Baby M" case.[2] In this instance, the surrogate mother, Mary Beth Whitehead, was required by contract completely to separate pregnancy from motherhood; surrogate motherhood, at least as far as Judge Harvey Sorkow's initial decision in the case applied, requires the severing of the relationship between bearing and rearing a child. Although I have argued that a distinction between bearing (pregnancy as such) and rearing (in the social sense) is desirable, Sorkow's decision severed the connection.

2. This case posed the problem of the enforceability of a surrogate motherhood contract: Could Mary Beth Whitehead reclaim her right to custody of the child she bore after giving up this right by signing a contract? For a discussion of the case, see Ellen Goodman, "Surrogate Contract Limited the Choice: Baby M Trial," *Philadelphia Inquirer*, 24 March 1987, p. A11; Mary Gordon, "'Baby M,'" *Ms.* 15 (June 1987): 25–28; Barbara Kantrowitz, "Who Keeps 'Baby M'?" *Newsweek* 109 (19 January 1987): 44–49; Murray Kempton, "The Contract for 'Baby M,'" *New York Review of Books* 34 (9 April 1987): 44; and Katha Pollitt, "The Strange Case of Baby M," *Nation* 244 (23 May 1987): 682–88.

Distinguishing pregnancy from motherhood is different from severing the connection between the two. Distinguishing recognizes a relationship between pregnancy and motherhood; severing the connection does not. Distinguishing enhances equality between the sexes; severing the connection does just the opposite, given present inequities between women and men. In the end, severing the connection between pregnancy and motherhood forces a woman such as Whitehead to give up her baby to its "natural" father, despite her strong objection, because her choices are set *within* phallocratic discourse. In the phallocratic view, one is either the mother—the bearer *and* rearer of a child are one and the same—or one is not the mother. A surrogate mother *only* bears a child; hence, she is not the *real* mother. The sperm supplier *is* the father, and the wife of the supplier, who rears the child, becomes the mother.

Judge Sorkow's decision was framed within a phallocratic discourse that assisted William Stern, the baby's biological father, in claiming paternal power. As such, this decision reaffirmed present inequality between the sexes. According to Sorkow, Whitehead irrevocably waived her rights as a mother when she signed the surrogacy contract.[3] In fact, Whitehead gave up many rights in that contract. She assumed all risk, including the risk of death. If she miscarried within the first five months, she would receive no compensation whatsoever. If amniocentesis detected abnormalities in the fetus, Stern could demand she abort the pregnancy. This was not a contract between equals; rather, it was a contract that established Stern's rights as father.

Sorkow's decision, however, was reversed by the New Jersey Supreme Court. Justice C. J. Wilentz, writing for the unanimous court, found the surrogacy contract invalid and unenforceable, although the supreme court sustained the trial court's grant of custody to the biological father. Wilentz stated for the court: "We find the payment of money to a surrogate mother illegal, perhaps criminal, and potentially degrading to women." This decision privileges the biological mother against the adoptive mother, Elizabeth Stern. The decision does not, however, extend this privilege to

3. See Judge Sorkow's decision in the "Baby M" case: 13 FLR 2001, 7 April 1987, and 217 N.J. Sup. 313 (1987). See also Trial Brief of Amicus Curiae, Nadine Taub, Rutgers Women's Rights Litigation Clinic, Newark, N.J.

contest the rights of the biological father. In other words, the biological mother is defined as the "real" mother in contrast to the adoptive mother, but the "real" and preferred parent—when custody is contested—is the father. A troublesome aspect in this ruling is that the court adopted the discourse of sex equality. While granting custody to Stern, the court argued that the "natural" mother and the "natural" father are entitled to equal weight in custody matters.[4]

Treating the biological father as equal in importance to the biological mother in questions of custody may seem like a progressive shifting of the discourse of sex equality. But in this instance, such treatment can be only partially interpreted as progressive, because surrogacy is constructed within an engendered legal and social system. In surrogacy arrangements thus far, the phallus takes the form of the economically privileged father as the more able parent. This will probably most often be the case when women are hired to bear men's children. This issue demonstrates a truth about all sex-specific legislation: we cannot talk about distinguishing the female from the mother's body in abstraction, that is, outside the context of power that constructs a woman's options.

This point about political context must remain at the forefront of discussions about surrogate motherhood if feminists are to be able to sort out the radical *and* the reactionary potential of surrogacy contracts. Surrogacy arrangements may appear potentially liberating in that they allow us to pluralize the notion of motherhood beyond the biological and pregnant female. But these same arrangements are potentially reactionary in that they require the enforced, contractual severing of the biological mother from parenthood, and they establish this requirement within a series of unequal economic relationships.

Pluralizing the notion of motherhood is in part what feminism is about. But feminists need to remember that it is a science and a technology which is already engendered that has created the possibility of surrogacy. The issue we must continue to sort through is whether surrogacy is where we want to begin to locate a radically pluralist notion of parenting.

4. Quotations from *New Jersey Law Journal* 121 (11 February 1988): 32, 37.

Sexually Specified Equality

Let us briefly review the debate over special sex-specific legislation and the controversy about sex equality that surrounds it. Feminist litigators are slowly coming to recognize that legislation committed to sex equality must address the particular and unique reproductive aspects of being female. The problem in this discussion, as we shall see, is that a misleadingly neat line is drawn between sex-specific law that is acceptable and sex-specific law that is not. Although the distinction between laws based on biological sex and those based on gender can be helpful as we sort through the question of sex equality, it is also problematic in its neatness. Sex-specific law directly related to pregnancy is often assumed in liberal law to be necessary to establish equality; other gendered aspects of women's lives, those more related to child rearing, are not reified in law.

Pregnancy is viewed within liberalism as a problem *because,* of course, the phallus cannot get pregnant. Its uniqueness is interpreted as a handicap.[5] Legislation that recognizes pregnancy as different is termed "special" or "protective." Some feminist litigators argue, as I discussed in Chapter 3, that special legislation is used to deny women their equality rather than to assist them in attaining it. Wendy Williams poses the question this way: "Do we want equality of the sexes—or do we want justice for two kinds of human beings who are fundamentally different?"[6] She recognizes that the choices are not so clear-cut in regard to pregnancy, but she notes that considering pregnancy a special case permits unfavorable, as well as favorable, treatment.[7] Williams is concerned with the possibly unfavorable ramifications of special treatment given the neoconservative climate of the 1980s. She speculates that if the Rehnquist Court is free to interpret sex-specific legislation, it will address the question of gender conservatively.[8] For Williams, so-

5. See Ann Scales, "Towards a Feminist Jurisprudence," *Indiana Law Journal* 56 (Spring 1981): 435.

6. Wendy Williams, "The Equality Crisis: Some Reflections on Culture, Courts, and Feminism," *Women's Rights Law Reporter* 7 (Spring 1982): 200.

7. See ibid., p. 196.

8. As Williams stated at the Feminist Legal Strategies meeting Perspectives

called sex-neutral law is not sufficient, but special legislation and
special exception are not viable alternatives. She favors neutral
rules but recognizes the disproportionate impact neutral rules
often have on women. Williams does not acknowledge that interpretation remains a key problem and goes beyond the conservatism of the Rehnquist Court.

In contrast, and in defense of sex-specific legislation, Sylvia Law
argues that we must be careful to distinguish between "laws drawing explicit sex-based lines and laws governing reproductive biology."[9] Laws regulating reproductive biology raise serious questions
about sex equality, but Law is skeptical of both a concept of equality that does not recognize the particularity of woman and one that
is supposedly neutral.[10] Herma Hill Kay, while critical of certain
forms of protective legislation, also argues that equal treatment is
insufficient for establishing sex equality. She believes that "a just
society needs to recognize and accommodate sex differences in order to neutralize them as barriers to equal opportunity for personal
achievement."[11] She favors carefully demarcated sex-specific legislation for pregnancy. As I discussed in Chapter 3, she views pregnancy as episodic: women should be treated as the same as men
when not pregnant and treated differently when they are pregnant.

The problem with this perspective is that the pregnant body is
also the mother's body, and motherhood encompasses more than a
short episode in a woman's life. Therefore, legislation that treats
women as unique only during pregnancy does not take into account aspects of gender difference that are, and have been, constructed as derivative of the pregnant body. Kay's recognition of
the sexual specificity of pregnancy and its episodic nature is an
important attempt to develop a politics of sex equality that neither
is premised in sameness nor relegates woman to her engendered

---

on Feminism: Past, Present, Future, sponsored by the National Women and the
Law Association, Washington, D.C., 16–17 October 1986.

9. Sylvia Law, "Rethinking Sex and the Constitution," *University of Pennsylvania Law Review* 132 (June 1984): 1007.

10. See ibid., p. 955.

11. Herma Hill Kay, "Models of Equality," *University of Illinois Law Review*
1985, no. 1 (1985): 44. And see her "Equality and Difference: The Case of Pregnancy," *Berkeley Women's Law Journal* 1 (Fall 1985): 1–38.

"difference." However, the view of pregnancy as episodic leaves us trying to limit and deny the long-term effects of pregnancy on women's lives in the hope of establishing the fact that women are more similar to than "different" from men. This view leaves the phallocratic stance intact at the same time that it appears to challenge the domination of that stance. To sever pregnancy from early infant care is to deny the way sex and gender operate in society today. Society need not operate so, but the fact that it does—and the fact that feminists, in the hope of changing it, feel compelled to deny that it should operate so—represent the dilemma of the sex/gender system.

Kay's argument—that special legislation must be limited to the term of pregnancy because any other form of sex-specific policy will be used against women—is a strategic one. The issue remains whether the categorization of pregnancy as biological—as more amenable to scientific, objective definition—makes it easier to legislate without the necessity of interpretation, which can be used to engender women's lives further. Pregnancy seems easier to define than (engendered) motherhood because pregnancy is by and large a biological condition. But it is important to remain cautious about construing pregnancy as completely biological and hence scientifically and objectively definable. Pregnancy is defined in and through phallocratic discourse, as is the science that establishes its definition. Pregnancy is a value-laden construct, mediated through a culture that is defined by gender.

Pregnancy poses the dilemma between the individuality of the female who has the capacity to become pregnant and her relegation to her engendered sex-class status as mother. Specialized pregnancy legislation is open to both interpretations: recognition of the biological female and her reproductive needs *and* restriction of women to this meaning alone. Once again sex and gender are not completely separable.

Pregnancy is *the* hard issue to resolve because it combines specificity and engendered "difference." There is no escaping the specificity of the female body when we speak of pregnancy or the unique capacity of woman as biological reproducer and mother. Yet if we want to deny the engendered "difference" of woman without denying her body, the easiest resolution seems to be to see her body as like man's body, to see pregnancy as like any other disability. We need to deal with pregnancy as it is: the pregnant body is more unique than it is similar to a man's body because the pregnant body is engendered as the mother's body. Therefore, we need special legislation that recognizes the specificity of pregnancy and creates equality *through* it, not in spite of it. Liberalism and its abstract (nonspecific) theory of equality cannot create sex equality for the pregnant body, as was shown in the "Baby M" case. This critique moves us beyond liberalism. The abstract individualism of the male body and/or the father as the common denominator of what it means to be equal cannot suffice.

My discussion here is directed to feminists who are interested in transforming the way equality is conceptualized. In this context, it goes without saying that pregnancy need not be incapacitating or all consuming. A woman can easily choose to bear a child at the same time that she remains absorbed by other work. A woman can be pregnant and yet not feel maternal. In other words, the pregnant woman can be much more similar to a man than to the notion of the engendered mother. With all this said, it is also true that pregnancy *can* be much less episodic than is generally thought. The view of pregnancy as episodic leaves us constrained by a homogeneous standard. Instead of weighing a multiplicity of options when considering how pregnancies affect women, we are left denying the various effects of pregnancy on women's lives. The woman with a difficult pregnancy may need leave not only during pregnancy but after the birth. If a woman has an easy pregnancy, without complication, she still may want a leave from her job *after* the pregnancy. It is after the pregnancy, during the process of becoming a *mother,* that women's bodies most often need rest, given the emotional and physical constraints on them at this time. Pregnancy does not end with the birth of the child, because it does not simply begin there; it is already engendered.

In trying to confine the meaning of "difference" in pregnancy, we can end up setting limits on women's biological potential. And if we believe that woman's reproductive uniqueness should have no inherent meaning—leading neither to her inequality nor to her superiority—then reproductive uniqueness needs room to be expressed and developed. If a person's biological sex will always be expressed through cultural intervention, then we must consider what kind of relationship we want to establish between biology and culture. We need to keep sex distinct from gender if we are to avoid equating pregnancy and motherhood. The question is how distinct we want to make them, and how do we make them distinct within the constraints of the phallocratic definition of equality.

In the debate over special (treating women differently) or same-sex (treating women as like men) legislation, the phallus continues to set the context. Therefore, the best we can do is leave the discussion of sex-specific legislation open. Treating pregnancy as episodic treats women both differently from men and as the same as men *at the same time*. In the long run, we can only hope that similar treatment will be replaced by a radical sex/gender pluralism that will reconstitute the meaning of equality. Until then, the demand for sameness of treatment remains, in part, radical. And so does sex-specific legislation, because it challenges the phallocratic underpinnings of sameness doctrine. That is why, at least at present, both equal (sameness) and special (difference) legislation will be appropriate in different instances.

Linda Krieger and Patricia Cooney argue for sex-specific legislation in the belief that American jurisprudence has not "developed a construct of equality that actually facilitates equality of effect in the context of functional heterogeneity between the sexes."[12] They therefore rightly reject the liberal phallocratic attempts to embrace equality through sameness doctrine. They do so, however, without recognizing that the notion of sameness implies a radical critique of the phallus, inasmuch as a woman is supposed to be "different" from a man. Sameness denies woman her particularity and makes her less than her uniqueness, but it also denies her engendered "difference." Sameness and "difference" can each be used either to undercut or to support phallocratic discourse. When woman is treated as the same as man, she challenges man's representation of specificity and is also denied her own specificity; when she is treated as "different," she is made the "other"; when her specificity is defined while her "difference" is denied, she moves toward equality, beyond the phallus. It is when we deny the opposition between sameness and difference that we decenter the phallus as well as the notion of a "center" itself.

12. Linda Krieger and Patricia Cooney, "The Miller-Wohl Controversy: Equal Treatment, Positive Action, and the Meaning of Women's Equality," *Golden Gate Law Review* 13 (1983): 556.

If sex equality is to encompass particularity, it will have to do so under the recognition that the oppositions between sex and gender, nature and culture, and biology and society are both false and real. Their meanings remain open and evasive. Helen Lambert, a feminist biologist, speaks to this point eloquently.

In brief, arguments about sex equality often get stuck on whether sex differences are socially or biologically caused. This battleground, which feminists generally have not chosen, is strategically unwise. In many cases the question is unanswerable. . . . We would more profitably use our energies devising practical measures to achieve greater social equality in ways which are compatible even with presently observed sex differences. . . . If a particular sex difference is incompatible with important aspects of social equality, we should argue for compensatory measures. . . . No doubt greater social equality will, in itself, tend to decrease sex differences to a biological minimum[,] . . . but equality will be slower in coming if we appear to have our demands in the proposition that sex differences are due wholly to nurture rather than partially to nature.[13]

A commitment to equality cannot deny the existence of sex and gender differences. It can, however, require that these differences not be used in restrictive ways. The key point for me, one that distinguishes an egalitarian argument (which recognizes biological specificity) from a "difference" approach (which assumes engendered beings), is the attempt to distinguish rather than collapse (or completely sever) sex and gender, however problematic it may be to do so. The contours of these positions are not always easy to locate, so it is best not to *over*draw them. Although a New Right or neoconservative politics based on engendered sex "difference" can be easily distinguished from a feminist egalitarianism, the various positions surrounding the debate on sex-specific legislation are not always so clear-cut. This has very much been true of the debates over protective legislation. Some feminists have argued that because protective legislation is sex specific, it is antiegalitarian; that protective legislation limits women to their "difference" and therefore denies them equality of opportunity. But this position clearly does not represent the whole story.

13. Helen Lambert, "Biology and Equality: A Perspective on Sex Differences," *Signs* 4 (Autumn 1978): 116–17.

Sex/Gender "Difference" and
Protective Legislation

The issue of protective legislation and its relation to women's struggle for equality has a long history. There are fundamentally two types of protective legislation. According to Alice Kessler Harris, the first kind attempts to provide safe, clean working conditions for all workers.[14] It established the minimum wage, shorter working hours, reduction of health hazards, compensation to workers for on-the-job accidents, and the like. The second kind of protective legislation attempts to exclude some workers from certain kinds of work and is partially to blame for institutionalizing a sexual division of labor in the work force. This form of restrictive sex/gender-specific legislation is at issue in the feminist debates surrounding protection because it singles out women workers.

Protective legislation limited the number of hours a woman could work in a day, instituted legal restrictions on compulsory overtime and nighttime work, required rest periods and chairs for resting, limited the weight women were expected to lift, and excluded women altogether from certain jobs (such as mining and tending bar).[15] Protective legislation involved both the restriction of women and the establishment of some benefits for them. The first such law was passed in 1881 in California, and it denied women the right to work in places that sold alcoholic beverages. The first legal restrictions on women doing night work were passed in Massachusetts in 1890. Between 1909 and 1917, nineteen states passed laws restricting the number of hours women could work per day. By 1914, twenty-seven states had passed some type of protective legislation (see *OW*, p. 187).

In *Lochner* v. *New York* (1905), the Supreme Court ruled that

14. See Alice Kessler Harris, *Out to Work: A History of Wage-Earning Women in the United States* (New York: Oxford Univ. Press, 1982); all further references to this work, abbreviated as *OW*, will be included in the text. See also Elizabeth Baker, *Protective Labor Legislation* (New York: Columbia Univ. Press, 1925); and William Chafe, *The American Woman: Her Changing Social, Economic, and Political Roles, 1920–1970* (New York: Oxford Univ. Press, 1972), esp. ch. 2.

15. See Barbara Brown, Thomas Emerson, Gail Falk, and Ann Freedman, "The E.R.A.: A Constitutional Basis for Equal Rights for Women," *Yale Law Review* 80 (April 1971): 922–23. See also Roxanne Barton Conlin, "Equal Protection vs. Equal Rights Amendment—Where Are We Now?" *Drake Law Review* 24 (Winter 1975): 259–335.

protective legislation was an interference with the right of workers to contract freely for work. In *Muller* v. *Oregon* (1908), the Court upheld the constitutionality of protective legislation requiring shorter working hours for women. The Court obviously has not been unified on this issue. In *Bunting* v. *Oregon* (1917), it upheld a maximum-hours law for men, and in *Adkins* v. *Children's Hospital of the District of Columbia* (1923), it struck down a minimum-wage law for women. In this decision, unlike the *Muller* case, the Court found the maternal function argument an insufficient defense for the restrictions on women workers. Nevertheless, the Court reversed itself both in *West Coast Hotel Co.* v. *Parrish* (1937), when it upheld a state minimum-wage law for women, and in *Goesart* v. *Cleary* (1948), when it upheld a Michigan protective labor law for women that excluded them from tending bar.[16]

Protective legislation has been challenged by Title VII, and throughout the 1970s the Supreme Court rarely upheld sex/gender-specific classifications, holding that women are entitled to the same rights and duties as men. The 1971 ruling of the California Supreme Court in *Sail'er Inn Inc.* v. *Kirby*, which challenged bartending restrictions for women, sums up this position. "The pedestal upon which women have been placed has all too often, upon closer inspection been revealed as a cage. We conclude that the sexual classifications are properly treated as suspect, particularly when those classifications are made with regard to a fundamental interest such as employment."[17]

At its peak, in the early 1930s, only one-third of women workers were covered by protective legislation. It did not include all kinds of work at first—it applied primarily to factory, laundry, restaurant, and cannery work; domestic workers were excluded (see "PWW," pp. 260–65). For those to whom protective legislation applied, its results were mixed. Often the restrictions were used as just that: women were prevented from competing equally for jobs. The impact of protective legislation varied greatly with fluctuations in the labor force (see *OW*, p. 180). Because it operates in a labor context

16. See Ann Corinne Hill, "Protection of Women Workers and the Courts: A Legal Case History," *Feminist Studies* 5 (Summer 1979): 247–73; all further references to this work, abbreviated as "PWW," will be included in the text. See also Conlin, "Equal Protection vs. Equal Rights Amendment."

17. 95 Cal. Rptr. 329, 341 (1971).

in which sex segregation and sex discrimination *already* exist, the impact of protective legislation is sometimes difficult to assess. It appears to be as much an effect as a cause in establishing discriminatory practices against women (see "PWW," pp. 247–48). But there are those who argue that protective legislation legitimates discrimination; that it institutionalizes sex/gender "difference" in the labor force; that it is more dangerous than helpful to have sex-specific law; that so-called protection is merely a guise for treating women unequally—that is, as "different."

The prevailing discourse on protective legislation in the late nineteenth century was firmly grounded in the idea of woman as mother. Woman was viewed as compassionate, nurturant, and unfit for the competition of the market. Legislation was needed to preserve and protect woman's purity; it "claimed special privilege for the home and motherhood" (*OW*, p. 185). According to Kessler Harris, some protective legislation did improve the lives of married women who were not entirely dependent on their own earnings. Traditional views of motherhood prevailed in the early twentieth century and underlay the protective legislation of this time, "releasing some women from some of the misery of toil, but simultaneously confirming their places in those jobs most conducive to exploitation" (*OW*, p. 214).

In this period the National Women's party, the militant wing of the suffrage movement led by Alice Paul, argued vehemently against protection and for equality. The two were opposed, as far as the party members were concerned. They therefore committed themselves in 1923 to an Equal Rights Amendment (ERA), which would in effect outlaw special sex-specific legislation. In their minds, the early-twentieth-century acceptance of protective legislation was merely an endorsement of women's primary responsibilities as wives and mothers. The NWA party members did not want protection to enable them to fulfill these roles. Instead, they desired equality, which for them meant being treated as the same as men. They did recognize some of the positive effects protective legislation had on wage-earning women, but they believed more strongly that it consigned women to a "status as a separate group of workers" (*OW*, p. 213).

The contemporary parallel to this argument could be the ACLU Women's Rights Project's position on sex-specific legislation. In its

1984 amicus curiae brief, which I discussed in Chapter 3, it opposed as unconstitutional the singling out of pregnant workers for special treatment, even if such treatment appears beneficial. The ACLU used its indictment of past protective legislation as justification for this position. It noted that although some benefits have resulted from it, on the whole such legislation has been used to exclude women from "male" occupations. In addition, it has been used to justify separate sexual spheres. "The notion of biologically based difference, so essential to protectionism, fueled a pervasive ideology which relegated women to a separate sphere of home and family." The ACLU views protective legislation in somewhat causal terms, believing that it creates and "supports the notion that woman's place is in the home."[18]

The ACLU's position, which blames the sex-specific treatment of pregnancy for discrimination against women workers, does not take into careful enough account the fact that sex segregation has existed in the labor force without recognizing pregnancy as sex specific. Singling women out for special legislation related to pregnancy is hardly what makes them "different." What makes women "different" is the engendered nature of pregnancy. In the eyes of an employer, a woman is a potential mother whether or not she is pregnant. Pregnancy affects a woman's options in the labor force either by its absence (she is not pregnant now but she may become pregnant) or by its presence. Recognition of pregnancy through sex-specific legislation undermines discrimination at least as much as, if not more than, it enforces it. Such recognition means if a woman has obtained a job and then gets pregnant, she will be protected against discrimination on the basis of her pregnancy. It is true that with such legislation in place, some employers will think twice about hiring a woman, but many of them think twice about doing so anyhow.

Although the ACLU's brief argues that "protectionist laws reflect an ideology which values women most highly for their childbearing and nurturing roles,"[19] it does not recognize that the discourse surrounding such legislation has shifted from the late

18. *California Federal Savings and Loan Association et al.* v. *Mark Guerra et al.*, Brief of the American Civil Liberties Union et al., Amici Curiae, Supreme Court of the United States, October term, 1985, No. 85-494, pp. 17–18, 19.
    19. Ibid., p. 7.

nineteenth century to the present. The issue of special sex/gender-specific legislation exists within a series of discourses, only some of which relegate women to motherhood. Even the neoconservatives recognize the "working mother," with her dual commitments to home and market.

I can understand discomfort with sex-specific legislation, given the New Right stance on protection and the neoconservative assault on equality on the basis of sex "difference." But New Right and neoconservative protectionist politics are not hegemonic. Their antiegalitarian discourse conflicts with the liberal feminist consciousness of the majority of the American public, which applauds equal treatment before the law for women and men. It also conflicts with the needs of the majority of married women, who are in the labor force.

I do not want to overstate my criticism of the ACLU's position. There are instances in which the doctrine of equal treatment/same treatment is the better option for women. But either way, sex-neutral law or sex-specific law, the phallus is not irrelevant. In the first instance, the phallus remains the standard, and women have to be seen as like men in order to be treated as equal to them. The phallus is allowed to remain cloaked in this case. In the second instance, the phallus remains relevant in the sense that sex/gender-specific law regards woman as the special case, man as the general case. But when legislation makes the specificity of women obvious, the abstract privilege of the phallus becomes obvious as well. Sex-specific equality legislation recognizes women's uniqueness while trying to reject engendered inequity. The problem is that it is often impossible to completely separate the two.

The complex interconnectedness of sex and gender works both ways. It can be used against women to say they are one and the same with their bodies, or it can be used to distinguish between women's physicality and their gender, which requires a critical stance toward the male/man standard. There are risks in both approaches, because each standpoint—equality as sameness *or* special sex-specified—is a construction constrained by contemporary discourse; neither exists outside those constraints. Both standpoints therefore need to be assessed in terms of the particular issues at hand, for their strategic effect. Sameness doctrine remains a significant obstacle to phallocratic privilege, but it is largely a defensive tactic. Eventually, we must establish an equality that recognizes the richness of differences and not accept an equality based in dualistic oppositions.

To conclude: sex/gender-specific legislation is not inherently problematic or progressive. It is made so by its aim and its political context. Some of the earliest sex-specific legislation led to real gains for particular groups of women, even though some of these gains were later turned against women and became more restrictive. Protective legislation can be discriminatory against women, yet women have moved (even if unevenly) toward equality because of it.[20] Sex-specific law is not just sex specific—it is sex/gendered specific. Therefore, it assumes woman's engendered inequality at the same time that it is supposed to challenge it.[21] Because there is no way to resolve this tension, we must be careful not to deny it but instead must use it as a measure against which to judge restrictiveness of legislation.

We can use the tension between the positive and negative aspects of gender to rethink the meaning of woman's unique qualities as a mix of her biology and her place in the family. In this process, we must remain critical of the cultural interpretations of sex and gender, which have been used to deny women their equality without allowing this to be the last word on the issue. Kessler Harris helps us imagine how this kind of new feminist standpoint might transform the focus of special legislation.

These new arguments from difference suggest that a woman's sense of morality and responsibility, and her behavioral codes (including those that derive from her sense of family and her childbearing capacity)[,] are as much a public as a private resource and they insist as a matter of social policy that the work force recognize and make room for these alternative approaches to human relationships. Far from believing that women can act like men at work, this position asserts women's differences proudly, insisting that the workplace accommodate to women's biology as well as society's need for these less individualistic qualities of personality and relationship that are her strength.[22]

20. See Patricia Zelman, *Women, Work, and National Policy: The Kennedy-Johnson Years* (Ann Arbor: Univ. of Michigan Research Press, 1980), p. 11.
21. See ibid., p. 14.
22. Alice Kessler Harris, "Recognizing Difference: The Debate over Equality for Women in the Workplace," in *Women and Work: An Annual Review*, vol. 1,

Specified legislation can be used to instigate changes in the workplace that would recognize women's lives in terms of their unique place in the family. "Because this position accepts domestic life as a necessary part of the wage-work process, it encourages innovative thought in regard to housing programs, transportation systems, child care, and the allocation of community resources."[23] Instead of trying to restrict the aspects of gender that have been a source of both the specialness and the oppressiveness of women's lives, this type of legislation focuses on the positive aspects of gender and uses them to transform the workplace. By attending to the workplace through the family and women's place in it, we can begin to shift the centered phallus. The question this kind of legislation presents is whether we can focus on gendered differences without reproducing the inequities of an engendered society.

Legislation that attempts to reorganize the workplace in light of sex/gender-specific needs moves beyond its specificity to effect change for both men and women. Men would gain the specificity of women, which is a first step in decentering the phallus. The next step would allow multiple plurality, which would deny the significance of being treated as "like" another, which always assumes a silent privileged referent, whether it be male or female. But we are nowhere near this step; we need to remain with the earlier attempt of shifting the phallus. If the female rather than the male body is our starting point, then legislation that takes into account the biological uniqueness of the female body need not be seen as inherently protectionist. Naming such legislation protectionist presumes woman's engendered differentiation: it presumes a weaker party in need of assistance.

Let us return to the issue of the pregnant body and "protective" legislation for a moment. The depiction of the pregnant body as weaker than the nonpregnant body is part of the way the engendered definition of pregnancy establishes woman's "difference." The pregnant body per se is not necessarily in need of protection— nor is it always as "different" as it is said to be—nor is it very often weak or disabled. It does, however, have specific needs. Language

---

ed. Laurie Larwood, Ann H. Stromberg, and Barbara A. Gluck (Beverly Hills, Calif.: Sage Publications, 1986), p. 157.

23. Ibid., pp. 157–58.

matters here: it sets up the way we think about these issues. And specificity—recognizing the richness of difference—is not the same thing as protectionism—assuming that difference means inequality.

Specific legislation should not be termed "special" or "protective." Nor does the way we consider pregnancy, especially in relation to the workplace, need to be so exclusively female specific. This is not to say that men and women have comparable needs in regard to pregnancy, but men and women are not as completely different as "special" legislation treats them. If the concern with pregnancy in the workplace is *in part* related to the desire for healthy infants, then the male worker's health is very much an issue as well. The workplace affects the male reproductive system, and legislation needs to take this fact into account. In this instance, sex-specific, though not identical, legislation for both women and men can be used to transform the workplace toward equality.

According to Wendy Chavkin, "Policies that focus solely on women flagrantly ignore the known facts of reproductive physiology. Men do indeed play a role in reproduction."[24] Michael Wright argues that "many of the substances claimed to be harmful to the fetus may be just as harmful to the unborn via the male reproductive system. None of these companies are talking about protecting the male reproductive system, or even assessing adequately the potential for male reproductive damage."[25] Instead, companies focus on the placental transmission of harmful substances and evade the question of the male body.[26] Exclusionary policies related to pregnancy have been used mainly to limit the number of women

24. Wendy Chavkin, Introduction to pt. 2 of *Double Exposure: Women's Health Hazards on the Job and at Home*, ed. Wendy Chavkin (New York: Monthly Review Press, 1984), p. 155. For a critique of Chavkin's position, see Joan Bertin, review of *Double Exposure: Women's Health Hazards on the Job and at Home*, by Wendy Chavkin, *Women's Rights Law Reporter* 9 (Winter 1986): 89–93.

25. Michael Wright, "Reproductive Hazards and 'Protective' Discrimination," *Feminist Studies* 5 (Summer 1979): 302.

26. See Rosalind Petchesky, "Workers, Reproductive Hazards, and the Politics of Protection: An Introduction," *Feminist Studies* 5 (Summer 1979): 351. See also Carolyn Marshall, "Fetal Protection Policies: An Excuse for Workplace Hazard," *Nation* 244 (25 April 1987): 532–34; Jeanne Stellman and Susan Daum, *Work Is Dangerous to Your Health* (New York: Pantheon Books, 1973); and Jeanne M. Stellman, *Women's Work, Women's Health: Myths and Realities* (New York: Pantheon Books, 1977).

in traditionally male jobs, for instance, in the metals and chemicals industries. Such policies have not been applied in traditionally female jobs, in settings such as laundries, hospitals, or automated offices. "Women beauticians are exposed to halogenated hydrocarbon hairspray propellants[;] . . . women in the dry cleaning industry are exposed to tetrachloroethylene, a mutagen. Airline flight attendants are exposed to higher than average levels of radiation."[27] This criticism of the inadequate scope and restrictive enforcement of special legislation related to pregnancy need not be used to reject such legislation altogether. Rather, the scope of the legislation needs to be broadened and policies put into effect in all workplaces.

Because the female body's health affects the fetus not just at conception but throughout pregnancy, legislation for men and women will not be identical. The argument that work-related legislation to protect the health of fetuses needs to apply to men as well as women does not depend on adopting the equality (meaning sameness) argument that women must be treated as like men. Instead, it contends that men need to be treated more as like women (but not necessarily as exactly the same) in this regard. While recognizing sex specificity, we can move our point of reference toward the pregnant body but not remain there.

Recognizing the pregnant body in the workplace is only one step toward creating sex equality legislation. We must construct a postpregnancy policy as well: parental leave, infant care, child day care, child sick-care leave, and so on. This legislation would be needed no matter how few women participated in the labor force. The United States Census Bureau reports that 87 percent of the nation's 50 million wage-earning women are likely to become pregnant during their wage-earning years. Today, when a majority of women with children are in the work force, child-care-related legislation is an utter necessity. Fifty-five percent of American women participated in the labor force in 1986; half of all mothers with children under three years of age were in the labor force at that time. Mothers of infants and toddlers make up a substantial part of the increased participation of women in the market since 1970. Most employed women work at full-time jobs, including about 73 per-

27. Wright, "Reproductive Hazards and 'Protective' Discrimination," pp. 304–5.

cent of all employed mothers of school-age children and 67 percent of mothers of preschoolers.[28] The labor-force participation rate of mothers with school-age children rose from 64 to 74 percent between 1980 and 1986, and by March 1987, 52 percent of mothers with children one year old or younger were in the labor force.[29] Because a woman is most often pregnant before becoming a mother and is most often a mother after being pregnant, and because a majority of women work in the labor force and are also pregnant and/or mothers, any commitment to sex equality must acknowledge these realities.

Pregnancy Leave, Day Care, and Equality

Equality before the law is necessary but insufficient. Women *need* sex equality. Unfortunately, given existing legal interpretation, all current public policy legislation has failed to ascertain this distinction, between sex equality and equality. The Equal Pay Act of 1963 and Title VII of the Civil Rights Act of 1964 both mandate nondiscrimination but do not recognize the need for sex-specific law in order to establish equality. More recent legislation, such as the Economic Equity Bill (H.R. 2472) sponsored by Representative Patricia Schroeder, is similar in form. It is supposed to ensure economic equity for American women by "providing retirement security for women as workers and as divorced or surviving spouses; making quality dependent care available to all working families; ending discrimination in insurance on the basis of race, color, religion, national origin or sex, and improving health care coverage for displaced homemakers; providing equal employment opportunity and pay equity for women;" and so forth.[30] Opportunities are supposed to exist for women as they do for men. Nondiscrimination on the basis of sex underlies the meaning of opportunity but it poses a problem for sex equality. Recognition of women, of their specificity, and of their uniqueness is needed to create sex equality. *Non*discrimination is necessary but not sufficient.

28. See U.S. Dept. of Labor, *News Bulletin* 84-321 (July 1984): 1.

29. See U.S. Dept. of Labor, *News Bulletin* 87-345 (August 1987): 1. This specific increase is considerable: five years earlier the proportion was 43 percent, and ten years before that, it was only 32 percent.

30. See Ruth Bader Ginsburg, "Gender and the Constitution," *University of Cincinnati Law Review* 44 (1975): 9; quotation from pt. 1, H.R. 2472.

The equal protection clause of the Fourteenth Amendment reflects this same problem. It protects individuals from discrimination that is based on their membership in a disadvantaged group. But this current doctrine "offers women no protection against discrimination that is based on real biological differences between men and women, and in fact denies that such discrimination is sex-based. Women are granted equal protection of the laws only to the extent that they are 'similarly situated' to men."[31] The clause is progressive, as far as it goes, but it does not go far enough: nondiscrimination assumes that women must be treated as like men, so it remains an insufficient guide. Its partial meaning can be used most effectively in establishing economic equality between the sexes. But economic (and legal) equality is only a part of what sex equality is about. The doctrine of nondiscrimination cannot address the uniqueness of the female body.

The ERA falls within this category of nondiscriminatory doctrine. It requires that "equality of rights under the law shall not be abridged by the United States or by any state on account of sex." Equality here means sameness of treatment before the law. Women are to be treated as individuals and not as an engendered sex class, making differentiation on the basis of sex legally suspect if not illegal. Unfortunately, the standard of equality remains the male standard. Ruth Bader Ginsburg interprets the amendment somewhat more generously. According to her, the Senate Judiciary Committee's majority report assumes that the ERA would still allow for the recognition of bodily privacy, for instance, in sex-segregated bathrooms and sleeping arrangements for the military. In her opinion, it also would allow for the recognition of physical characteristics unique to one sex through legislation that would support financing for pre- and postnatal maternal health clinics.[32] Given this interpretation, the ERA would allow an equality recognizing various specificities.

In part as a reaction to the insufficiency of existing law and the Supreme Court decision to classify pregnancy as a non-sex-specific

31. Dawn Johnsen, "The Creation of Fetal Rights: Conflicts with Women's Constitutional Rights to Liberty, Privacy, and Equal Protection," *Yale Law Journal* 95 (January 1986): 620–21.

32. See Ruth Bader Ginsburg, "Sexual Equality under the Fourteenth and Equal Rights Amendments," *Washington University Law Quarterly* no. 1 (Winter 1979): 175.

category existing outside the purview of Title VII, Congress passed the Pregnancy Disability Act (PDA) in 1978. The PDA amends Title VII explicitly to include pregnancy as a classification within its definition of sex discrimination. "The PDA establishes that pregnancy classifications are sex based because the condition affects only women."[33] It thus becomes possible in this view to argue that "the denial of benefits to pregnant employees, comparable to those given male and nonpregnant female employees, constitutes sex discrimination."[34] Although men and women are to be treated as alike, in the end the PDA is not a sex-neutral approach to equality. The statute calls for employers to recognize the distinctness of the sexes, as a mode of establishing equality. According to Andrew Weismann, the PDA "offers a useful model for giving legal significance to both the differences between the two sexes and their equality. Thus an employer who adopts a sex-blind no-leave-of-absence policy discriminates against women by failing to recognize and compensate for the different reproductive roles of the sexes."[35]

Not all legal experts agree with Weismann's view, however. The PDA is still regarded by some as limited by the sameness doctrine. According to Krieger and Cooney, the pregnant woman is protected only against less favorable treatment than a man; she is not granted any affirmative accommodation for pregnancy. "The pregnant employee has only the right not to be treated *worse* than male, or non-pregnant female employees."[36] The PDA needs to move beyond the notion that equal treatment means equality: sex equality need not mean identical treatment of dissimilar individu-

33. Andrew Weismann, "Sexual Equality under the Pregnancy Discrimination Act," *Columbia Law Review* 83 (April 1983): 692. And see Patricia Ann Boling, "Pregnancy Benefits, Benign Sex Discrimination, and Justice: Why Does It Matter How We Ask the Question?" *Golden Gate University Law Review* 11 (Summer 1981): 981–99; David Pannick, "Sex Discrimination and Pregnancy: Anatomy Is Not Destiny," *Oxford Journal of Legal Studies* 30 (Spring 1983): 1–21; and Reva Siegel, "Employment Equality under the Pregnancy Discrimination Act of 1978," *Yale Law Review* 94 (1985): 929–56.

34. Sheila Kamerman, Alfred Kahn, and Paul Kingston, *Maternity Policies and Working Women* (New York: Columbia Univ. Press, 1983), p. 40. And see Sheila Kamerman, "Work and Family in Industrialized Societies," *Signs* 4 (Summer 1979): 632–50.

35. Weismann, "Sexual Equality under the Pregnancy Discrimination Act," p. 726.

36. Krieger and Cooney, "The Miller-Wohl Controversy," p. 518.

als, nor should benefits to pregnant employees be seen as comparable to benefits to male or nonpregnant employees. If a standard must be used, it should be that of the pregnant female, precisely because this is a more inclusive standard.

The United States is the only advanced industrial nation that does not have a national pregnancy policy. In 1983 more than one hundred countries had mandatory maternity policies with an average of five months paid leave. The average length of maternity leave among the 127 countries with national legislation is between twelve and fourteen weeks.[37] The United States lags well behind a number of countries—some of which have far fewer financial resources from which to provide paid leave, among them Iraq, the Netherlands, the Federal Republic of Germany, Uganda, Argentina, Nepal, and Pakistan, to name a few. Each of these countries has full-pay pregnancy leave. Most industrial countries provide paid maternity leave, usually wage related, and health insurance benefits covering a minimum of three months. Five or six months leave is increasingly characteristic for much of Northern Europe. Most countries provide unpaid job-protected leaves for up to one or two years.[38] In Italy a woman can take five months paid leave at 80 percent of her salary and then elect for six more months at 30 percent. In Sweden either parent can receive 90 percent of his or her earnings for nine months.

Legislation to establish greater equality between the sexes and to provide for the health and well-being of children began in the mid-1930s in Sweden. The accepted discourse established the idea of equality of opportunity in the home and the market: in 1982, 77 percent of all women between the ages of twenty and sixty-four held paid jobs, even though many of those jobs were part-time and

37. See Rosalie Ducommun, Fumiko Hakoyama, and Madeleine Zeller, comps., *Maternity Benefits in the Eighties: An International Labor Office Global Survey, 1964–1984* (Geneva: International Labor Office, 1985), p. 1. See also W. W. Daniel, *Maternity Rights: The Experience of Women* (London: Policy Studies Institute, 1980); Sheila Kamerman and Alfred Kahn, *Social Services in the United States: Policies and Programs* (Philadelphia: Temple Univ. Press, 1976); and Jeanne M. Stellman, *Maternity and Pregnancy Provisions: U.S. and Abroad*, Trade Union Women's Studies Series [New York State School of Industrial and Labor Relations, Cornell University] (January 1976).

38. See Kamerman, "Work and Family in Industrialized Societies," pp. 647–49.

on the low end of the pay scale. Economic equality is hardly a reality for Swedish women. But legislation that makes wage-earning mothers' work lives more flexible exists alongside this economic inequality. Parents of children under age eight can work six instead of eight hours a day at reduced pay.[39] In 1974 legislation was passed that entitled Swedish fathers to a ten-day leave when their child was born, established parental leave during the child's first year, and permitted either parent up to sixty days leave per year per child if the child or his or her regular caretaker was ill. Such legislation is only a first step toward creating sex equality, but it is at least that.

By 1972 pregnant Swedish workers could not be fired for pregnancy, they had the right to a six-month leave of absence, and they could receive free advice and treatment at a maternity center. Obstetric care was free, and mothers were to receive a maternity allowance through the national insurance system.[40] As of January 1984, either the father or the mother is entitled to a leave with an allowance of 90 percent of income for 180 days after the birth of a child. Either the father or the mother is allowed to stay home to take care of the child (full-, half-, or one-quarter time) for an additional 180 days, and either parent can take time off work to care for sick children.[41] I do not present the example of Sweden as a panacea, because aspects of the view of the engendered mother remain intact there: only 25 to 30 percent of fathers who were eligible for parental leave in the first year of a child's life took it, while 76 percent of all new fathers took work leave at the time of delivery.[42] In 1980, 43 percent of all preschool children were cared for by a parent in the home, and there was a great shortage of day care for children under age six. Nonetheless, Sweden shows how far the United States has to go just to catch up with other countries.

39. See Ruth Sidel, *Women and Children Last: The Plight of Poor Women in Affluent America* (New York: Viking Press, 1986), esp. ch. 9.

40. See Marianne Karre et al., "Social Rights in Sweden before School Starts," in *Child Care—Who Cares? Foreign and Domestic Infant and Early Childhood Policies*, ed. Pamela Roby (New York: Basic Books, 1973), p. 138.

41. See Wendy Williams, "Equality's Riddle: Pregnancy and the Equal Treatment/Special Treatment Debate," *New York University Review of Law and Social Change* 13 (1984–85): 377–78.

42. See Sidel, *Women and Children Last*, pp. 181–82.

According to Sheila Kamerman, through the 1960s and 1970s in the United States, the important legislative targets concerning pregnancy were elimination of mandatory leaves and protection of a pregnant worker's job benefits and seniority while she was on leave. The goal of this legislation was to have employers treat pregnancy and maternity as the same as any other illness or disability through existing health insurance, disability benefits, and job-protected child-care leaves.[43] The components of a maternity-leave policy would include a health insurance package covering the hospital and physical care of the mother and infant; a leave for a specified period with seniority, pension, and other entitlements protected; and full or partial wage replacement. At present about one-third of wage-earning women have no health insurance of their own, while 10 percent have no insurance at all. Some employers give two- to three-month unpaid leaves, whereas some states give six weeks paid leave; but there is no coherent or consistent policy. The United States has not moved much beyond its first federal legislation dealing with maternity—as a result of the 1946 amendment to the Federal Railroad Unemployment Insurance Act, pregnant employees became entitled to temporary disability insurance and weekly cash and sickness benefits for maternity.[44]

As we turn from the issue of pregnancy per se to examine parenting, we must endorse a sex/gender-neutral stance. It is, however, much harder to create such a stance. The Parental and Medical Leave Bill (H.R. 4300), also sponsored by Representative Schroeder, would allow workers up to eighteen unpaid weeks off in a two-year period in order to care for a newborn or newly adopted child, seriously ill children, or dependent parents. Workers could also take up to twenty-six weeks of unpaid medical leave. The pending bill would "establish a commission to study ways of providing salary replacement for employees who take any such leave."[45] Although this bill presumes to be sex neutral, in effect it

43. See Kamerman, Kahn, and Kingston, *Maternity Policies and Working Women*, p. 4.
44. See ibid., p. 35.
45. In the Senate, the Parental and Medical Leave Bill (S2238) is sponsored by Senator Christopher Dodd of Connecticut and Senator Paula Hawkins of Florida. For further discussion of parental leave, see John McMullen, "The New Proposals for Parental Leave and Leave for Family Reasons," *Company Lawyer* 7

is not. As long as white women continue to earn only sixty cents (and black women, fifty-four cents) to every dollar men earn, as long as women remain clustered in the low-paying end of the economic spectrum, and as long as a majority of women's wages hover around the poverty line, it will be women who will be expected to take unpaid leaves. For the woman who has no economic partner—a single parent, for instance—taking an unpaid leave is not a viable option. Single parents whatever their sex, unless independently wealthy, will be excluded by circumstances from eligibility for a leave. This kind of so-called sex-neutral legislation pretends to treat parenting as though it were gender neutral, but it actually reinforces existing gendered inequalities. In the name of sex neutrality, economic class privilege is simply institutionalized along sexual lines. This bill is a clear example of how policy initiatives can represent a significant shift in political discourse and still not be adequate to dislocate the present arrangements of power.

Economic class inequities and women's positioning within them are even more in evidence in the treatment of infant and child day care. When men and women both work in the labor force and have children, day care becomes a necessity. It is well documented that not all the children who need day care can get it. It is also well known that even those parents who have been able to make day-care arrangements for their children wish there were better alternatives available. Although there is a day-care crisis, the Reagan administration was almost completely silent about this issue: it failed to recognize day care as a policy concern of major proportion. There was some limited discussion about establishing a voucher system for working parents, and the question of state licensing of day-care facilities was occasionally raised. Otherwise, day care has been ignored, or even vilified for its purported association with sexual molestation.

In recent U.S. history, child-care programs have most often been defined as part of social-welfare policy, as in Project Head Start in the mid-1960s and the Work Incentive Program (WIN) in 1967. The idea of a federal program to support innovative child-

<hr />

(January 1986): 30–32; and Nadine Taub, "From Parental Leaves to Nurturing Leaves," *New York University Review of Law and Social Change* 13 (Spring 1985): 381–410. Quotation from pt. 1, H.R. 4300.

care programs for all working parents was rejected by President Nixon in 1971, and there has been no change in the federal government's position since.[46] Consequently, making acceptable arrangements for day care remains a concern for which families must find individual solutions, and most often the burden falls on the mother. This is especially true for single-parent families. Day care exists within an engendered marketplace. Day-care workers, who are primarily women, earn women's wages: two out of three center-based day-care workers earn below poverty wages, and these are the best-paid caregivers. According to Ruth Sidel, 87 percent of home-based day-care workers—women who care for other people's children in their own homes—earn below the minimum wage.[47] Single parents in the labor force, who are predominantly women to begin with, have the greatest need of day care but also the least available money to pay for it. The poverty of women feeds on itself in the day-care arena: a majority of women earn under $15,000 a year, and day-care workers are at the low end of that spectrum. It is not surprising that many of these underpaid day-care workers have children of their own who need daytime care.

It is difficult to imagine what sex equality can mean when this is the political context in which our thinking about it takes place. After all, if equality means freeing women from their engendered "difference"—and if that difference is in part defined by the pregnant body and in part defined by creating good options for the care of children—the issues of pregnancy-related and child-care needs become central policy concerns. This is different from saying that these are women's issues. Child care is—or should be—the concern of every parent. But for most people at present, it is considered a problem for women in a distinctly different way than it is for men. The difference is that when child care does not exist, its absence does not create a problem of equality for men, but it does

46. See Pamela Roby, "Young Children: Priorities or Problems? Issues and Goals for the Next Decade," in Roby, *Child Care: Who Cares?* p. 56; and Sidel, *Women and Children Last*, ch. 6.

47. See Sidel, *Women and Children Last*, p. 117. See also Marion Blum, *The Day Care Dilemma: Women and Children First* (Lexington, Mass.: Lexington Books, 1983); Suzanne Braun Levine, "Caring about Child Care," *Ms.* 15 (March 1987): 31; Karen Rubin, "Whose Job Is Child Care?" *Ms.* 15 (March 1987): 32–34; and Barbara Kantrowitz et al., "A Mother's Choice," *Newsweek* 107 (31 March 1986): 46–51.

create, as well as reflect, a problem of sex/gender equality for women.

This discussion would be incomplete if I did not note that a politics of sex equality—which recognizes the specificity of women and the varieties of ways this specificity is expressed—requires the freedom not to express one's specificity as well. This means that reproductive freedom and the right to abortion have to underlie a woman's choice to bear a child; otherwise, childbearing is not truly a choice. Sexual freedom that adopts a heterogeneous standpoint on sexual practices and preferences must underlie sex equality as well; this greater freedom recognizes the importance of sexual activity free from childbearing and/or heterosexual privilege.

A Politics of Sex Equality

I have argued throughout this book that an adequate theory and politics of sex equality have yet to be developed. The generalized and abstracted vision of equality that presently exists—that is, when it is not being rejected by neoconservatives—subsumes the inequality of women to men by means of women's engendered "difference." I have also argued, however, that the abstractness of this vision is not all bad. A generalized, nonspecified notion of equality allows for the radical critique of specific male privileges. "Equality is a platitudinous concept that practically everybody supports because it can be given any meaning we like. . . . Formal agreement on equality as a value masks the fact that we haven't a clue as to what is supposed to be equal to what, and in what way, or to what degree."[48] We can use the formal agreement over the importance of equality to try to define better its particular meaning and to give its symbolic meaning more significance.

Ronald Dworkin helps to untangle the confusion that surrounds the meaning(s) of the general theory of equality. He maintains that there are two dominant views of what equality requires. "The first is the right to *equal treatment*, which is the right to an equal distribution of some opportunity or resource or burden. . . . The second is the right to *treatment as an equal*, which is the right not to

48. Phillip E. Johnson, "Do You Sincerely Want to Be Radical?" *Stanford Law Review* 36 (January 1984): 289–90.

receive the same distribution of some burden or benefit, but to be treated with the same respect and concern as anyone else." For Dworkin, "in some circumstances the right to treatment as an equal will entail a right to equal treatment, but not, by any means, in all circumstances."[49] In other words, some instances call for unequal treatment; equality will not always entail the same treatment. For example, Dworkin hypothesizes, "If I have two children and one is dying from a disease that is making the other uncomfortable, I do not show equal concern if I flip a coin to decide which should have the remaining dose of the drug."[50] The first view reduces the notion of equality to sameness; the second recognizes that different treatment may be more egalitarian in the long run.

Treating pregnancy as the same as other disabilities may mean treating it as equal to other disabilities, but it does not necessarily mean that this is equivalent to treating the pregnant worker as equal to nonpregnant workers. Pregnancy may need to be treated differently from other disabilities in order to ensure that the pregnant worker will come out equal. Recognizing the need for different treatment, as affirmative action policy guidelines do, can help to establish equality; in fact, it is especially true in affirmative action policy that equality does not mean sameness of treatment. Dworkin specifically addresses this issue when he advises that we not use the equal protection clause to "cheat ourselves of equality." He argues that "in certain circumstances a policy which puts many individuals at a disadvantage is nevertheless justified because it makes the community as a whole better off."[51]

49. Ronald Dworkin, *Taking Rights Seriously* (Cambridge, Mass.: Harvard Univ. Press, 1977), p. 227.

50. Ronald Dworkin, "DeFunis v. Sweatt," in *Equality and Preferential Treatment,* ed. Marshall Cohen, Thomas Nagel, and Thomas Scanlon (Princeton, N.J.: Princeton Univ. Press, 1977), p. 68. And see "Pluralism and Its Discontents" (special issue), *Critical Inquiry* 12 (Spring 1986); "Winter Symposium: The Quest for Equality," *Washington University Law Quarterly* 1979 (Winter 1979), esp. Paul Freund, "The Philosophy of Equality," pp. 11–25; Peter Westen, "The Empty Idea of Equality," *Harvard Law Review* 95 (January 1982): 537–96; Stephanie Wildman, "Note: Toward a Redefinition of Sexual Equality," *Harvard Law Review* 95 (1981): 487–508; and Bertha Wison, "Law in Society: The Principle of Sexual Equality," *Manitoba Law Journal* 13 (Spring 1983): 221–33.

51. Dworkin, "DeFunis v. Sweatt," pp. 83, 73. For a discussion of the related problem of recognizing difference(s) within a feminist conception of equality, see

The same treatment of different individuals, or of individuals with differences, does not mean that the treatment is equal; sameness of treatment can just as easily mean unequal treatment. Difference and more particularly the plurality of existing differences are not inherently in opposition to equality. The apparent opposition is a social construction that establishes hierarchical privilege.

A woman who is nauseated in the first trimester of pregnancy may find it helpful to snack often rather than eat a meal at one sitting. She may therefore prefer a series of short breaks to a specified lunch hour. The pregnant worker with edema may need to keep her feet propped up on a stool to reduce the swelling of her legs. Both needs require that the pregnant worker be treated differently from other (i.e., nonpregnant) workers, but there is nothing inherently problematic about these accommodations unless different treatment is assumed to mean inequality. Nor is there an inherent problem in recognizing special needs for pregnant workers who have such needs and not recognizing them for pregnant workers who do not. My point is that a multiplicity of differences characterize the conditions and needs of pregnant workers and that these differences must be recognized as part of women's right to equality.

Specialized treatment constitutes a notion of equality that recognizes difference(s). The pregnant worker may have needs different from those of the nonpregnant worker; the nonpregnant worker may have needs different from those of the pregnant worker; the needs of individual pregnant workers may differ; pregnant and nonpregnant workers may have similar needs. These are all equal ways of being, if we dislocate the silent phallocratic referent.

The fact that sex-specific legislation, such as some forms of protective legislation, has been used to restrict women's options is a political and strategic problem. But this is no reason for us to lessen our commitment to an equality that recognizes diversity. We lose too much when we do so: we lose the recognition of the rich-

Carole Pateman and Elizabeth Gross, eds., *Feminist Challenges: Social and Political Theory* (Boston: Northeastern Univ. Press, 1986); and Anne Phillips, ed., *Feminism and Equality: Readings in Social and Political Theory* (Oxford: Blackwell, 1987).

ness of the multiplicity of variety. Those who choose to use woman's uniqueness against her are left free to do so while they endorse the sameness standard of equality that silences the plurality of expressions of this uniqueness. We are not free, however, to locate ourselves in the realm of plural differences, because the liberal theories of equality and abstract individualism set the political context in which the discussion of sex equality takes place. Its standard of sameness constrains us: it cannot be ignored, yet it cannot be given the last word. Sex equality will have to include similar *and* specific treatment. One *or* the other will not do.

Abstract generalizations about how and when equality requires particular treatment are problematic. We need to take into account the specificities of an individual's circumstances. It is not acceptable to treat a woman as pregnant when she is not, and it is not acceptable to treat the pregnant female as though she were not pregnant if her individual circumstances require specific treatment. The standpoint establishing sex equality will always have to be interpreted in terms of the particular situation. Needless to say, interpretation is a problem in and of itself. But this problem always exists, whether the standard is sameness, "difference," or a blending of the two that transforms each.

We are going to feel weary in this terrain. If the concept of difference(s) remains open to plural definition, it remains equally open to neoconservative construction and interpretation. The neoconservative defense of engendered sex "difference" is not just one of many discourses, it is one with significant power. Therefore, we must recognize that some of the power of neoconservatism derives from its identification with liberal discourse, revised though it may be, and we must use this neoconservative commitment to abstract individualism against neoconservatism itself. Individualism can be turned into a radical critique of neoconservatism in much the same way that the idea of equality has been used to radicalize liberalism. Individualism requires individuality, which involves the plurality of differences, not a homogeneous engendered "other."

I argue that equality must encompass generalization, abstraction, and homogeneity as well as individuality, specificity, and heterogeneity. The homogeneity of woman's "difference" from man is displaced by her plural specificities *and* similarities. Sex discrimination is redefined to mean the treatment of an individual woman as a member of a sex class that restricts her freedom of choice and self-determination while ignoring both her individual differences from members of her sex class and her similarities with men. Sameness is no longer equated with equality nor is specific legislation equated with discrimination. Once the oppositional differentiation of woman from man is replaced by a notion of sexual heterogeneity, equality cannot mean sameness. Difference is no longer oppositional. It does not mean less than, a lacking, or "other." A person can be different and (not un)equal.

Radical Pluralism and the Heterogeneity of Sameness

We need to adopt a radical pluralist method for thinking about how difference constitutes the meaning of equality. Such an approach assumes that differences and plurality constitute society but understands that hierarchy and unequal relations of power presently structure those differences. A feminism rooted in radical pluralism aims to destroy the hierarchy and the oppositions that hierarchy constructs, and it seeks to create a view that recognizes a multiplicity of individuals who are free to be equal and are equal in their freedom. Radical pluralism differs from liberal pluralism, which assumes through the process of abstraction and generalization that equality *already* exists. In liberal pluralism the silent male referent masks the hierarchy and inequality.

A radical pluralist and feminist theory of equality must recognize the specificity of the female body and the variety of ways this is expressed: individually (as in differences of health, age, body strength, and size) and in terms of a woman's race and economic class. The unique aspect of the female body—its capacity for childbearing—makes women a sex class, even though differences exist among them. The engendered meaning of the mother's body plays a large part in this designation. Neither the female body nor the pregnant body is uniform in kind or meaning. A middle-class, black, pregnant woman's body is not one and the same as a working-class, white, pregnant woman's body. The pregnant body of a woman in her midthirties is not identical to the pregnant body of a woman in her early twenties. A welfare woman's pregnant body may not be the same as an upper-middle-class woman's pregnant body, or a diabetic's pregnant body, or an inseminated lesbian's pregnant body, or a surrogate mother's pregnant body.

It is the engendered meaning of the woman's body that homogenizes her "difference" from men and constructs her similarity to other women. Because the engendered viewpoint treats sex and gender as one, gender establishes similarity among women. The unity of women as a sex class is located in the intersection between sex and gender: a place in between that defines heterogeneous females as a homogeneous class. The pregnant body is plural in and of itself, whereas the "idea" of the mother's body is one: diversity and unity, differences and sameness exist simultaneously.

Biology—as the body—is always mediated through its discourses. The meaning of the pregnant body is therefore established in and through the ideas and practices that define an individual's body. Instead of recognizing the heterogeneous expressions of pregnancy and motherhood along individual, economic class, sexual preference, and racial lines, phallocratic discourse abstracts the mother's body as middle class, heterosexual, and white, because acknowledging the plurality of differences among women would undercut the sameness/"difference" opposition. In part, this oppositional stance underlies present changes in child custody law and the tender years doctrine I discussed in Chapter 2. The dualistic privileging of the phallus is reproduced in these options at the same time that they begin to question the equations between femaleness and motherhood, sex and gender.

Policies of sex equality must recognize the pluralism of women's bodies. Neither their uniformity nor their differences are complete. In the hope of creating such a viewing, we need to argue for legislation that will push in the direction of radical pluralism. This, in part, means maintaining the legalization of abortion and extending its applicability to poor women, assuring jobs with a fair wage for all who seek them, instituting paid pregnancy leaves and creating child-care leaves for parents of both sexes with a guaranteed living wage, developing a child-care sick-day leave policy, building adequate day-care programs for the numbers who need them, and substantially increasing wages for day-care workers. Pregnancy and parental legislation should in no way be tied to the institution of marriage; a parent should not need to have a heterosexual partner to be eligible for these services and benefits. A child, and not necessarily even the parent's biological child, should be the sole requisite.

In this neoconservative period, when there is no easy way to talk about sex equality, these kinds of policy initiative keep at least the idea of sex equality alive. We remain caught between what exists and what we would like to exist. And in that small space, it is almost impossible to decipher what we might want from our bodies if they were not engendered or how we might envision sex without engendered inequality. It makes sense that women are hesitant to accept sex equality legislation that begins to deny the gendered relations of society, as the reversal of tender years doctrine does, while the constraints existing prior to the legislation remain.[52] Often law only affords women protection of their present engendered status. What happens if gender-specific law is changed in the name of equality, while the practice of gender inequality is allowed to continue? And how will law be changed to accommodate the new developments in reproductive technology, which will necessarily affect the relationship between sex and gender? Women, from their position on the margins, are right to be cautious about the long-term significance of these changes.

Phallocratic power—which is plural, dispersed, and sometimes incoherent as well as hierarchical and unequal in its dispersion—sets the limits of sex equality. The multiple existing political discourses regarding sex and gender *and* "difference" and sameness constitute and reflect these relations of power. They position our viewing of power in between ideas and practice, in between the truth and falsity of gender. If the pregnant body is both real (as a biological entity) and ideal (as a social construct), and therefore exists in between those realms, then the discourse of sex equality must remain in between as well—between sex and gender, differences and sameness, and between liberalism and the phallus on the one hand, and deconstruction and feminism(s) on the other. There is at present no place else to be.

52. See Ann Snitow, "The Paradox of Birth Technology," *Ms.* 15 (December 1986): 42–77, for an interesting discussion of the contradictory aspects of challenging the "naturalness" of motherhood.

Index

Compositor:	Graphic Composition
Text:	11/13 Caledonia
Display:	Caledonia
Printer:	Maple-Vail Book Manufacturing Group
Binder:	Maple-Vail Book Manufacturing Group